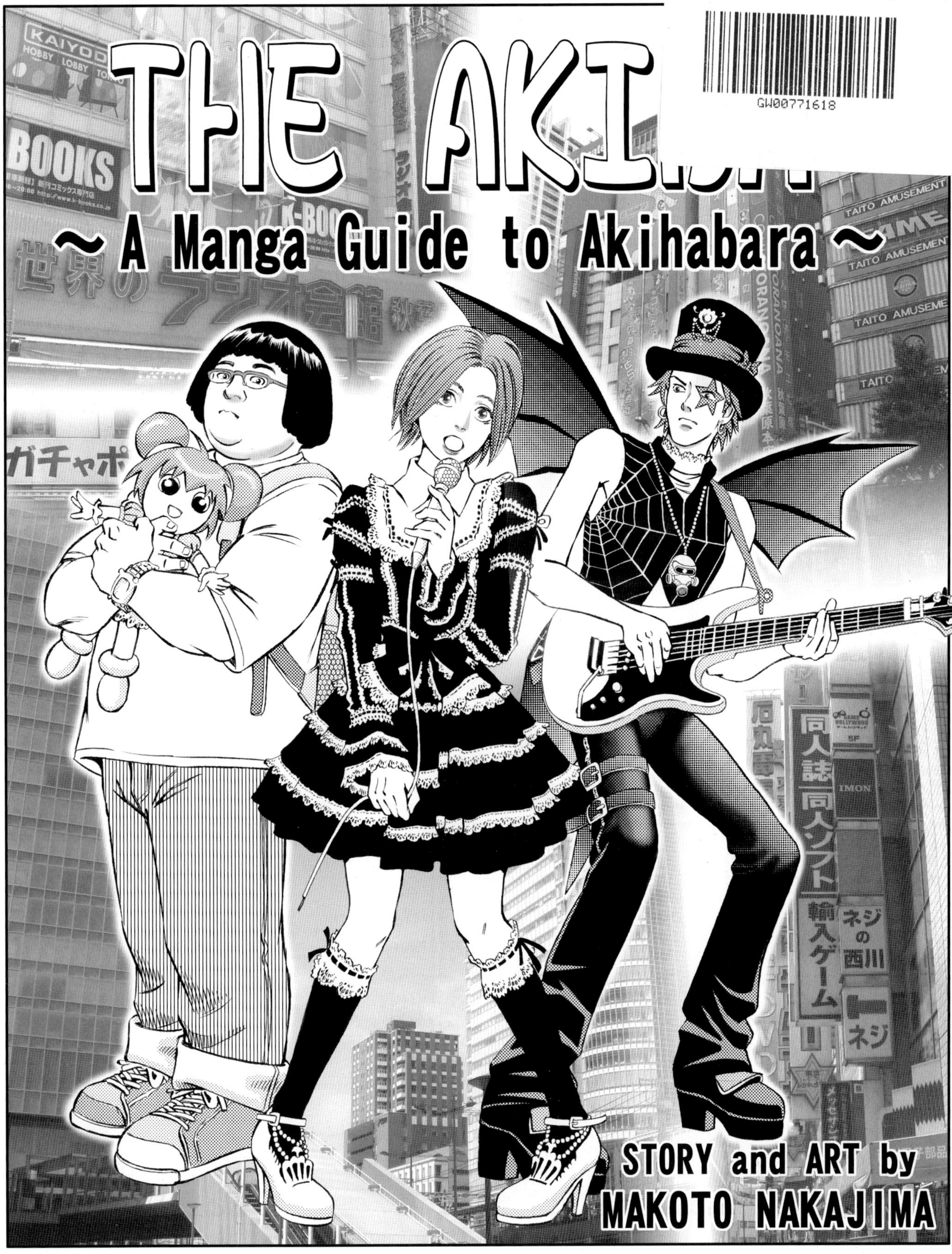
THE AKI
~A Manga Guide to Akihabara~
STORY and ART by
MAKOTO NAKAJIMA
KAIYODO
HOBBY LOBBY TOKYO
BOOKS
K-BOOKS
世界のラジオ会館
ガチャポ
TAITO AMUSEMENT
TAITO AMUSEMENT
TAITO AMUSEMENT
同人誌
同人ソフト
輸入ゲーム
ネジの西川
ネジ
IMON
5F

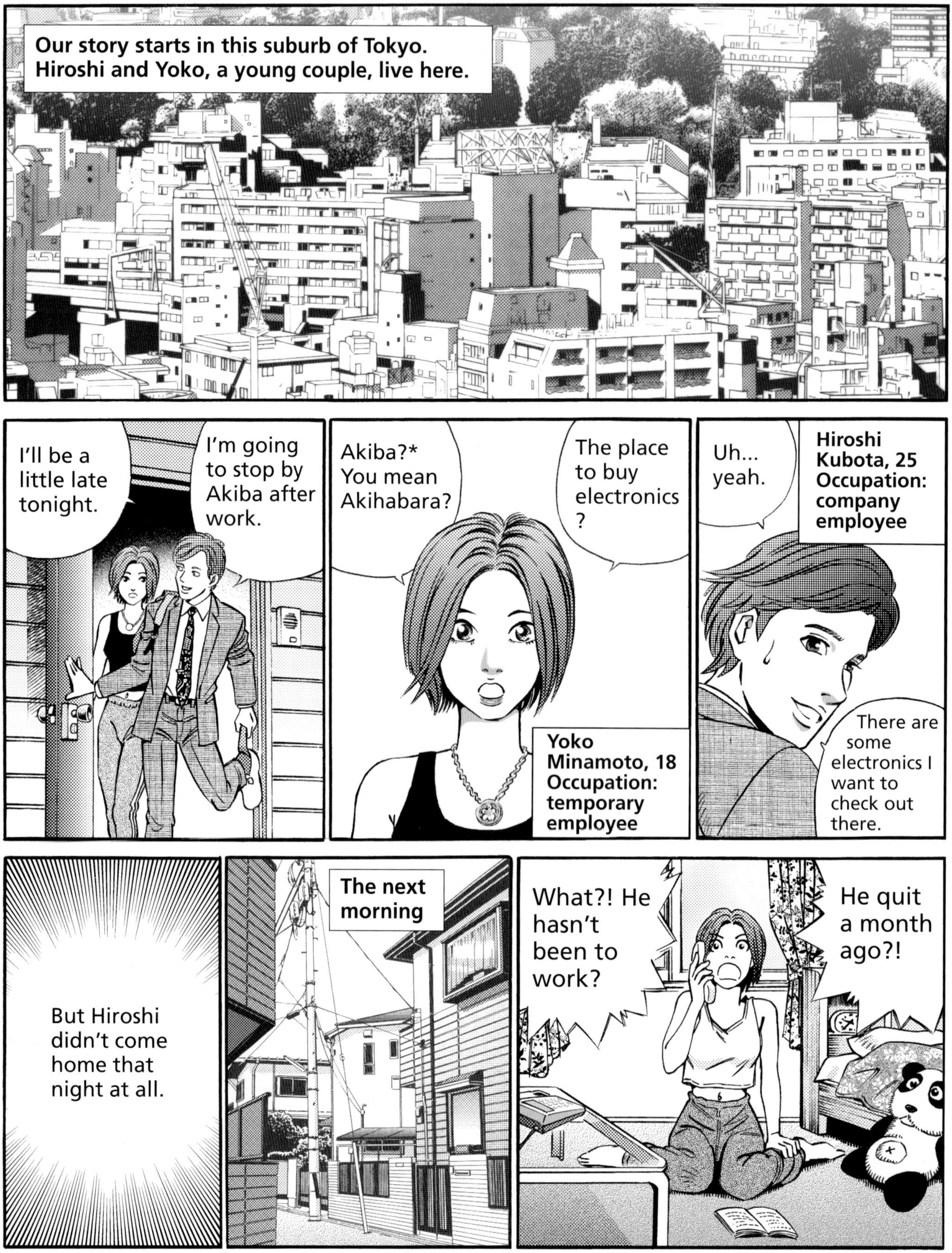
Our story starts in this suburb of Tokyo. Hiroshi and Yoko, a young couple, live here.
I'll be a little late tonight.
I'm going to stop by Akiba after work.
Akiba?* You mean Akihabara?
The place to buy electronics?
Yoko Minamoto, 18 Occupation: temporary employee
Uh... yeah.
Hiroshi Kubota, 25 Occupation: company employee
There are some electronics I want to check out there.
But Hiroshi didn't come home that night at all.
The next morning
What?! He hasn't been to work?
He quit a month ago?!

* Younger Japanese often shorten the place-name "Akihabara" to "Akiba."

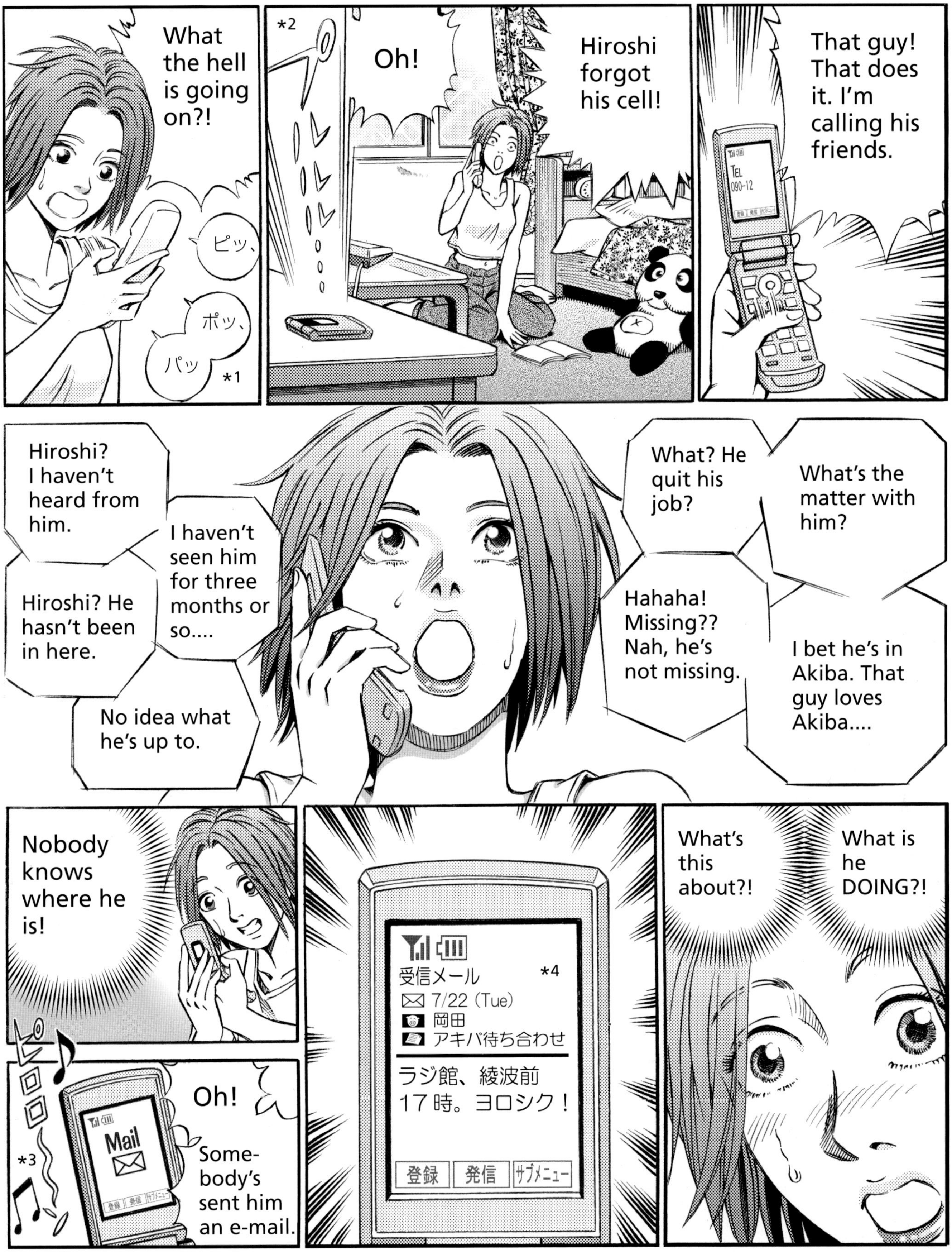
What the hell is going on?!
ピッ、
ポッ、
パッ *1
*2
Oh!
Hiroshi forgot his cell!
TEL 090-12
That guy! That does it. I'm calling his friends.
Hiroshi? I haven't heard from him.
I haven't seen him for three months or so....
Hiroshi? He hasn't been in here.
No idea what he's up to.
What? He quit his job?
What's the matter with him?
Hahaha! Missing?? Nah, he's not missing.
I bet he's in Akiba. That guy loves Akiba....
Nobody knows where he is!
ピロロロ *3
Mail
Oh!
Somebody's sent him an e-mail.
受信メール *4
7/22 (Tue)
岡田
アキバ待ち合わせ
ラジ館、綾波前
17時。ヨロシク！
登録 発信 サブメニュー
What's this about?!
What is he DOING?!

*1 Japanese onomatopoeia for the sound of dialing
*2 Ring, ring, ring!
*3 Incoming mail!
*4 Tuesday, July 22. From: Okada. Subject: Meeting in Akiba. See you at Raji-kan, in front of Ayanami, at 5:00 p.m.

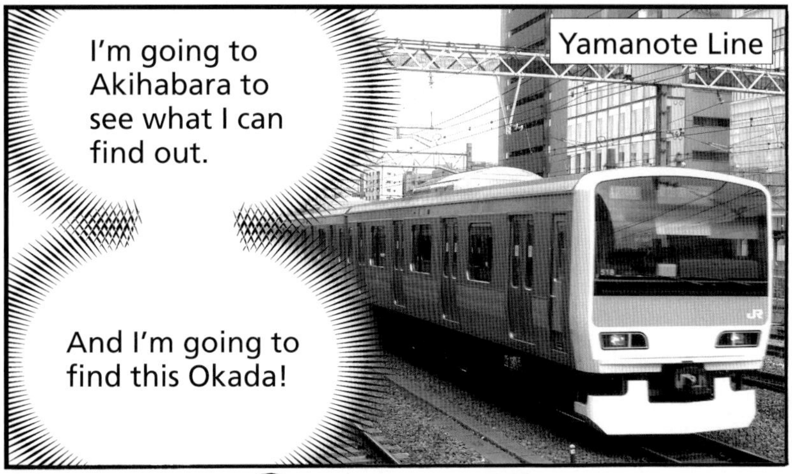
Yamanote Line
I'm going to Akihabara to see what I can find out.
And I'm going to find this Okada!

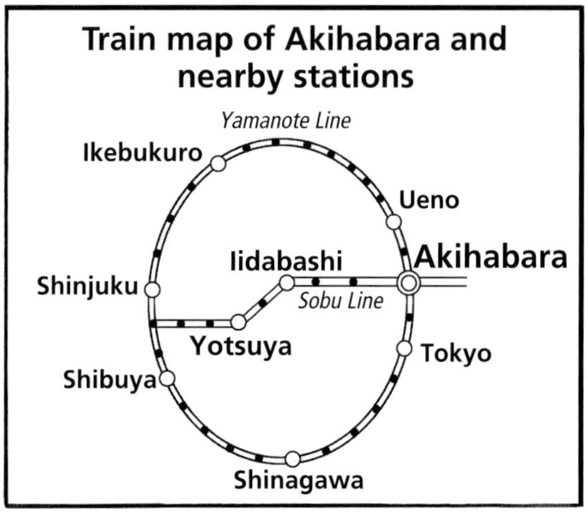
Train map of Akihabara and nearby stations
Yamanote Line
Ikebukuro
Ueno
Iidabashi
Akihabara
Shinjuku
Sobu Line
Yotsuya
Tokyo
Shibuya
Shinagawa

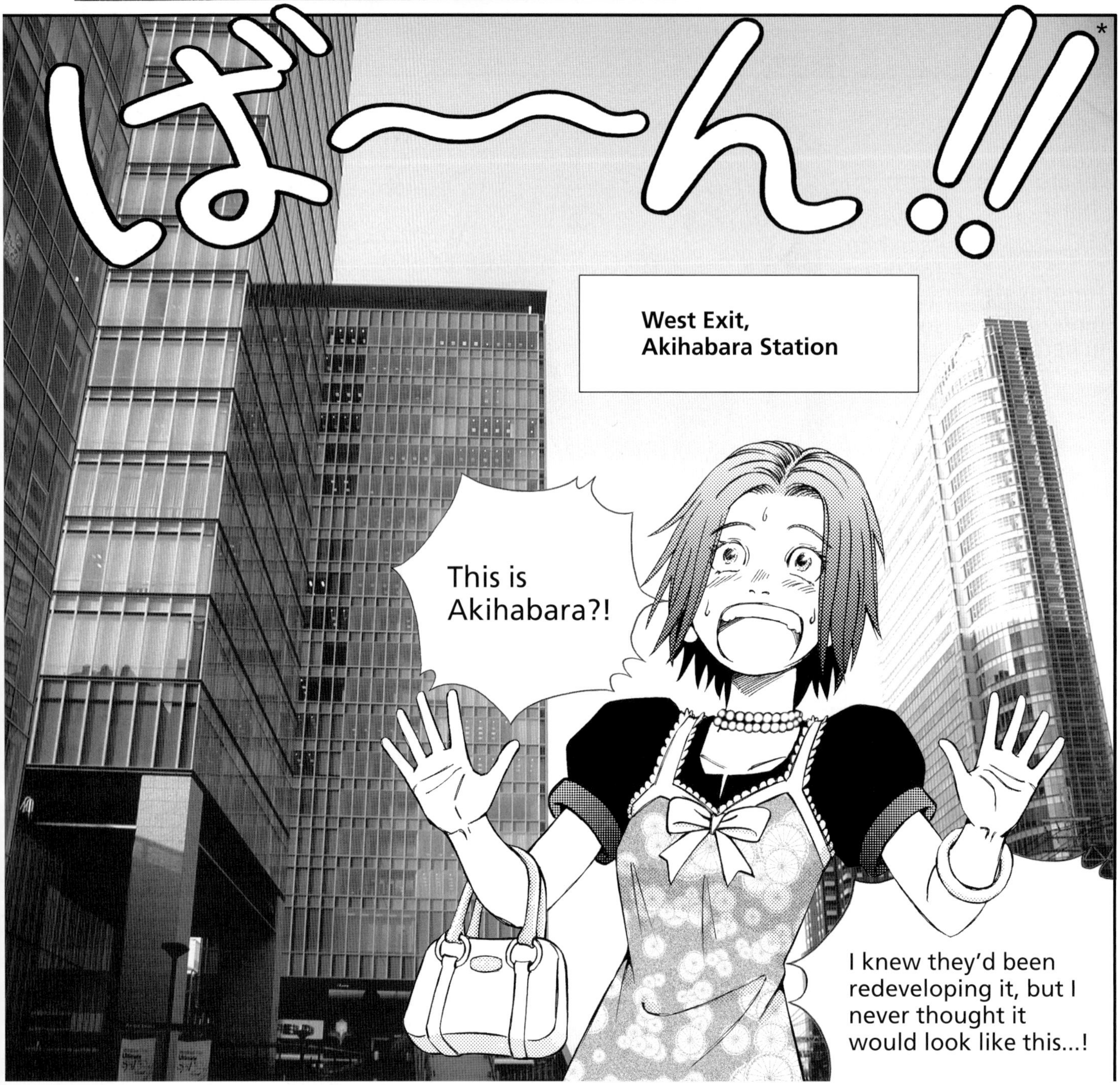
ば〜ん!!*
West Exit, Akihabara Station
This is Akihabara?!
I knew they'd been redeveloping it, but I never thought it would look like this...!

* Bam!

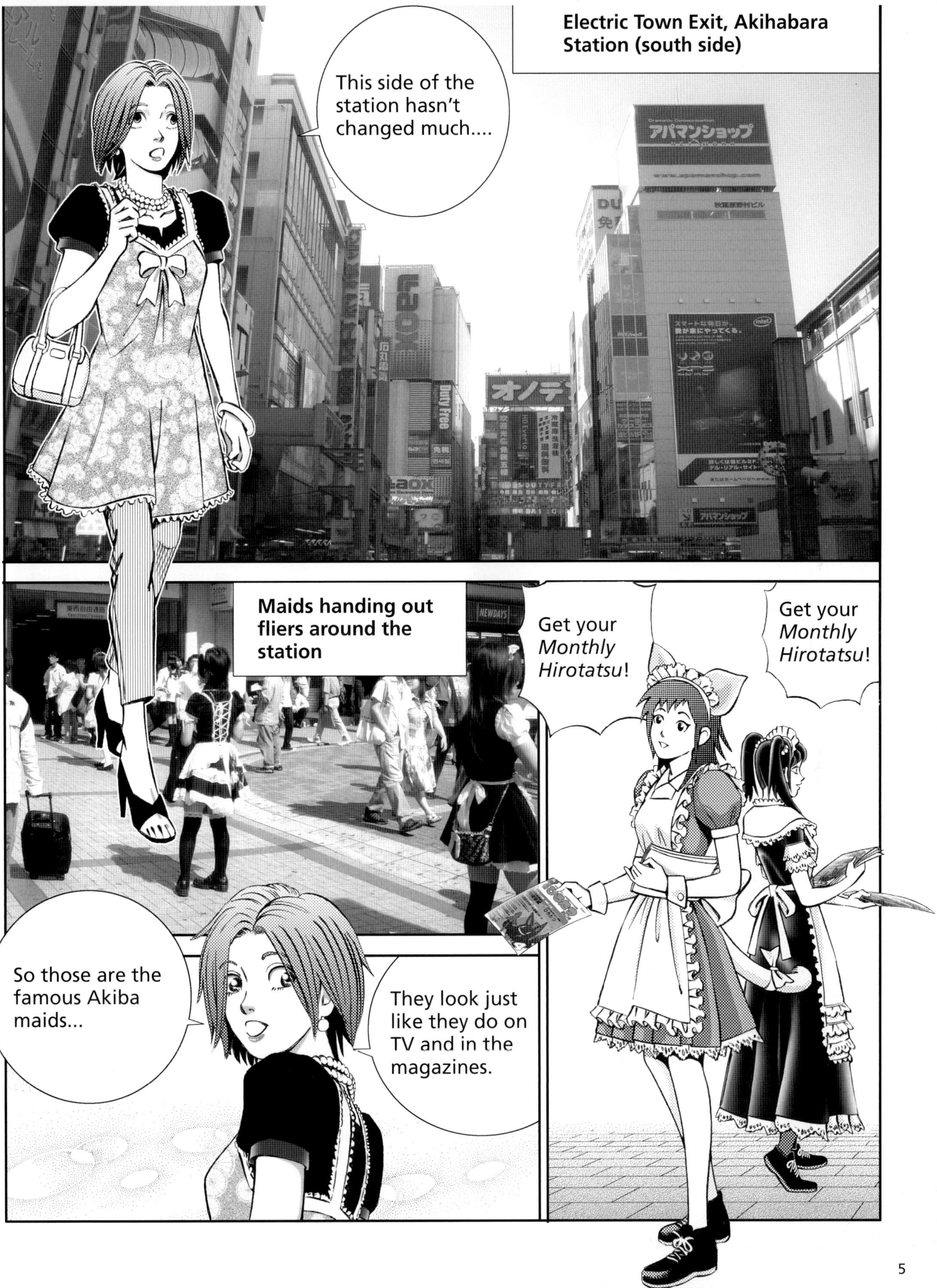

Electric Town Exit, Akihabara Station (south side)
This side of the station hasn't changed much....
Maids handing out fliers around the station
So those are the famous Akiba maids...
They look just like they do on TV and in the magazines.
Get your *Monthly Hirotatsu*!
Get your *Monthly Hirotatsu*!

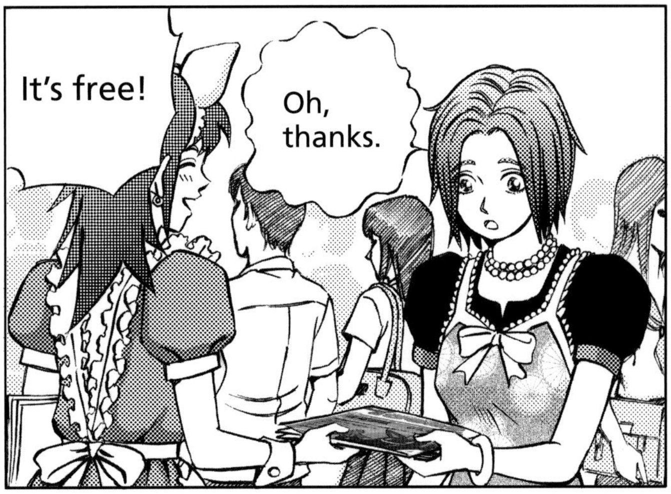
It's free!
Oh, thanks.

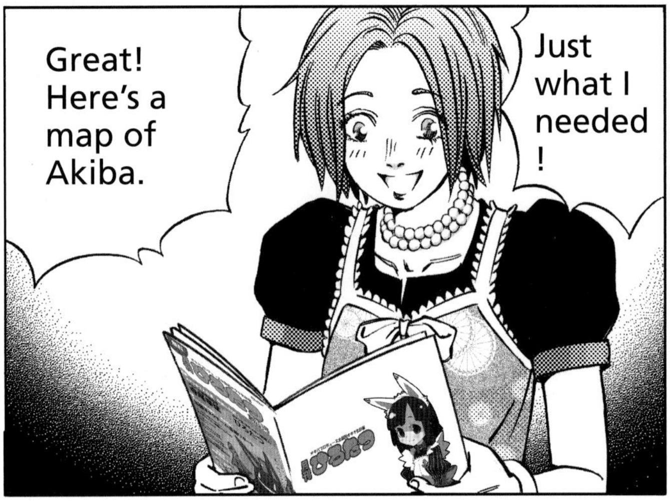
Great! Here's a map of Akiba.
Just what I needed!

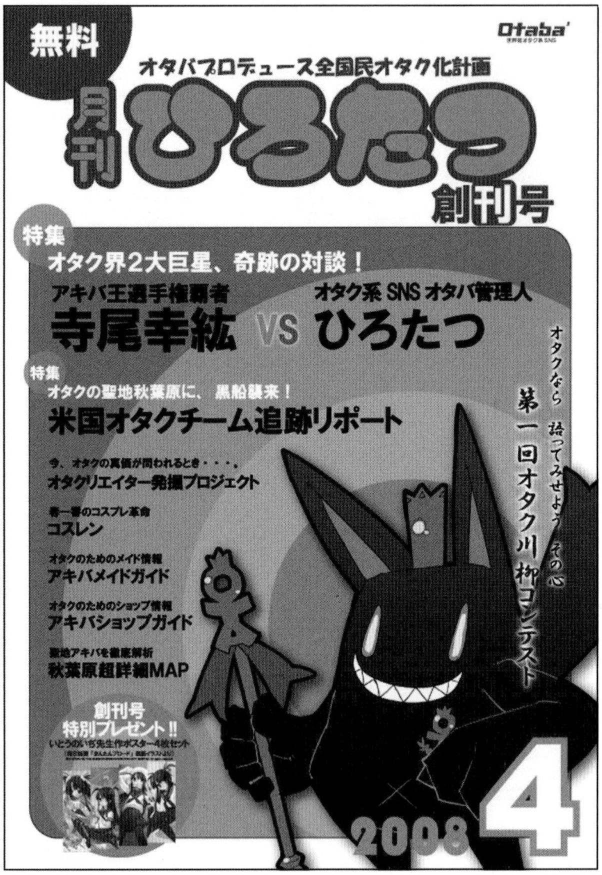
無料
Otaba'
オタバプロデュース全国民オタク化計画
月刊
ひろたつ
創刊号
特集
オタク界2大巨星、奇跡の対談！
アキバ王選手権覇者
寺尾幸紘
VS
オタク系 SNS オタバ管理人
ひろたつ
特集
オタクの聖地秋葉原に、黒船襲来！
米国オタクチーム追跡リポート
オタクリエイター発掘プロジェクト
コスレン
アキバメイドガイド
アキバショップガイド
秋葉原超詳細MAP
創刊号
特別プレゼント!!
オタクなら 語ってみせよう その心
第一回オタク川柳コンテスト
2008
4

Monthly Hirotatsu: A free newspaper promoting Akihabara's special dynamism and the maid culture published by Otaba, Inc., the world's first social networking service for otaku.

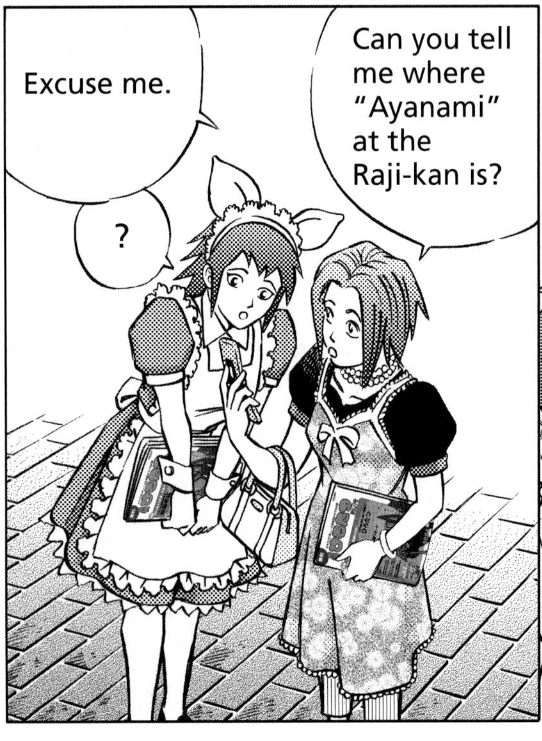
Excuse me.
Can you tell me where "Ayanami" at the Raji-kan is?
?

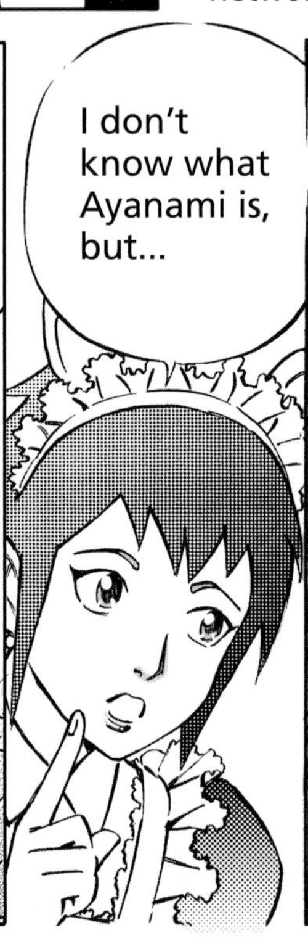
I don't know what Ayanami is, but...

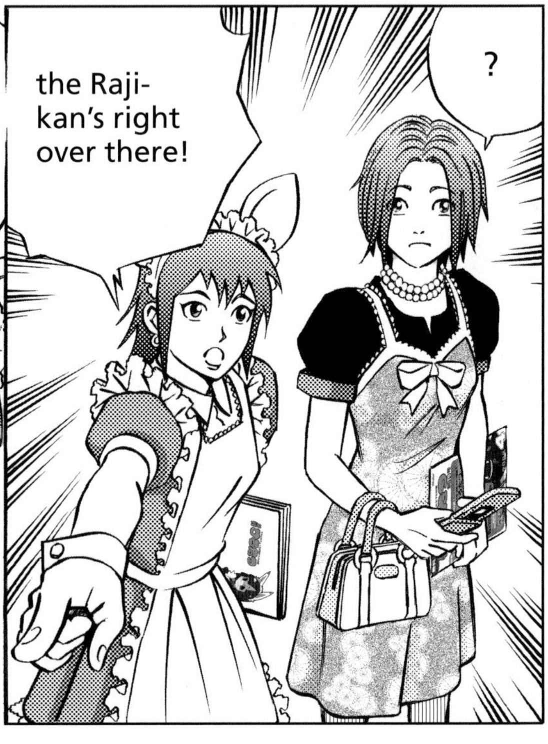
the Raji-kan's right over there!
?

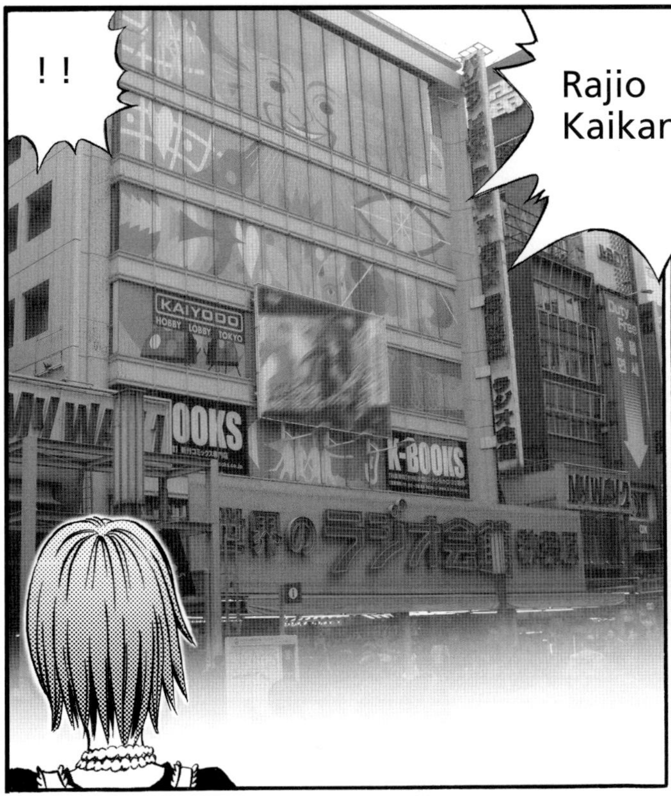
! !
Rajio Kaikan!?
KAIYODO
HOBBY LOBBY TOKYO
K-BOOKS

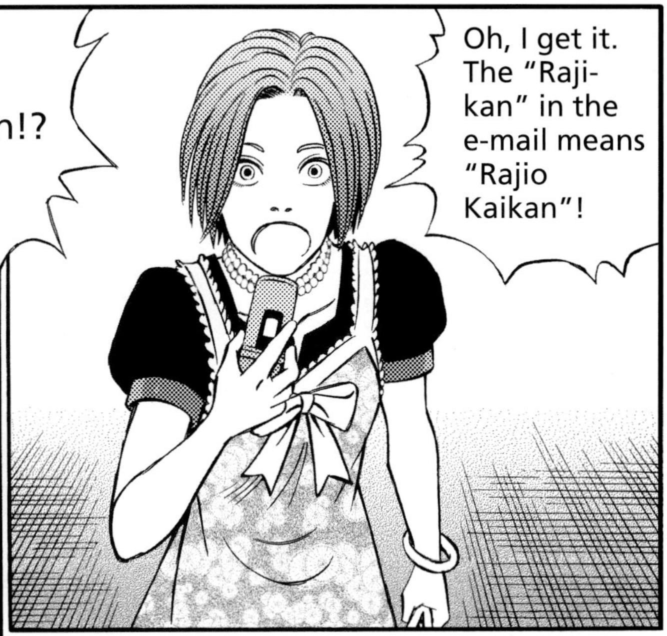
Oh, I get it. The "Raji-kan" in the e-mail means "Rajio Kaikan"!

Rajio Kaikan (Radio Hall) is the building that's right in front of you when you come out of the Electric Town Exit of Akihabara Station. Younger Japanese abbreviate "Rajio Kaikan" to "Raji-kan."

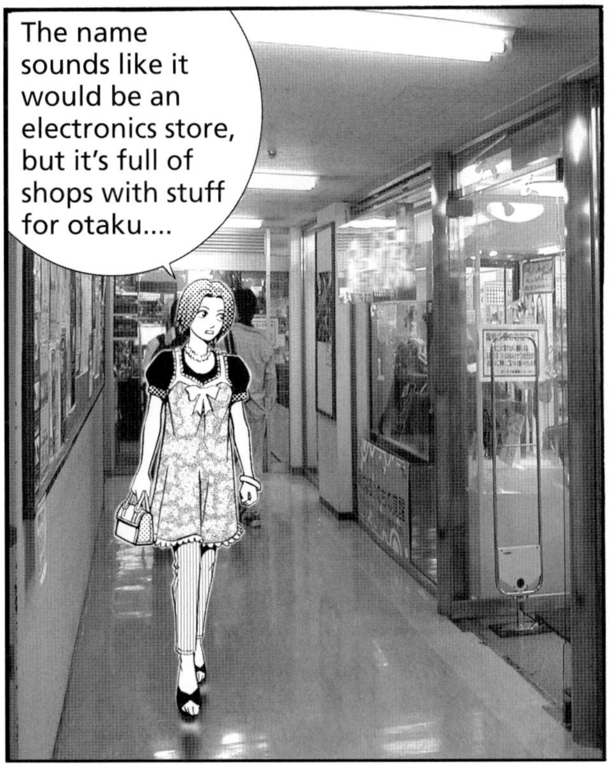
The name sounds like it would be an electronics store, but it's full of shops with stuff for otaku....

This building used to have lots of electronics specialty shops, but in 2000 a number of otaku specialty stores, including figure shops and manga bookstores, moved in.

K-BOOKS
(3rd floor)
Besides new and used manga and *dojin-shi* (self-published manga), K-BOOKS sells *anime*-related items as well.

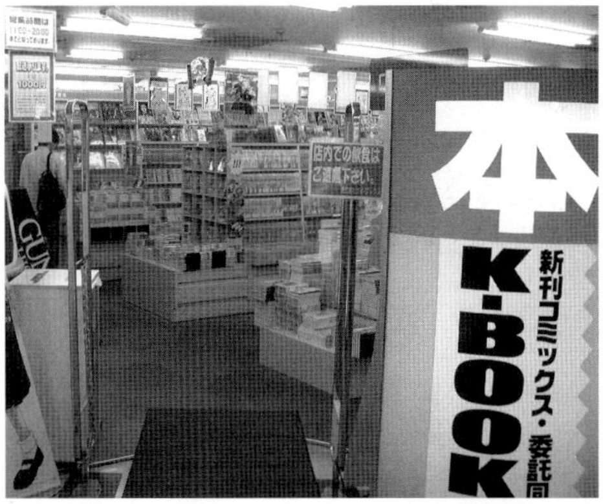
本
K-BOOK

Yellow Submarine
(4th & 7th floors)
This hobby shop sells figures, character items, game items and more.

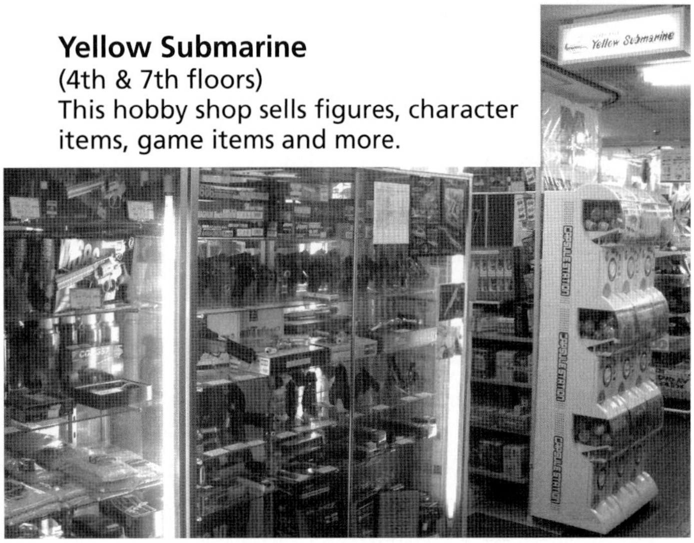
Yellow Submarine

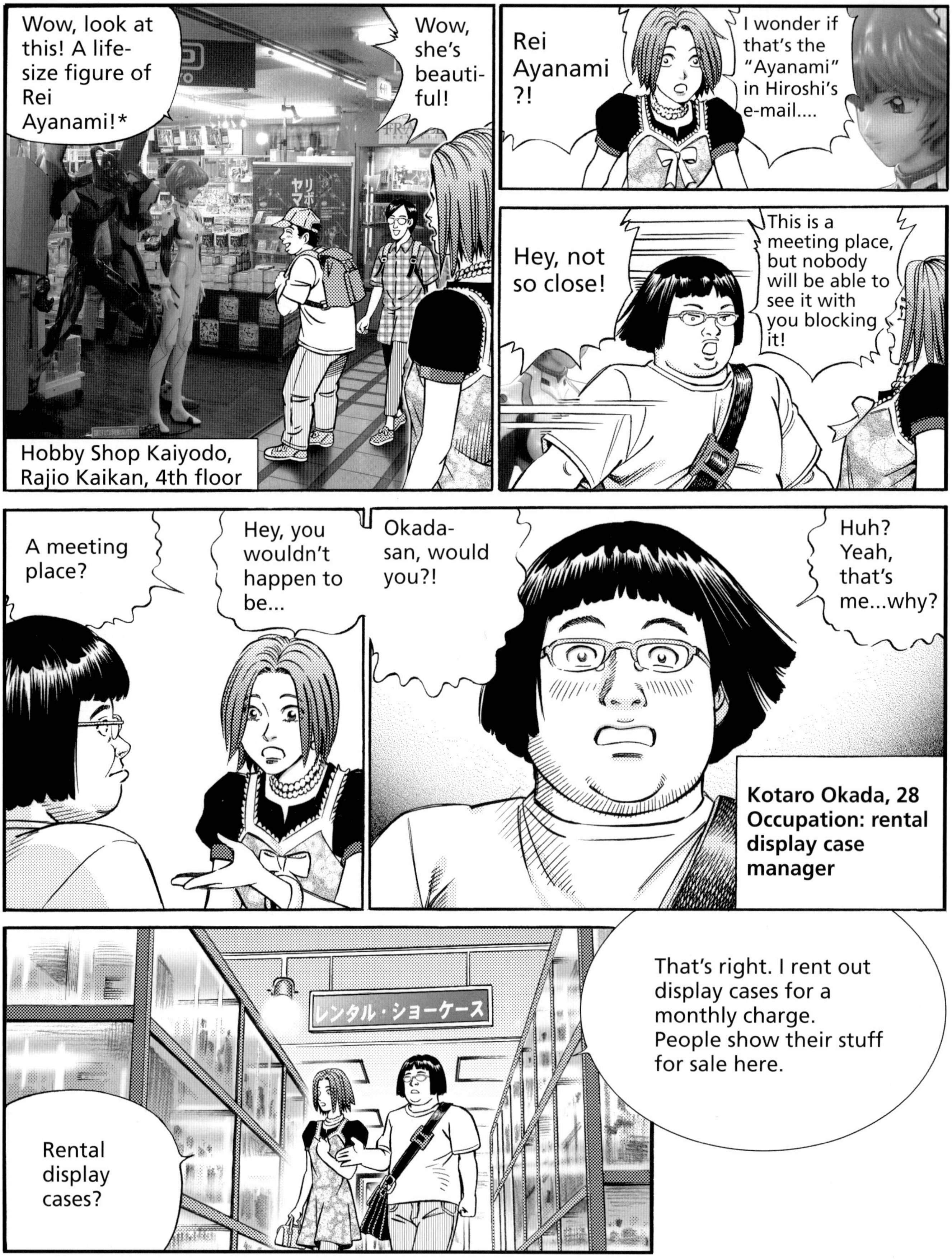
Wow, look at this! A life-size figure of Rei Ayanami!*
Wow, she's beauti-ful!
Hobby Shop Kaiyodo, Rajio Kaikan, 4th floor
Rei Ayanami ?!
I wonder if that's the "Ayanami" in Hiroshi's e-mail....
Hey, not so close!
This is a meeting place, but nobody will be able to see it with you blocking it!
A meeting place?
Hey, you wouldn't happen to be...
Okada-san, would you?!
Huh? Yeah, that's me...why?
Kotaro Okada, 28
Occupation: rental display case manager
Rental display cases?
レンタル・ショーケース
That's right. I rent out display cases for a monthly charge. People show their stuff for sale here.

* Rei Ayanami: A *bishojo* character appearing in the popular Japanese *anime Neon Genesis Evangelion.* ©GAINAX

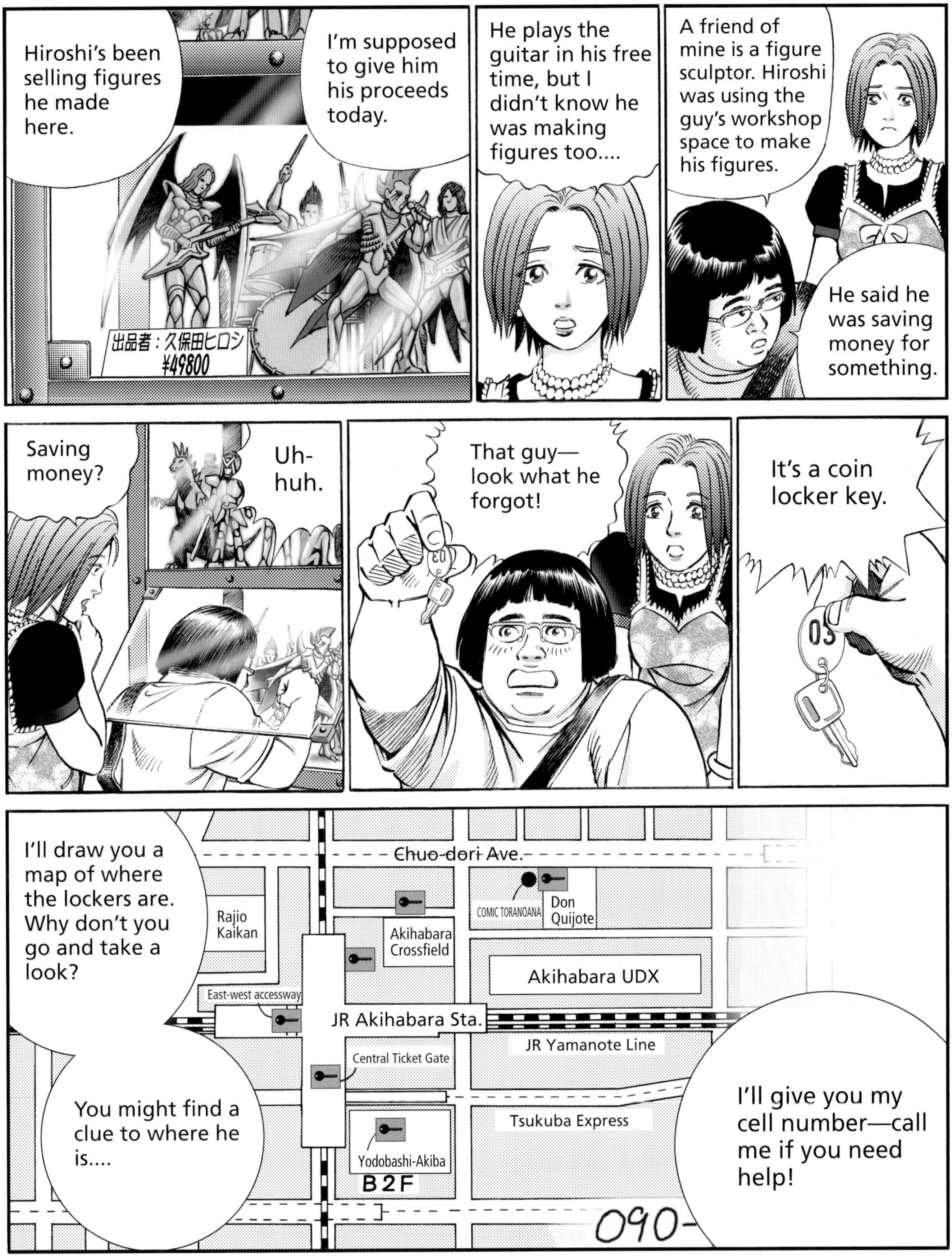
Hiroshi's been selling figures he made here.
I'm supposed to give him his proceeds today.
出品者：久保田ヒロシ ¥49800
He plays the guitar in his free time, but I didn't know he was making figures too....
A friend of mine is a figure sculptor. Hiroshi was using the guy's workshop space to make his figures.
He said he was saving money for something.
Saving money?
Uh-huh.
That guy—look what he forgot!
It's a coin locker key.
I'll draw you a map of where the lockers are. Why don't you go and take a look?
You might find a clue to where he is....
Chuo-dori Ave.
COMIC TORANOANA
Don Quijote
Rajio Kaikan
Akihabara Crossfield
Akihabara UDX
East-west accessway
JR Akihabara Sta.
JR Yamanote Line
Central Ticket Gate
Tsukuba Express
Yodobashi-Akiba
B2F
I'll give you my cell number—call me if you need help!
090-

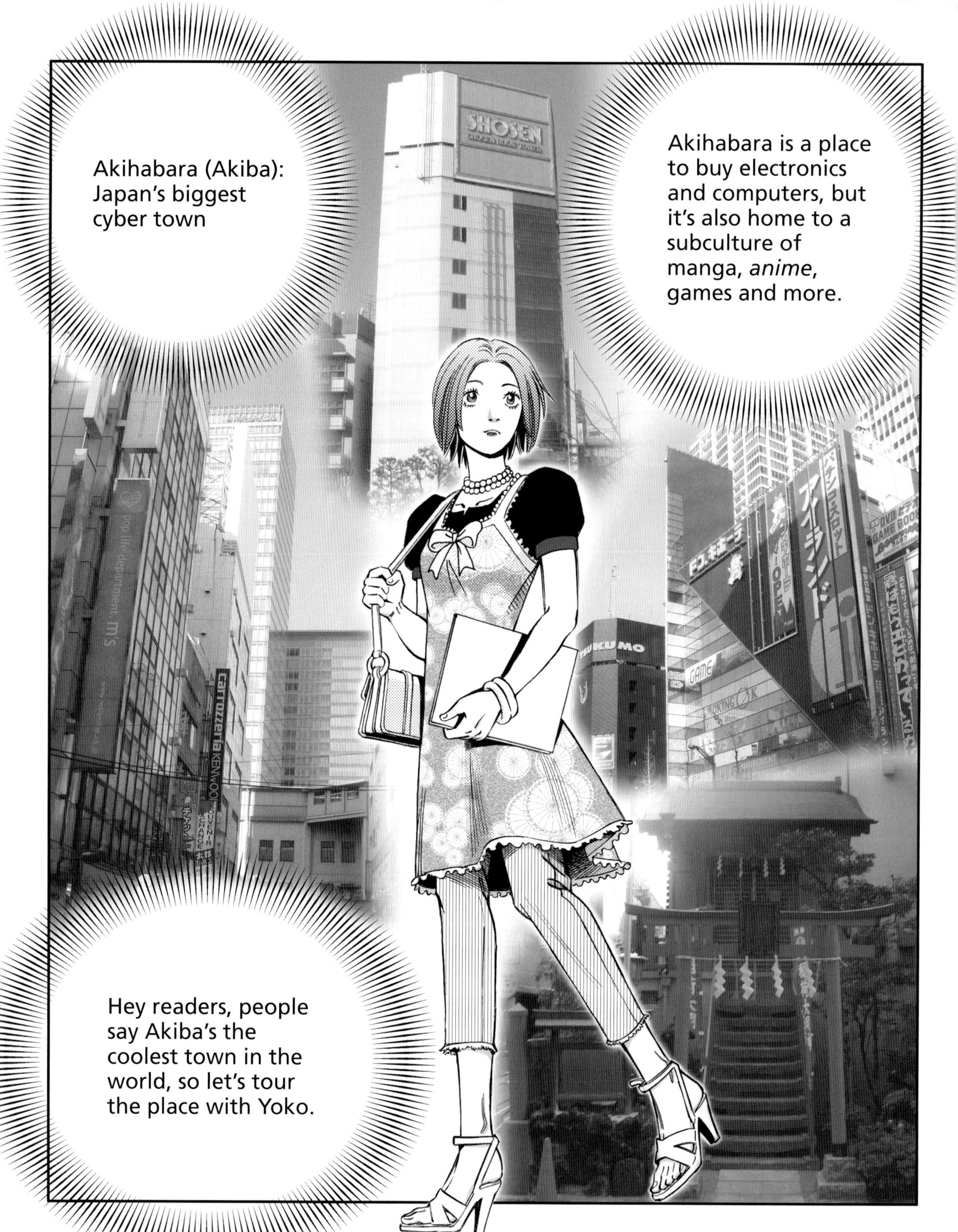
Akihabara (Akiba): Japan's biggest cyber town
Akihabara is a place to buy electronics and computers, but it's also home to a subculture of manga, *anime*, games and more.
SHOSEN
TSUKUMO
Hey readers, people say Akiba's the coolest town in the world, so let's tour the place with Yoko.

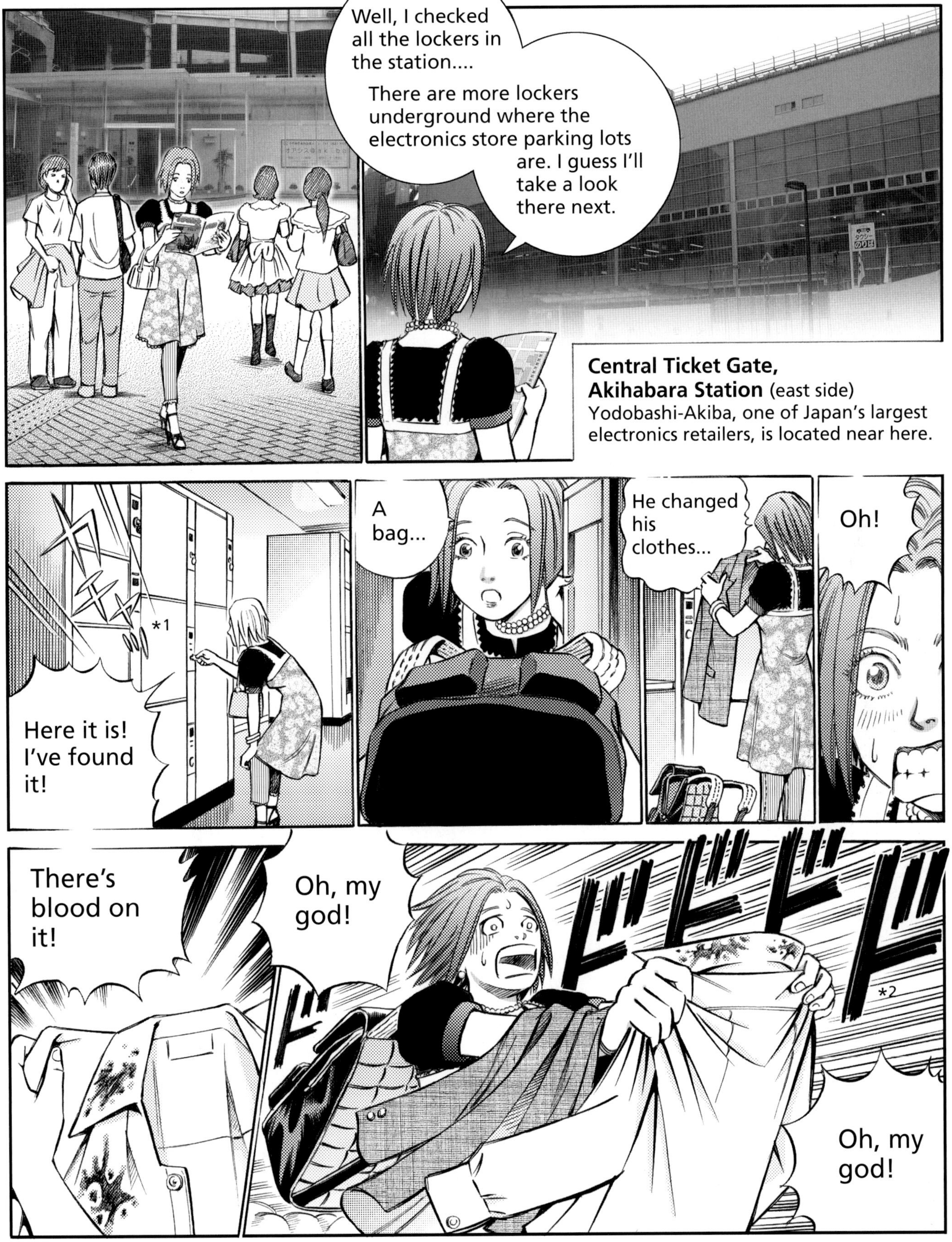
Well, I checked all the lockers in the station....
There are more lockers underground where the electronics store parking lots are. I guess I'll take a look there next.
Central Ticket Gate, Akihabara Station (east side)
Yodobashi-Akiba, one of Japan's largest electronics retailers, is located near here.
*1
Here it is! I've found it!
A bag...
He changed his clothes...
Oh!
There's blood on it!
Oh, my god!
*2
Oh, my god!

*1 Click, click
*2 Sound of running

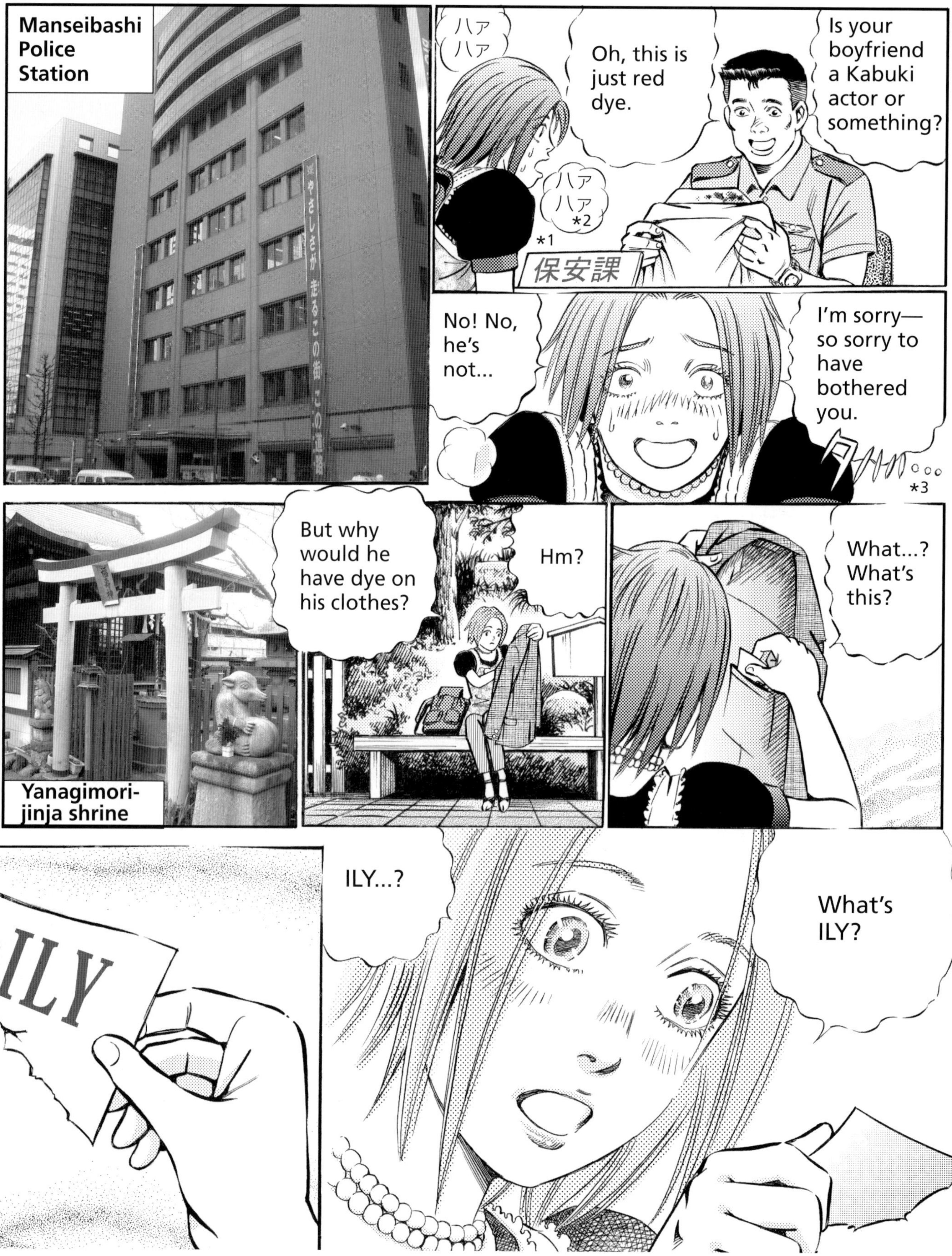
Manseibashi Police Station
やさしさが走るこの街この道路
ハァハァ
Oh, this is just red dye.
Is your boyfriend a Kabuki actor or something?
ハァハァ *2
*1
保安課
No! No, he's not...
I'm sorry— so sorry to have bothered you.
タハハ *3
Yanagimori-jinja shrine
But why would he have dye on his clothes?
Hm?
What...? What's this?
ILY
ILY...?
What's ILY?

*1 Security Section
*2 Huffing and puffing
*3 He-he

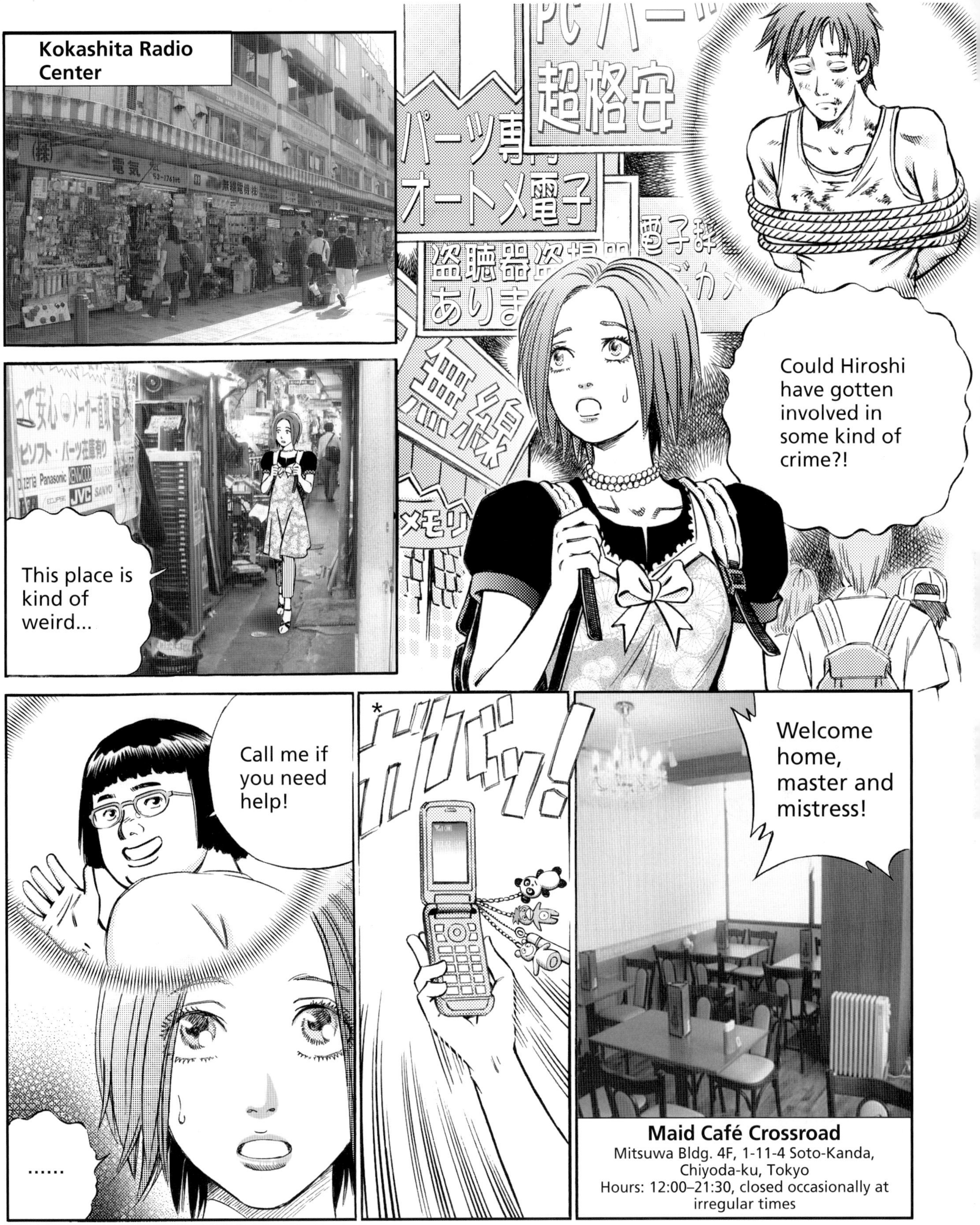
Kokashita Radio Center
This place is kind of weird...
Could Hiroshi have gotten involved in some kind of crime?!
Call me if you need help!
......
*
Welcome home, master and mistress!
Maid Café Crossroad
Mitsuwa Bldg. 4F, 1-11-4 Soto-Kanda, Chiyoda-ku, Tokyo
Hours: 12:00–21:30, closed occasionally at irregular times

* Clack!

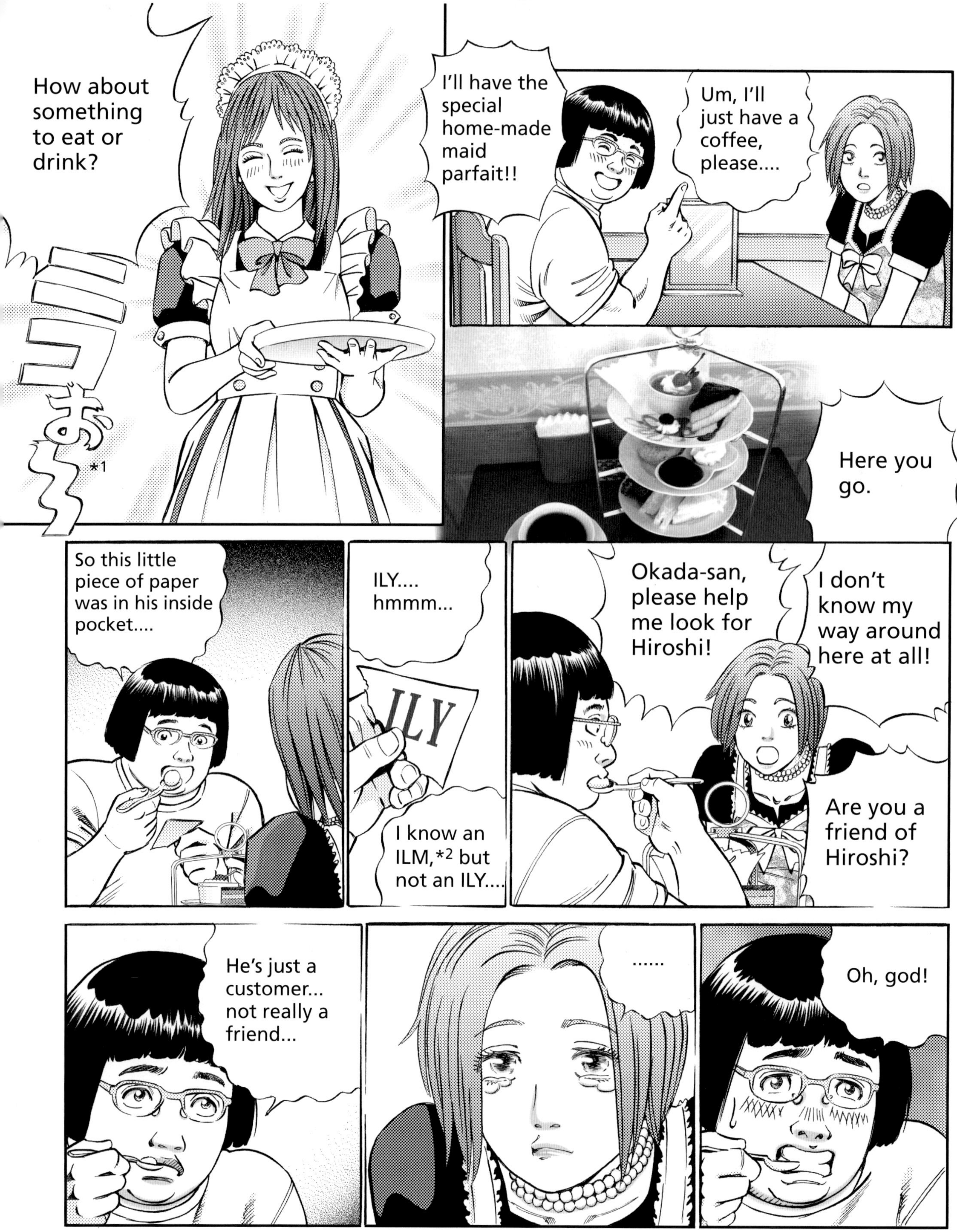
How about something to eat or drink?
ニコぉ〜 *1
I'll have the special home-made maid parfait!!
Um, I'll just have a coffee, please....
Here you go.
So this little piece of paper was in his inside pocket....
ILY.... hmmm...
ILY
I know an ILM,*2 but not an ILY....
Okada-san, please help me look for Hiroshi!
I don't know my way around here at all!
Are you a friend of Hiroshi?
He's just a customer... not really a friend...
......
Oh, god!

*1 Big smile
*2 ILM: Industrial Light & Magic. A U.S. special effects company

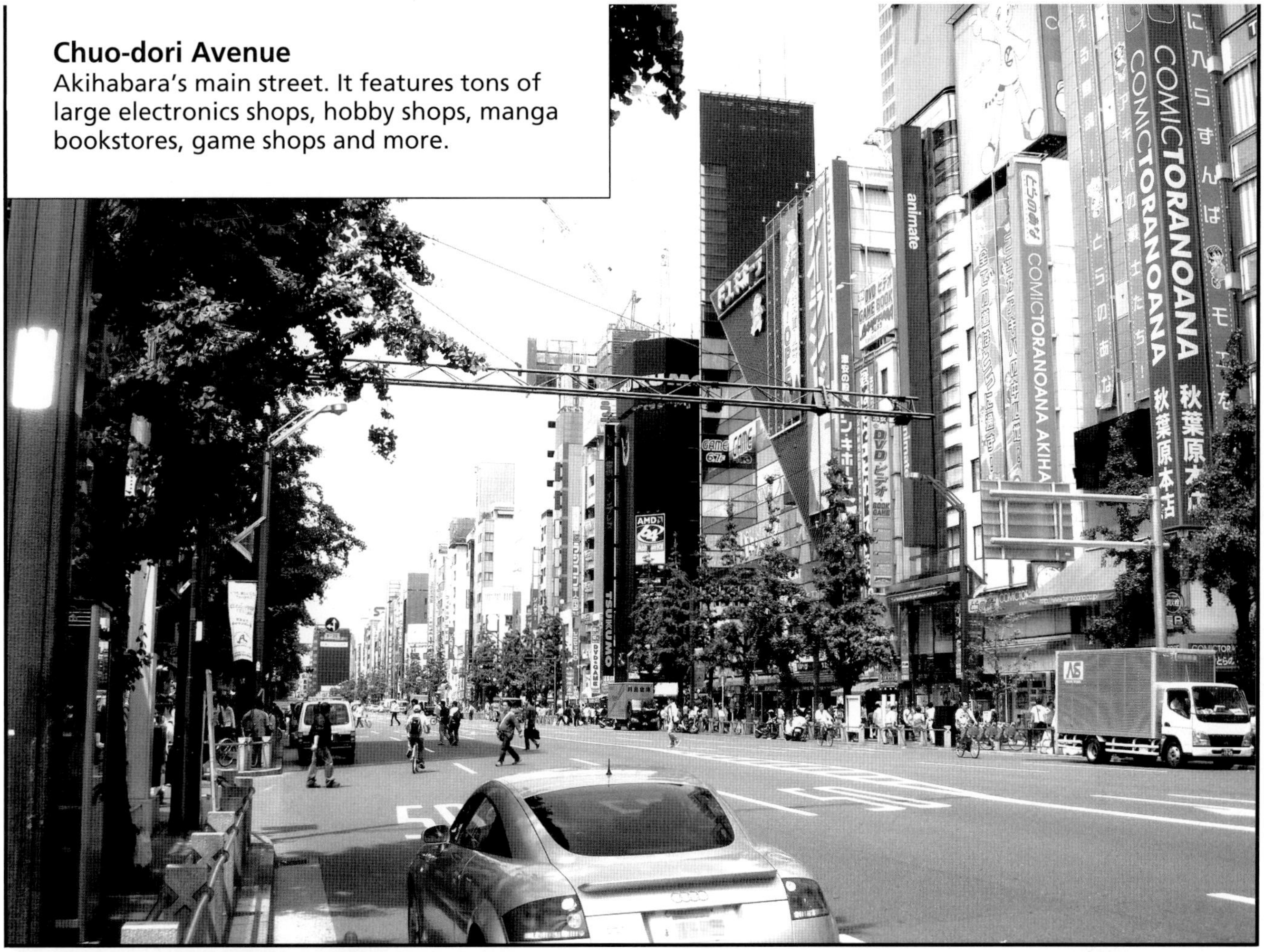
Chuo-dori Avenue
Akihabara's main street. It features tons of large electronics shops, hobby shops, manga bookstores, game shops and more.
animate
COMICTORANOANA
秋葉原本店

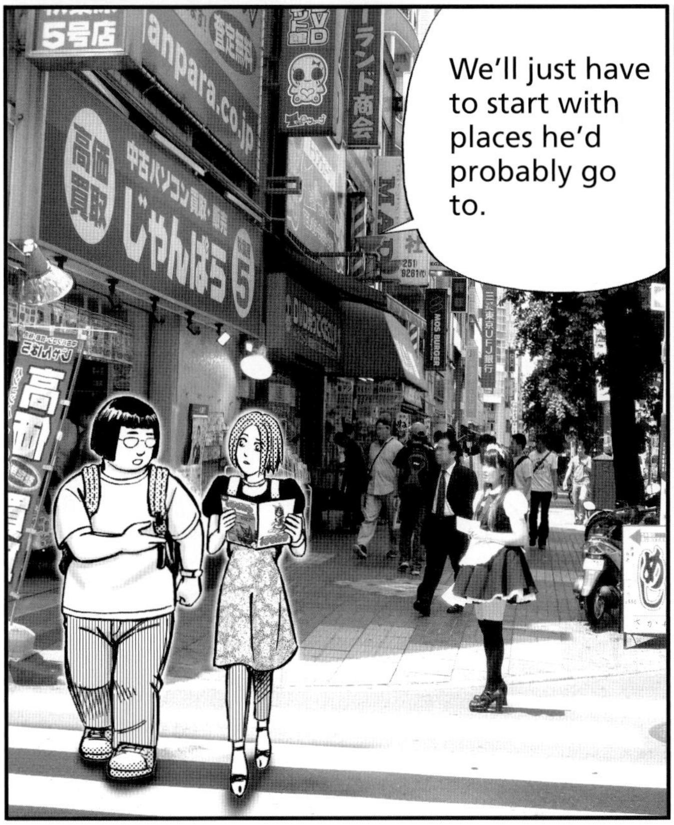
5号店
じゃんぱら
We'll just have to start with places he'd probably go to.

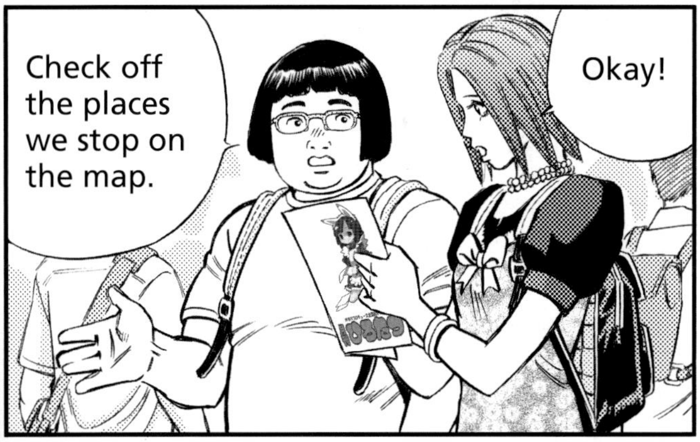
Check off the places we stop on the map.
Okay!

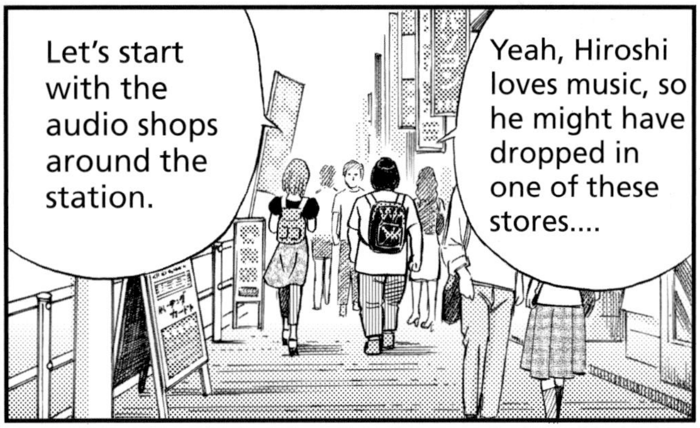
Let's start with the audio shops around the station.
Yeah, Hiroshi loves music, so he might have dropped in one of these stores....

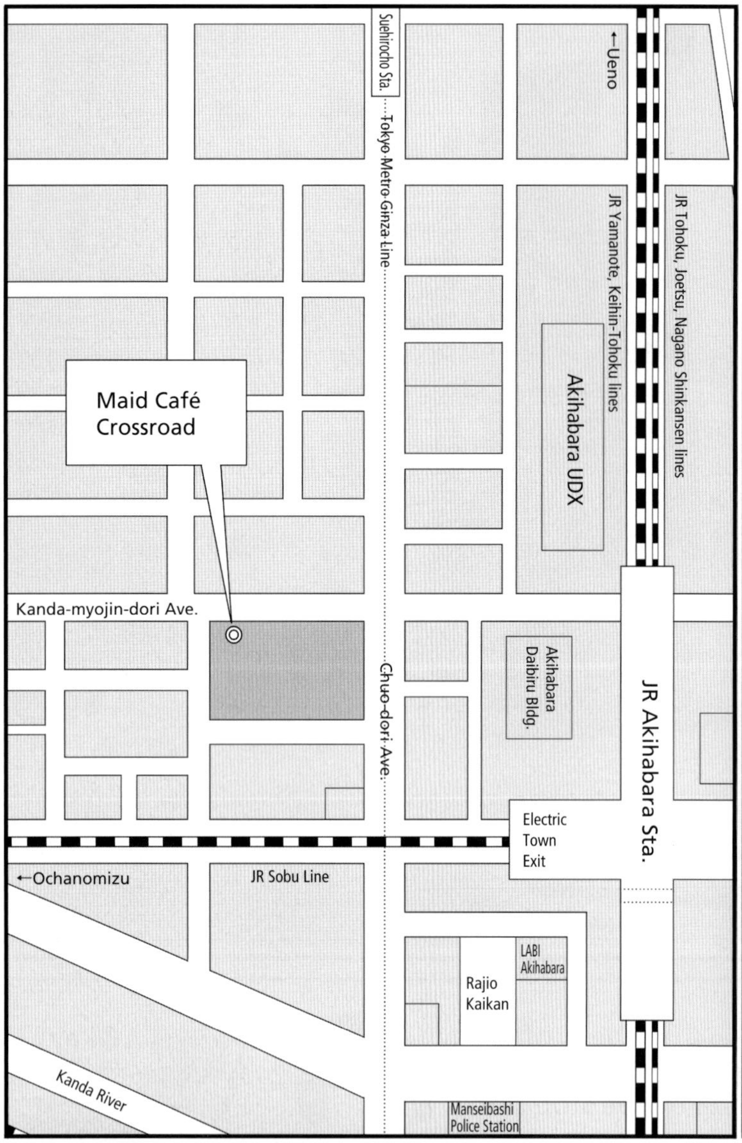
Suehirocho Sta.
Tokyo Metro Ginza Line
←Ueno
JR Yamanote, Keihin-Tohoku lines
JR Tohoku, Joetsu, Nagano Shinkansen lines
Akihabara UDX
Maid Café
Crossroad
Kanda-myojin-dori Ave.
Akihabara
Daibiru Bldg.
Chuo-dori Ave.
JR Akihabara Sta.
Electric
Town
Exit
←Ochanomizu
JR Sobu Line
LABI
Akihabara
Rajio
Kaikan
Kanda River
Manseibashi
Police Station

Consistent with its reputation as a great place to buy electronics, Akihabara has numerous audio equipment shops, but there are surprisingly few stores selling musical instruments. These tend to be near Ochanomizu Station, the next station over from Akihabara.

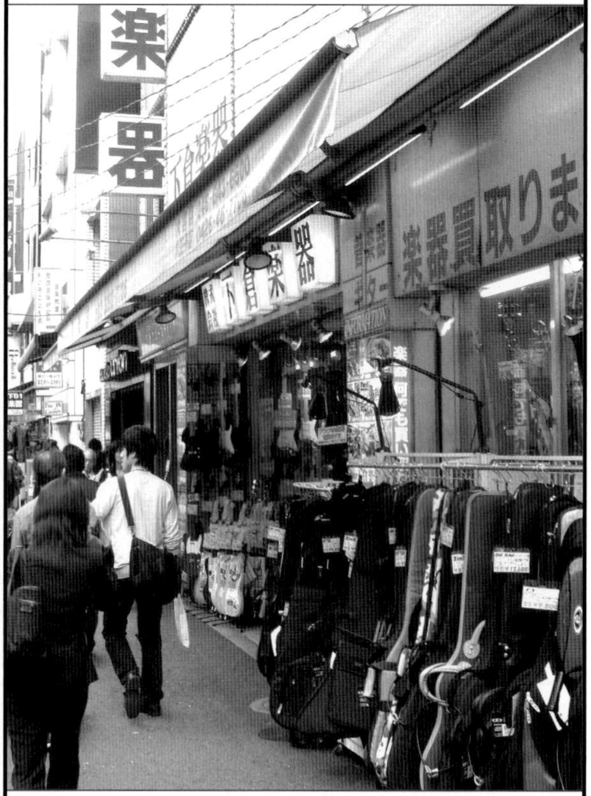

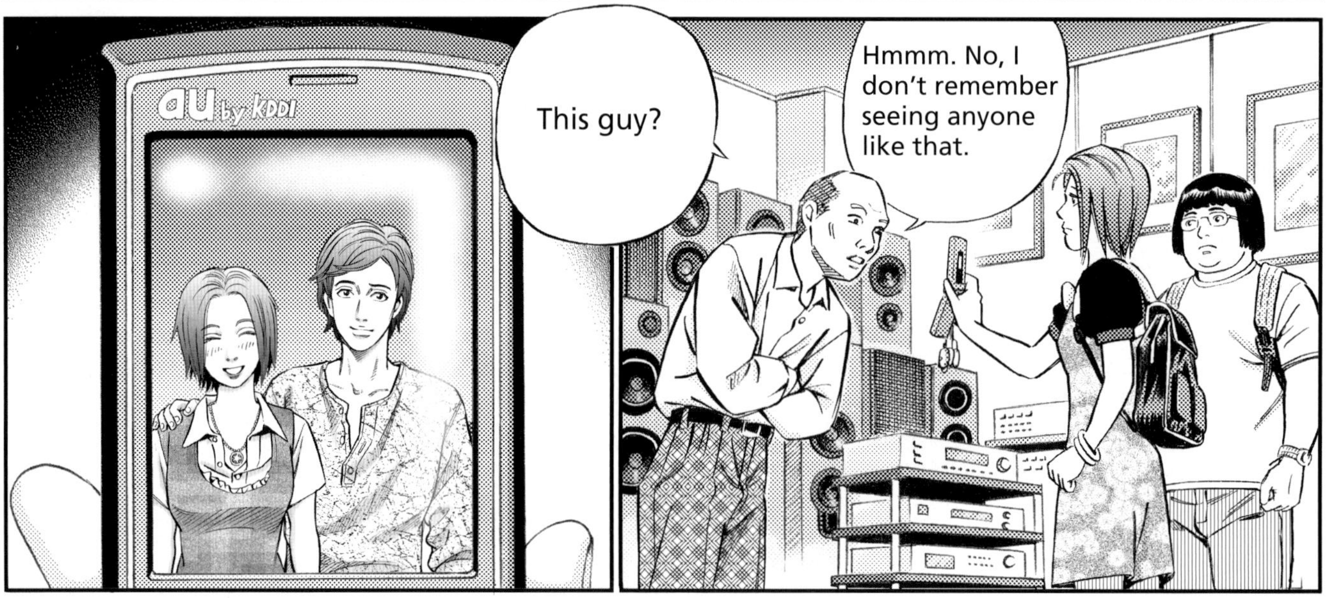
au by KDDI
This guy?
Hmmm. No, I don't remember seeing anyone like that.

Many young Japanese use a favorite photo or picture for their cell phone standby screen.

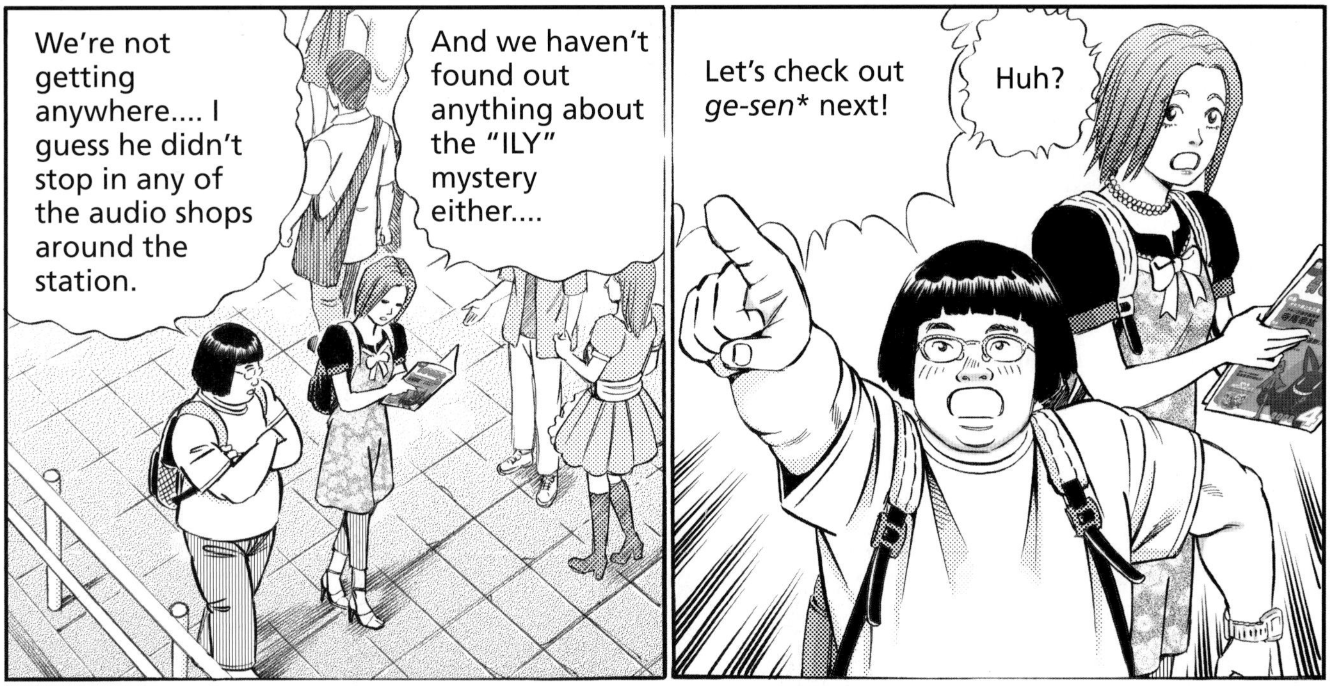
We're not getting anywhere.... I guess he didn't stop in any of the audio shops around the station.
And we haven't found out anything about the "ILY" mystery either....
Let's check out *ge-sen** next!
Huh?

↓ Club Sega
It's an old, established arcade along Chuo-dori Avenue.

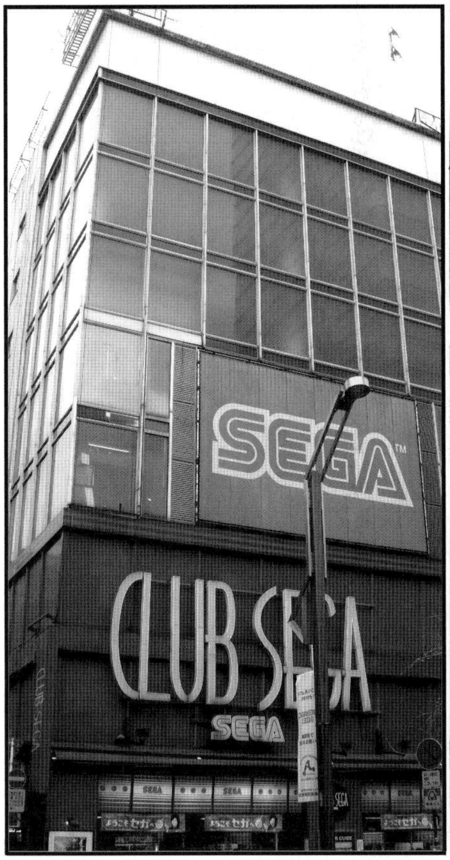
SEGA
CLUB SEGA
SEGA

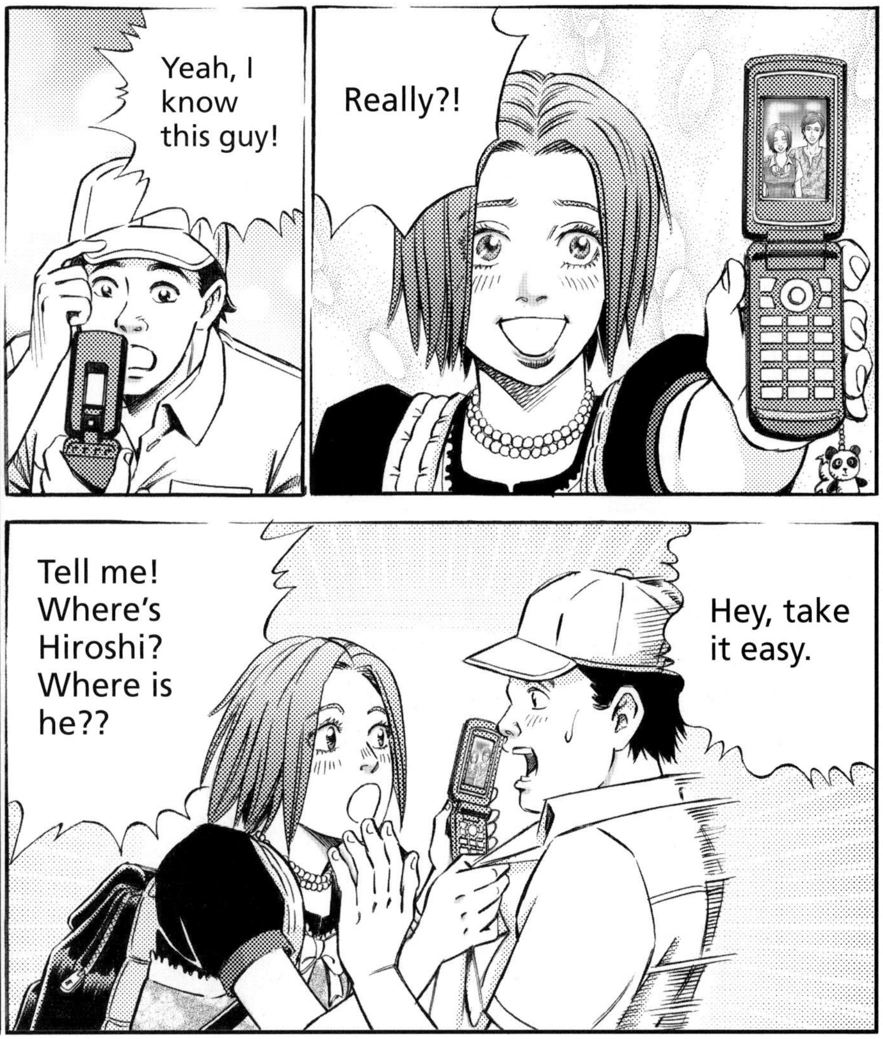
Yeah, I know this guy!
Really?!
Tell me! Where's Hiroshi? Where is he??
Hey, take it easy.

* Younger Japanese tend to shorten "game center," pronounced *"geimu senta"* in Japanese, to *"ge-sen."*

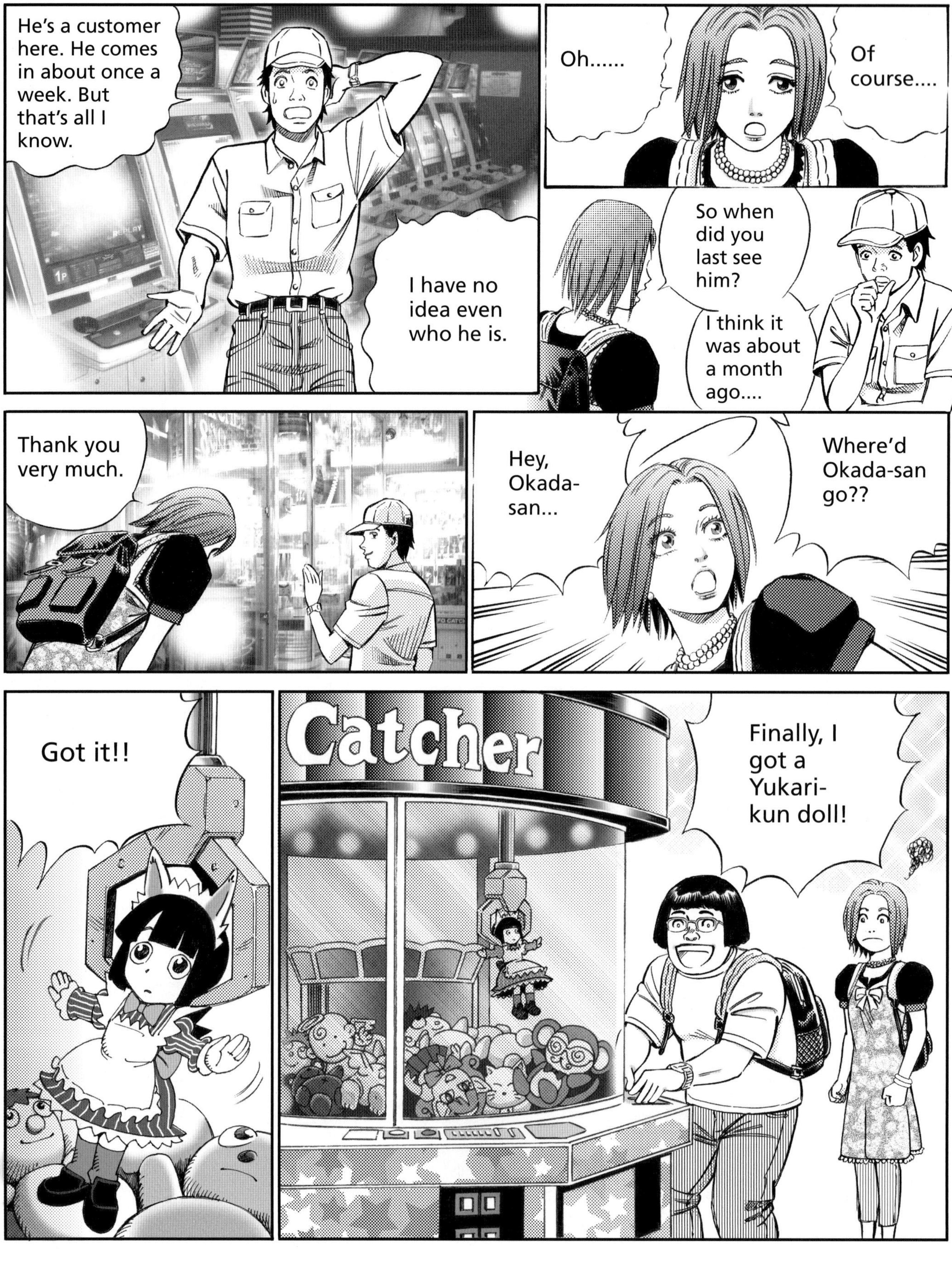
He's a customer here. He comes in about once a week. But that's all I know.
I have no idea even who he is.
Oh......
Of course....
So when did you last see him?
I think it was about a month ago....
Thank you very much.
Hey, Okada-san...
Where'd Okada-san go??
Got it!!
Catcher
Finally, I got a Yukari-kun doll!

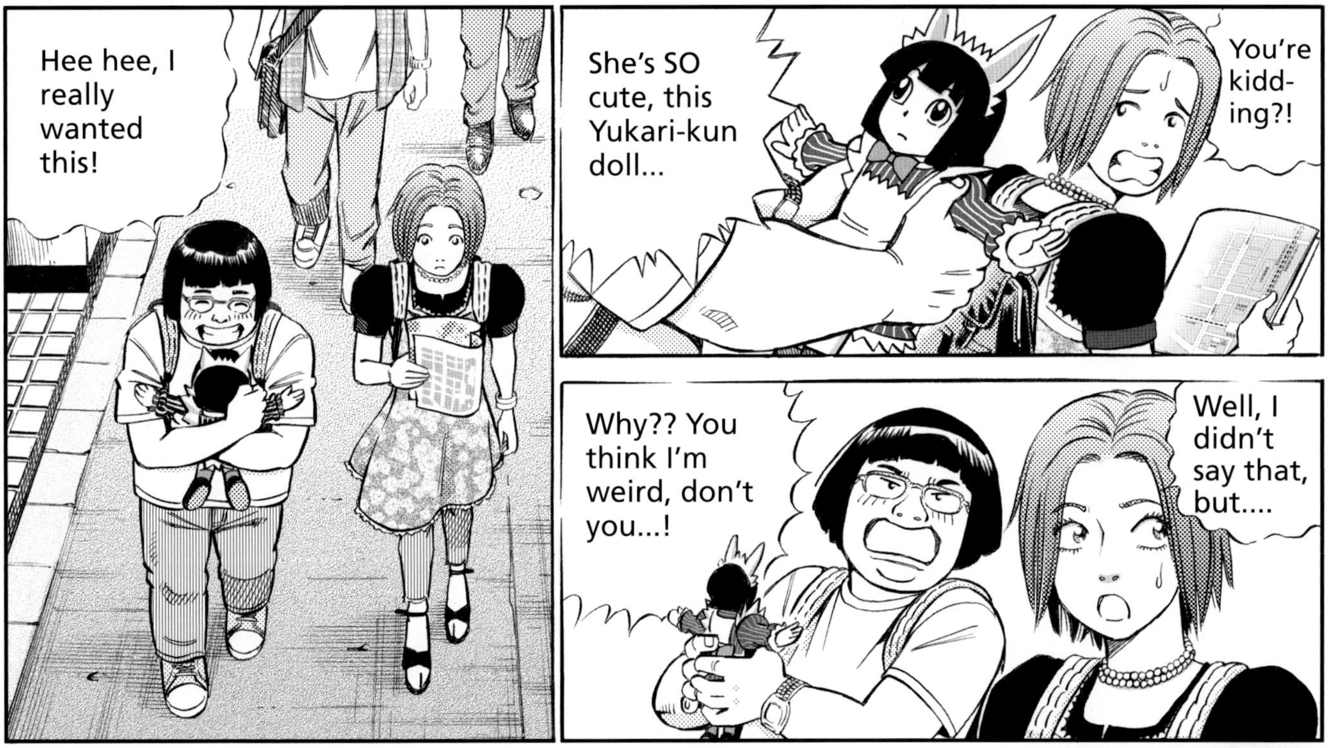
Hee hee, I really wanted this!
She's SO cute, this Yukari-kun doll...
You're kidd-ing?!
Why?? You think I'm weird, don't you...!
Well, I didn't say that, but....

↓ **COMIC TORANOANA**
A large retailer selling comic magazines, *dojinshi* (self-published manga), *anime* DVDs, CDs and more.
http://www.toranoana.co.jp

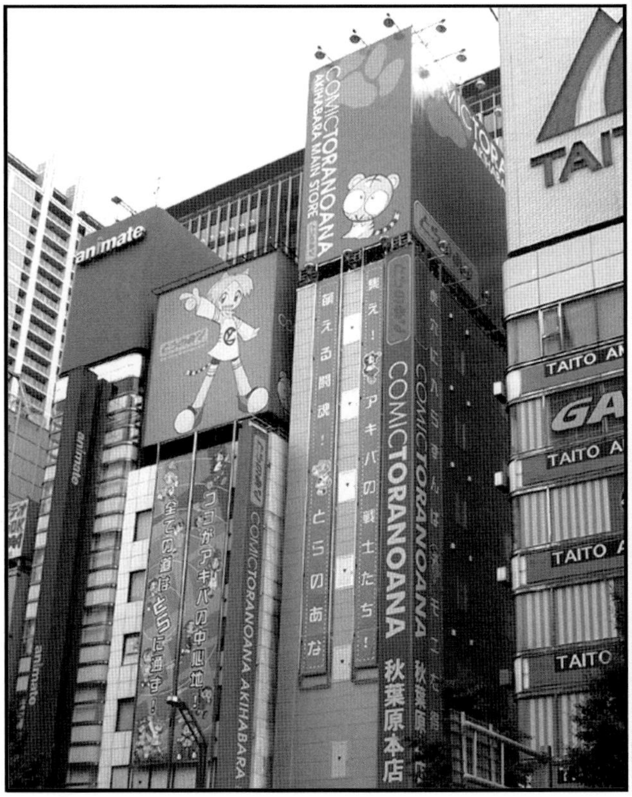
COMICTORANOANA
AKIHABARA MAIN STORE
animate
TAITO
COMICTORANOANA AKIHABARA
秋葉原本店

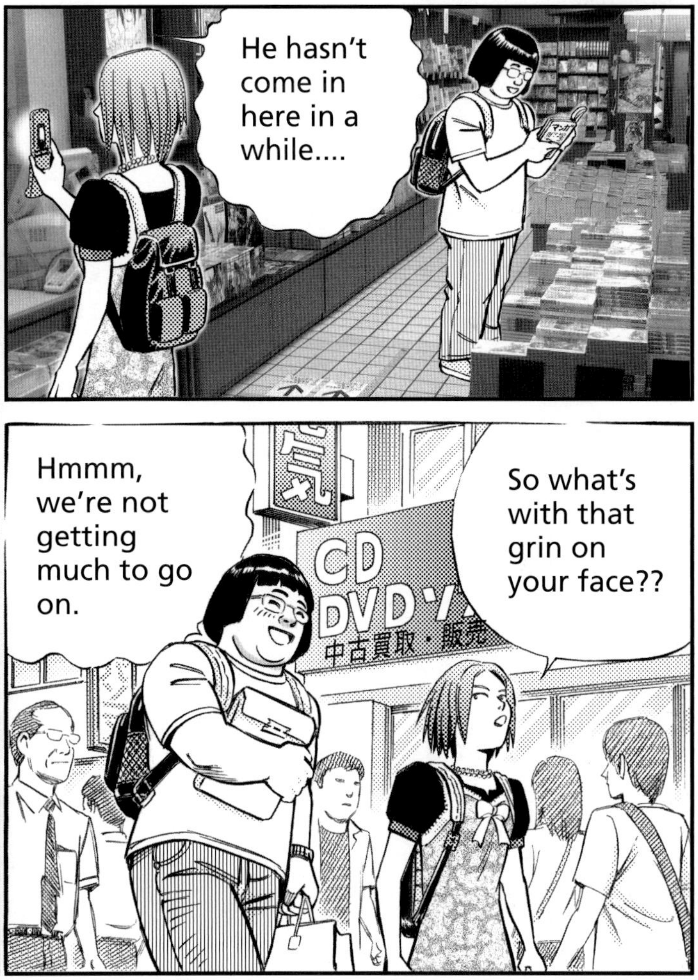
He hasn't come in here in a while....
Hmmm, we're not getting much to go on.
So what's with that grin on your face??
CD
DVD
中古買取・販売

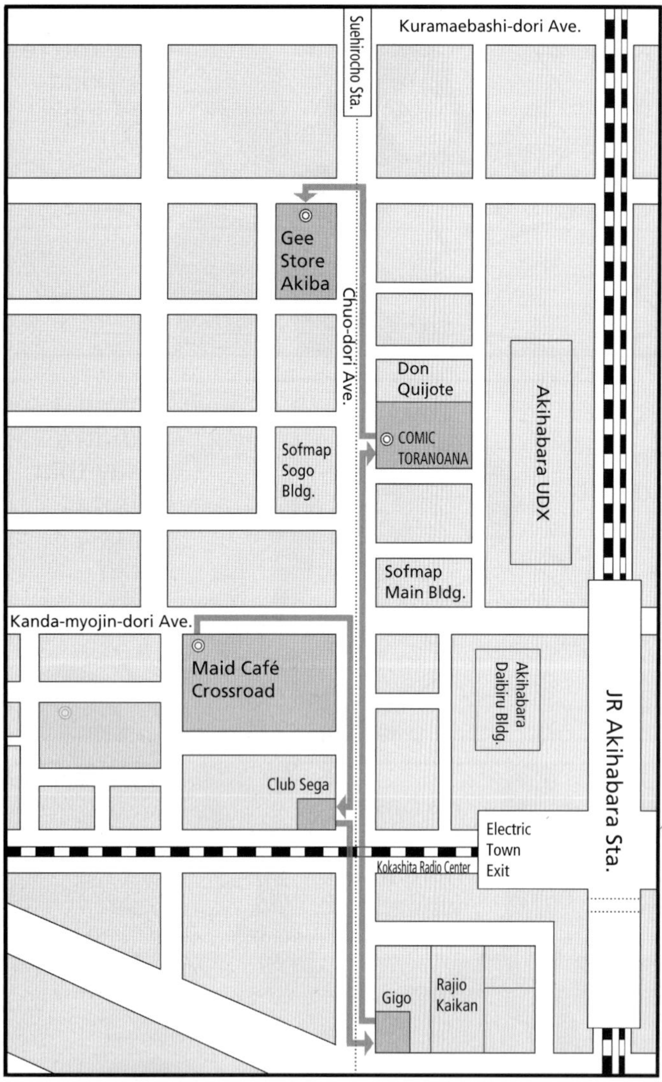
Suehirocho Sta.
Kuramaebashi-dori Ave.
Gee Store Akiba
Chuo-dori Ave.
Don Quijote
COMIC TORANOANA
Sofmap Sogo Bldg.
Akihabara UDX
Sofmap Main Bldg.
Kanda-myojin-dori Ave.
Maid Café Crossroad
Akihabara Daibiru Bldg.
JR Akihabara Sta.
Club Sega
Electric Town Exit
Kokashita Radio Center
Gigo
Rajio Kaikan

↓ **Gee Store Akiba**

Run by Cospa, manufacturer of character goods and apparel. The first floor features Gachapon Kaikan (Gachapon Hall), while the second to fifth floors house Cospa shops, figure shops and more. On the sixth floor is Cure Maid Café, a pioneer in the maid café business.

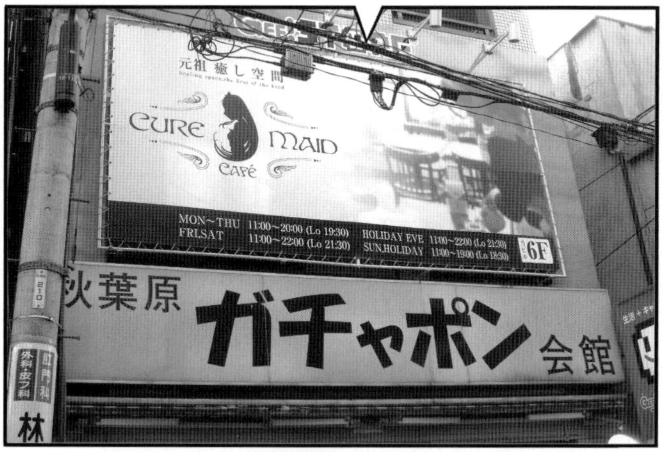
元祖癒し空間
CURE MAID CAFÉ
MON～THU 11:00～20:00 (Lo 19:30)
FRI.SAT 11:00～22:00 (Lo 21:30)
HOLIDAY EVE 11:00～22:00 (Lo 21:30)
SUN.HOLIDAY 11:00～19:00 (Lo 18:30)
6F
秋葉原
ガチャポン会館

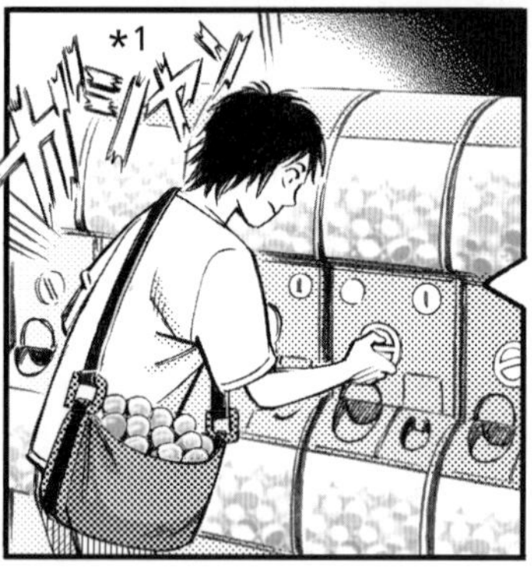
*1

Gachapon: These vending machines sell toys-in-a-capsule. Just put in a coin and pull the lever! Depending on the manufacturer, they're called *gachapon* or *gashapon*. Here at the Gachapon Kaikan, there are a total of more than 360 of these machines.

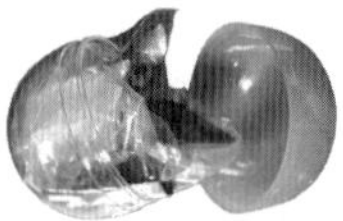

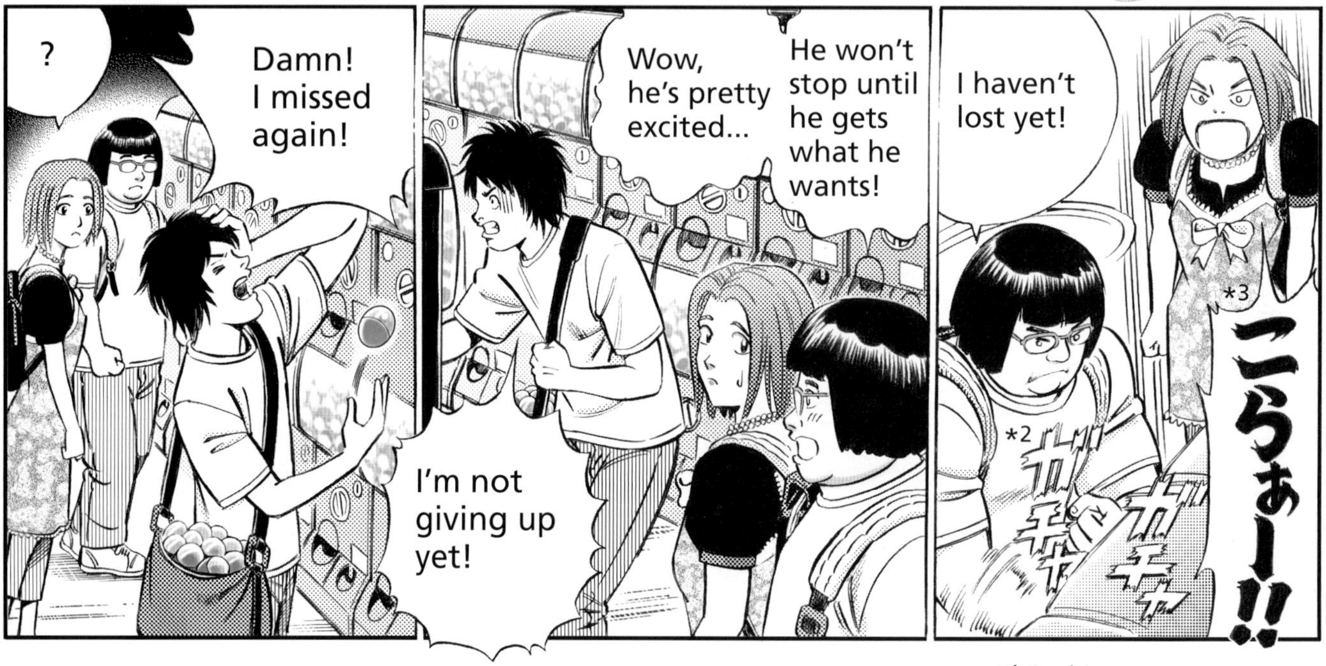
?
Damn! I missed again!
Wow, he's pretty excited...
He won't stop until he gets what he wants!
I'm not giving up yet!
I haven't lost yet!
*2
*3
こらぁー!!

*1 Crash!

*2 Clackety-clack!

*3 Hey!! What are you DOING?!

↓ **Cospa Gee Store Akiba**
Gee Store Akiba 2F. The specialty store offers character items from manga, *anime* and video games.

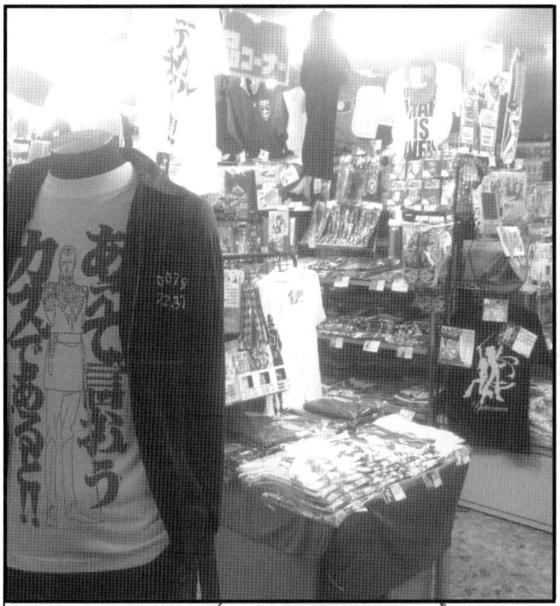

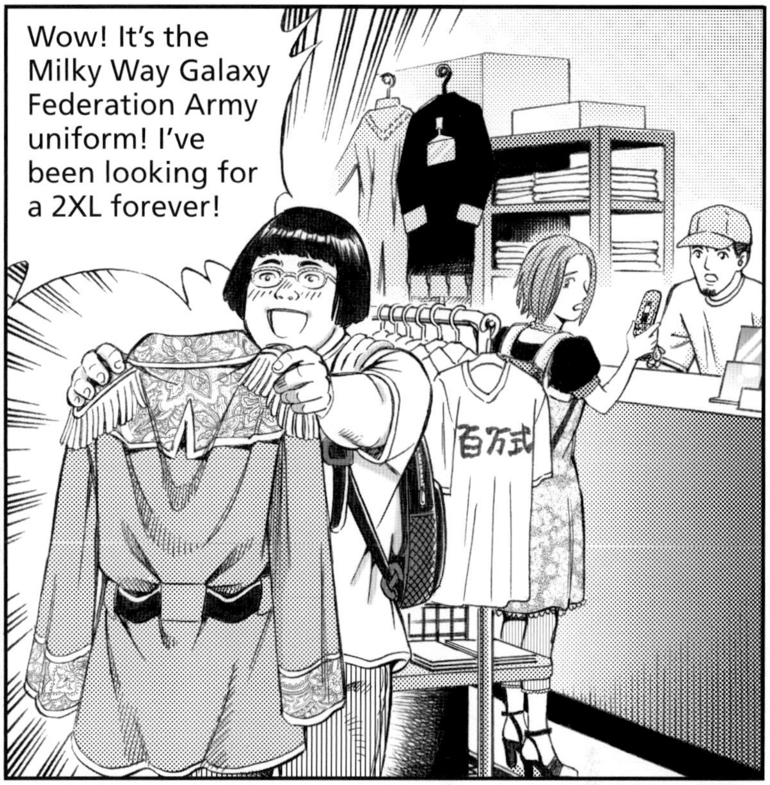
Wow! It's the Milky Way Galaxy Federation Army uniform! I've been looking for a 2XL forever!
百万式

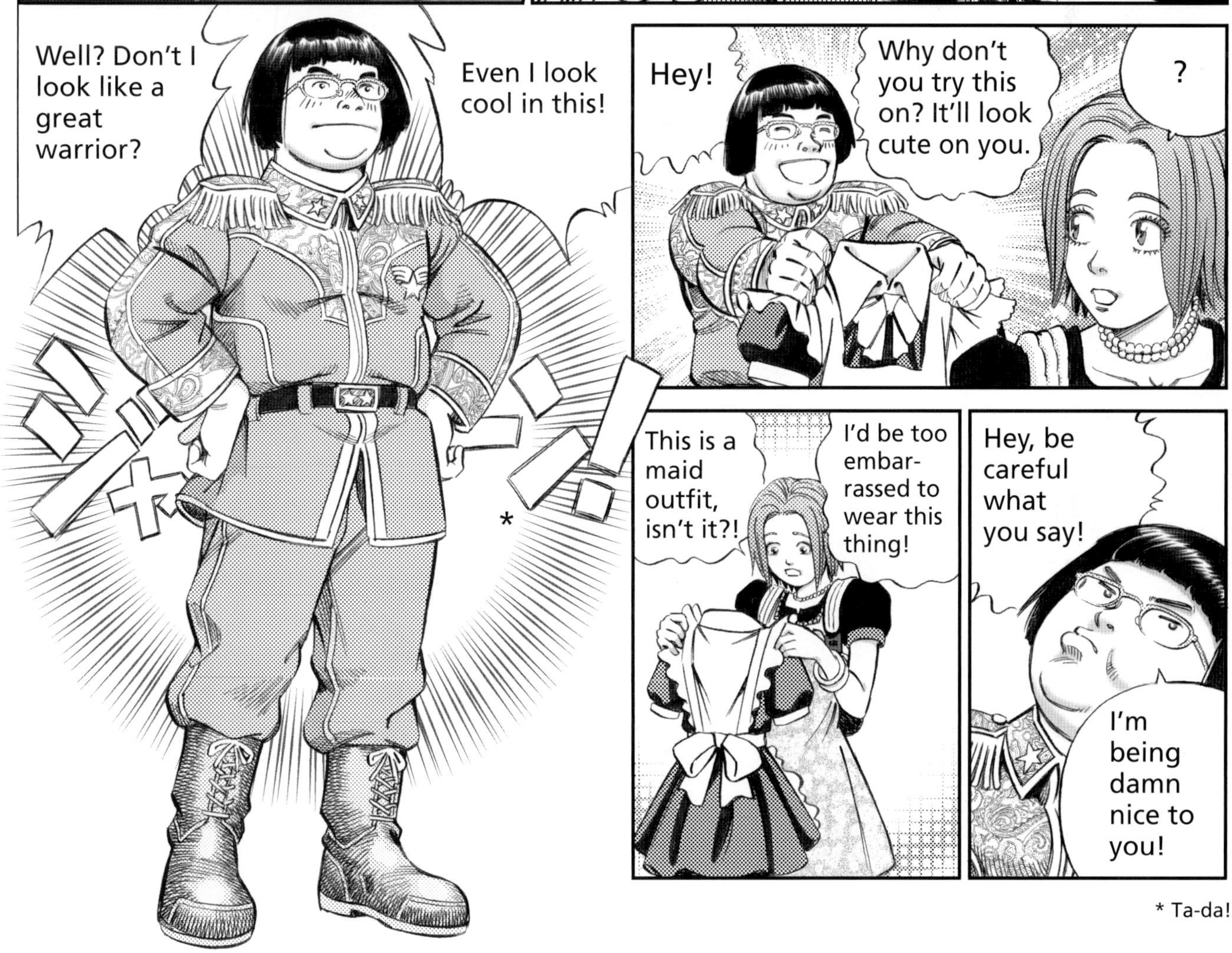
Well? Don't I look like a great warrior?
Even I look cool in this!
ジャーン!
*
Hey!
Why don't you try this on? It'll look cute on you.
?
This is a maid outfit, isn't it?!
I'd be too embar-rassed to wear this thing!
Hey, be careful what you say!
I'm being damn nice to you!

* Ta-da!

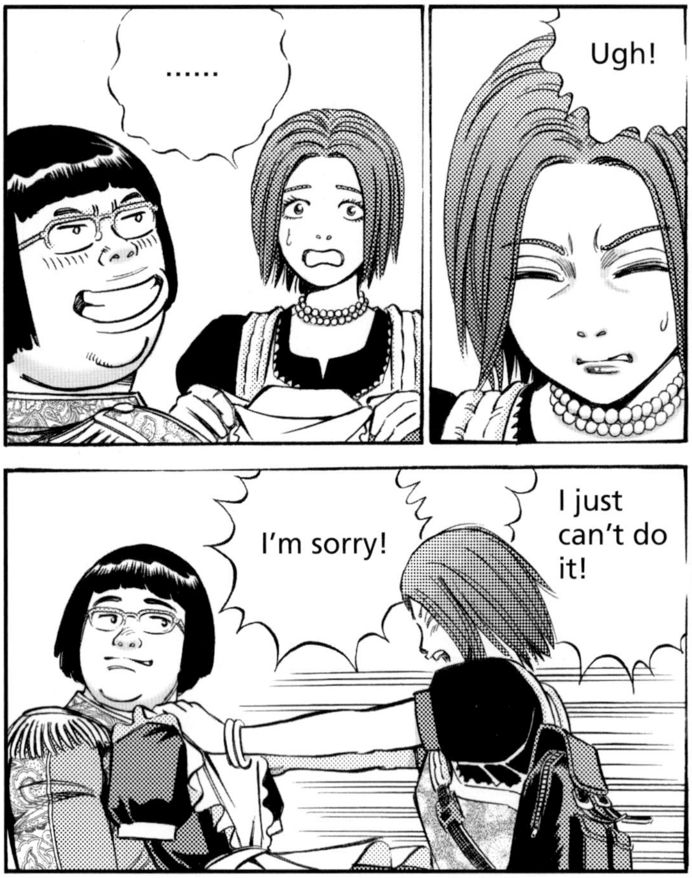
......
Ugh!
I'm sorry!
I just can't do it!

↓ Cure Maid Café
Opened in 2001, Cure Maid Café is a pioneer in the maid café business. Located on the sixth floor of Gee Store Akiba, it's a quiet, relaxed location.

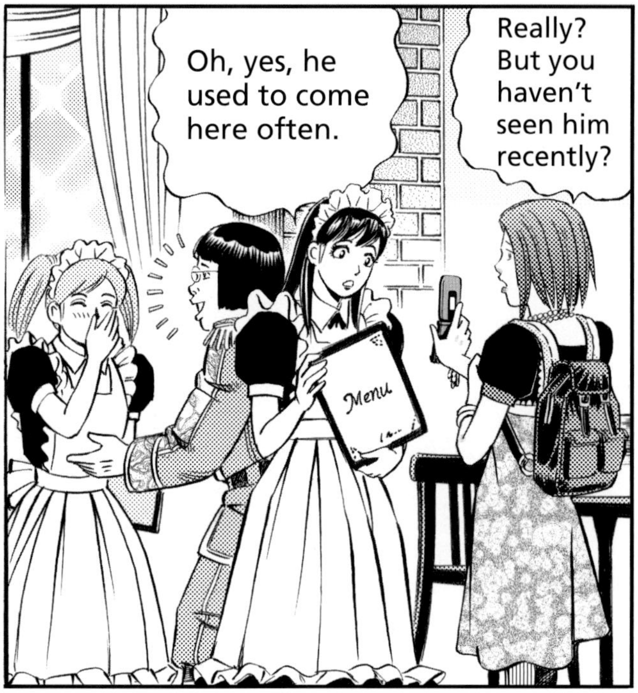
Oh, yes, he used to come here often.
Really? But you haven't seen him recently?
Menu

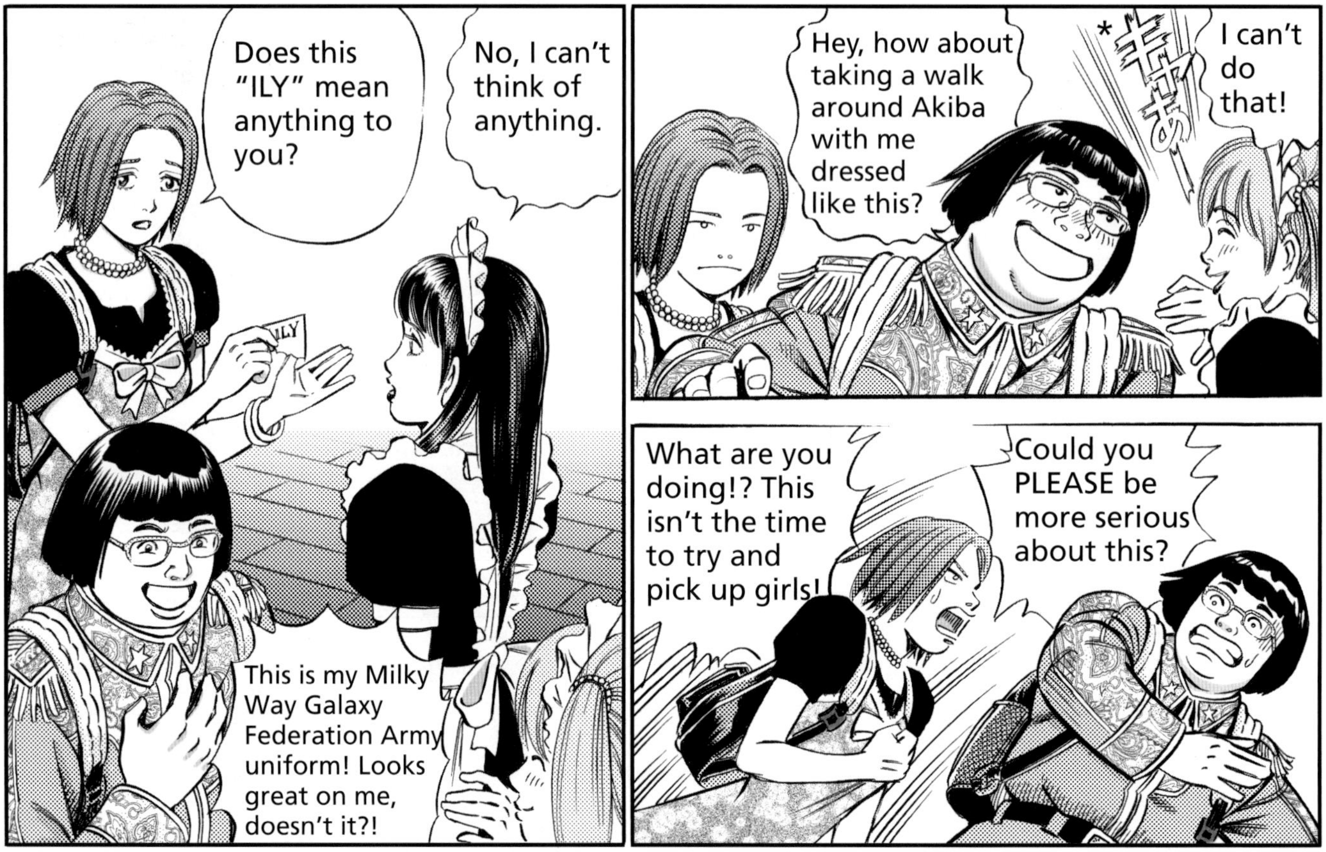
Does this "ILY" mean anything to you?
No, I can't think of anything.
This is my Milky Way Galaxy Federation Army uniform! Looks great on me, doesn't it?!
Hey, how about taking a walk around Akiba with me dressed like this?
*キャあ
I can't do that!
What are you doing!? This isn't the time to try and pick up girls!
Could you PLEASE be more serious about this?

*Eek!

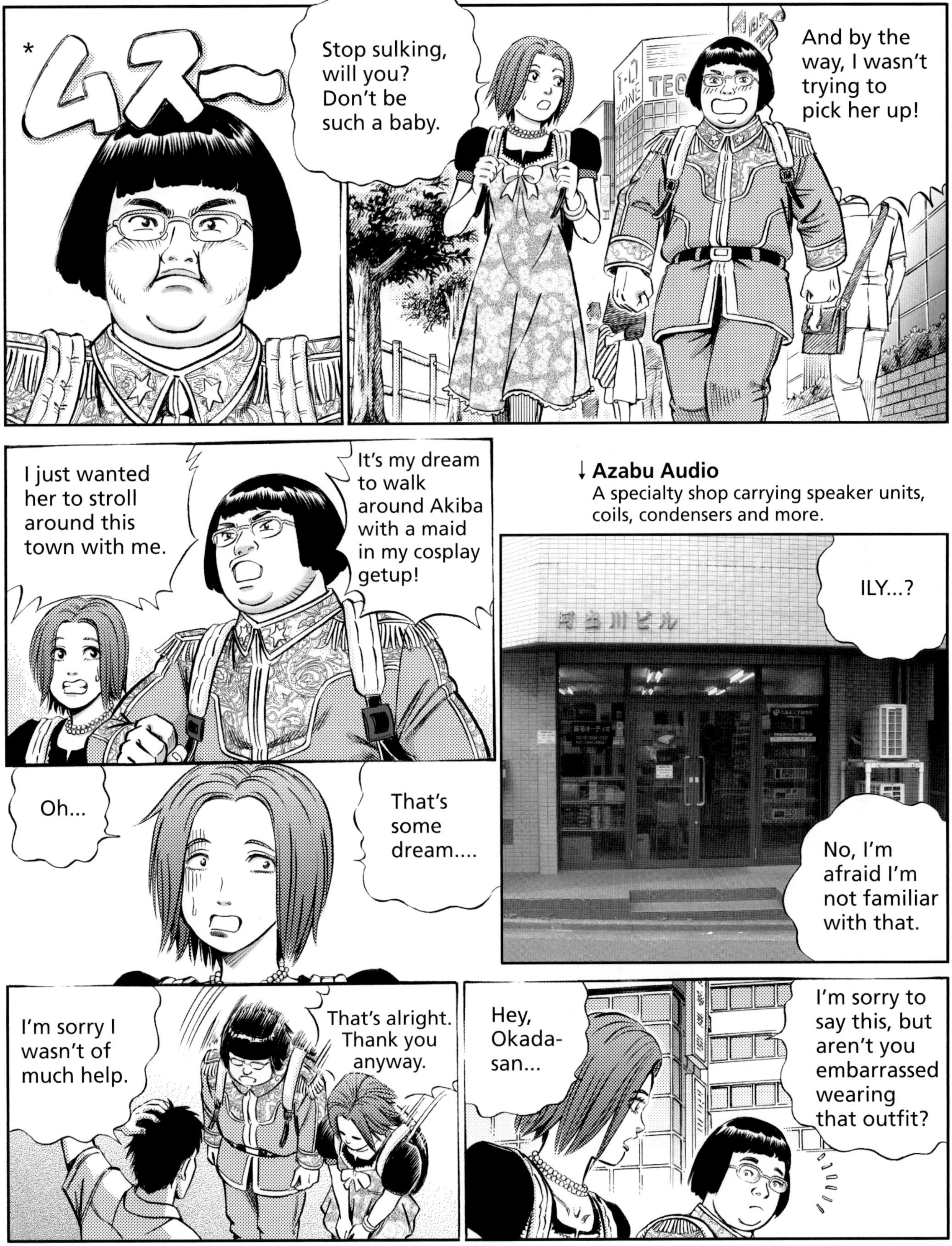

*
ムスー
Stop sulking, will you? Don't be such a baby.
And by the way, I wasn't trying to pick her up!
I just wanted her to stroll around this town with me.
It's my dream to walk around Akiba with a maid in my cosplay getup!
Oh...
That's some dream....
↓ Azabu Audio
A specialty shop carrying speaker units, coils, condensers and more.
ILY...?
No, I'm afraid I'm not familiar with that.
I'm sorry I wasn't of much help.
That's alright. Thank you anyway.
Hey, Okada-san...
I'm sorry to say this, but aren't you embarrassed wearing that outfit?

*Pouts

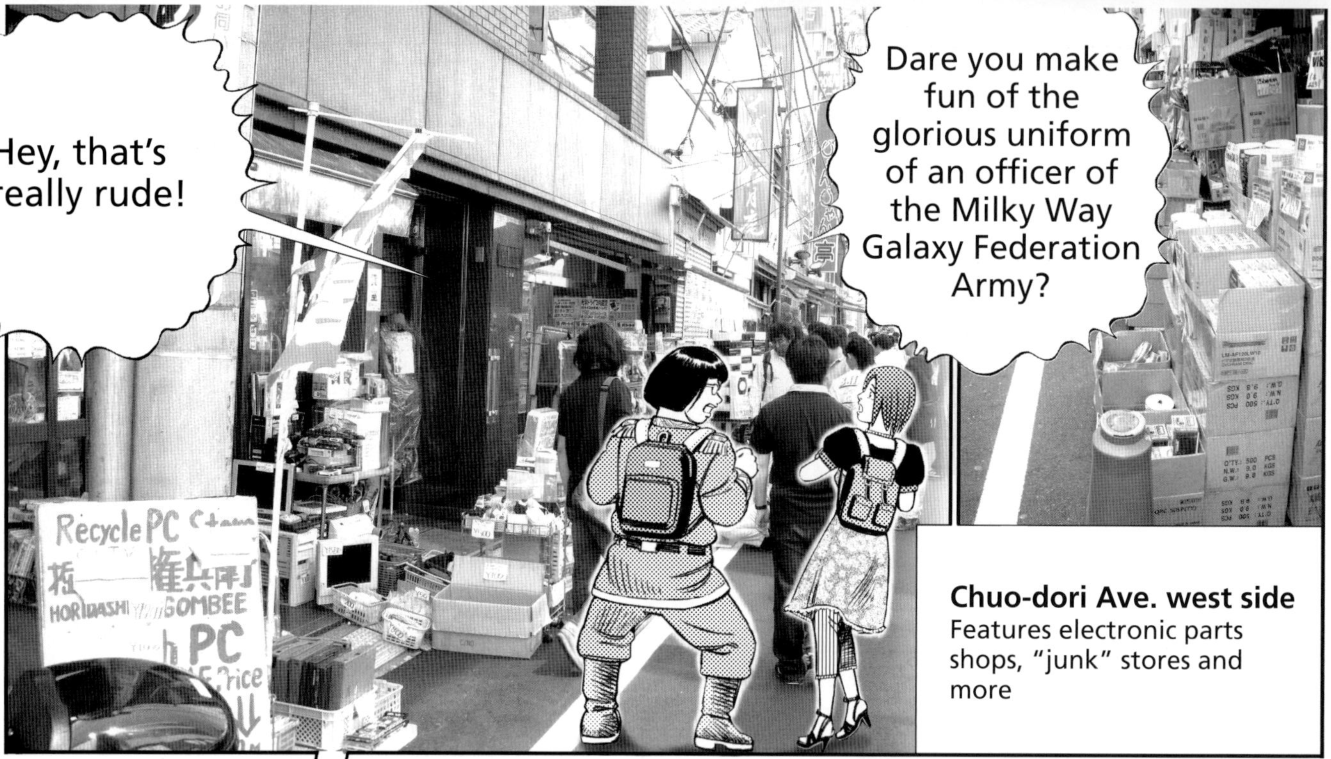
Hey, that's really rude!
Dare you make fun of the glorious uniform of an officer of the Milky Way Galaxy Federation Army?

Chuo-dori Ave. west side
Features electronic parts shops, "junk" stores and more

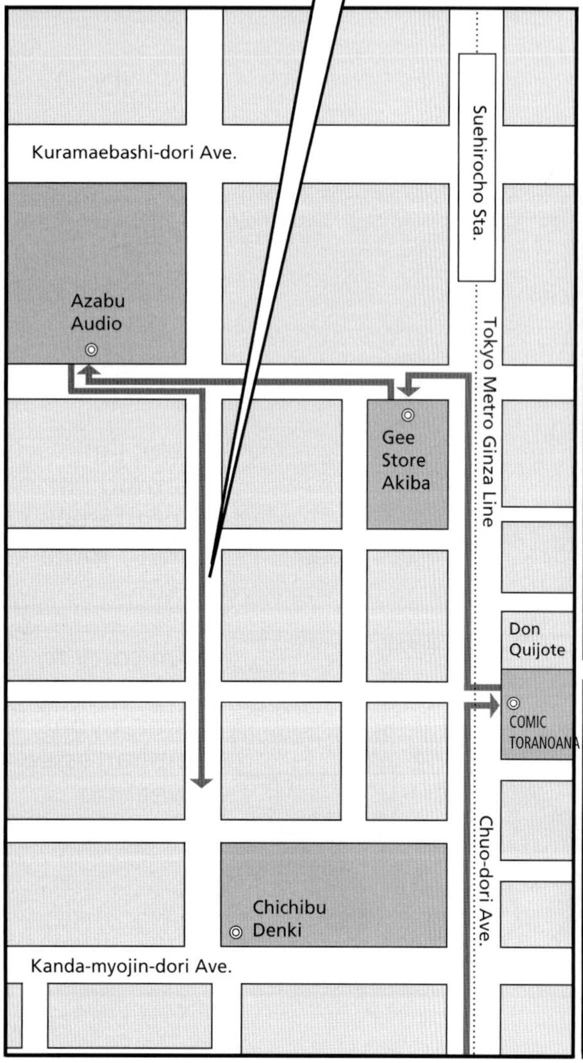
Kuramaebashi-dori Ave.
Suehirocho Sta.
Azabu Audio
Gee Store Akiba
Tokyo Metro Ginza Line
Don Quijote
COMIC TORANOANA
Chuo-dori Ave.
Chichibu Denki
Kanda-myojin-dori Ave.

↓ **Chichibu Denki**
A shop specializing in Toshiba's Libretto subnotebook computers. The store came to be known throughout Japan for the canned *oden* vending machines in front of it. *Oden* is a mildly seasoned stew of vegetables, *konnyaku* (alimentary yam paste), fish sausage, etc.

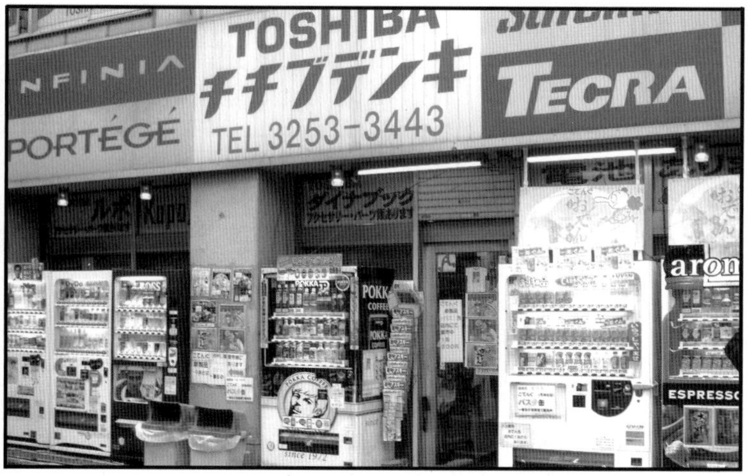
TOSHIBA
チチブデンキ
TEL 3253-3443
TECRA
PORTÉGÉ

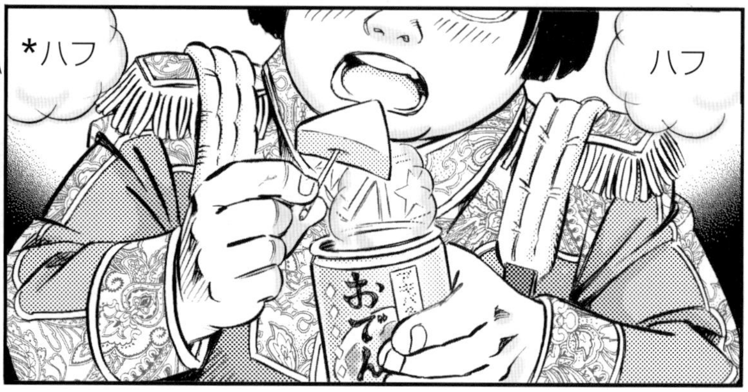
*ハフ
ハフ

*Chomp, chomp

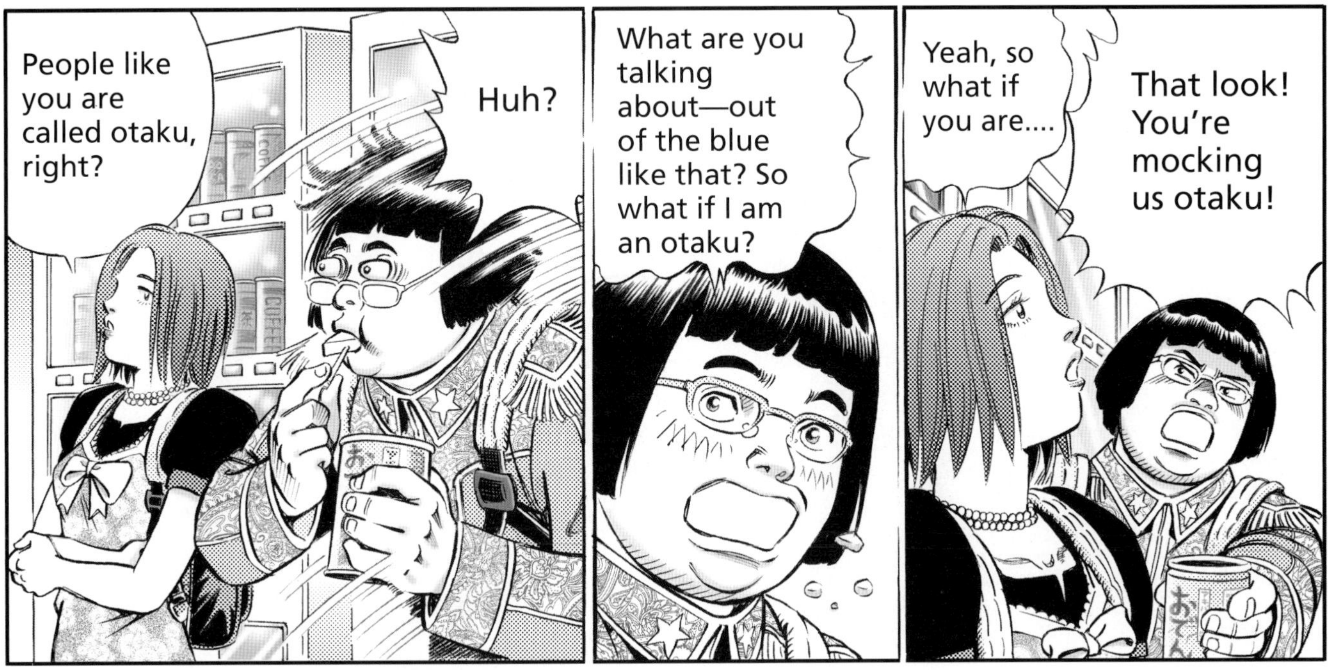
People like you are called otaku, right?
Huh?
What are you talking about—out of the blue like that? So what if I am an otaku?
Yeah, so what if you are....
That look! You're mocking us otaku!

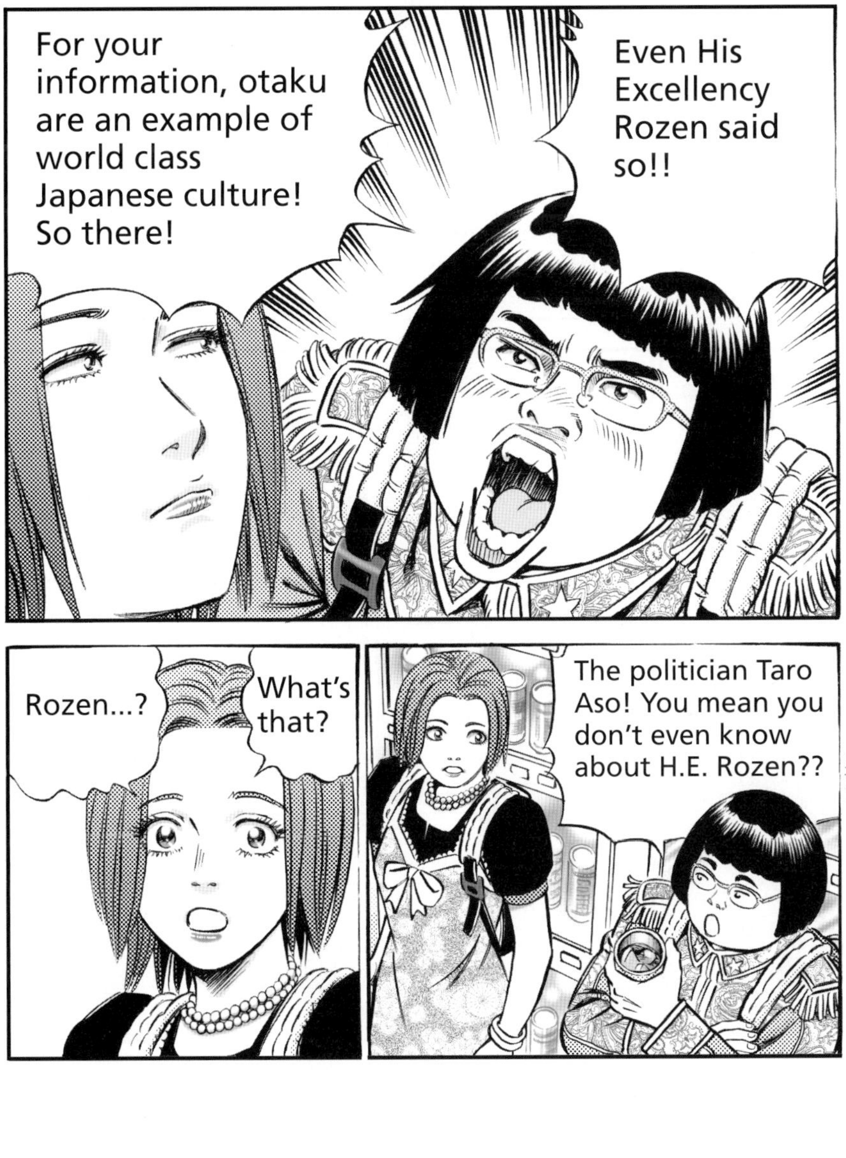
For your information, otaku are an example of world class Japanese culture! So there!
Even His Excellency Rozen said so!!
Rozen...?
What's that?
The politician Taro Aso! You mean you don't even know about H.E. Rozen??

Taro Aso

A prominent politician who served as the minister of public management, home affairs, posts and telecommunications, and as the minister of foreign affairs. Aso is the Japanese politician reputed to have the most complete understanding of the Japanese content industry.

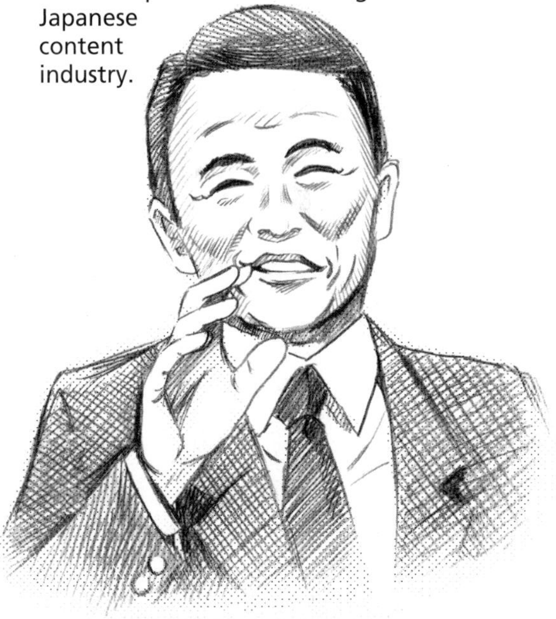

A rumor spread on the Internet that Taro Aso was reading the manga *Rozen Maiden* at the airport, and some Web users gave him the nickname "His Excellency Rozen."

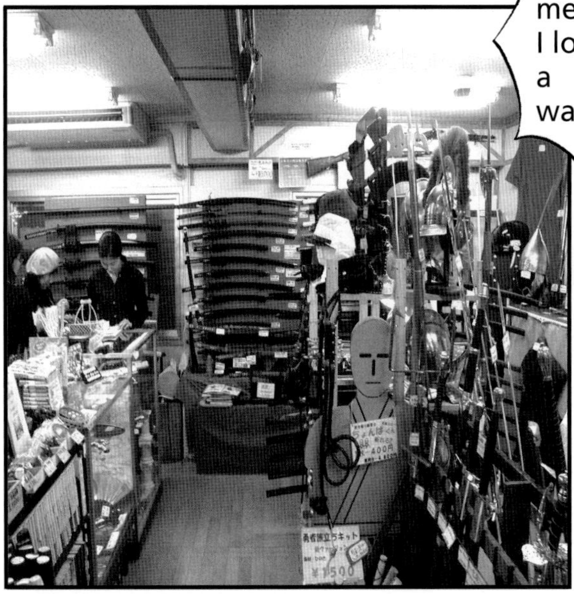

↑ **Bukiya**

One of Akiba's well-known stores, Bukiya offers a variety of items such as replica swords, protective gear, historical props and more. All "weapons" in the store are replicas, and none of the swords can actually be used for fighting.

http://www.wbr.co.jp

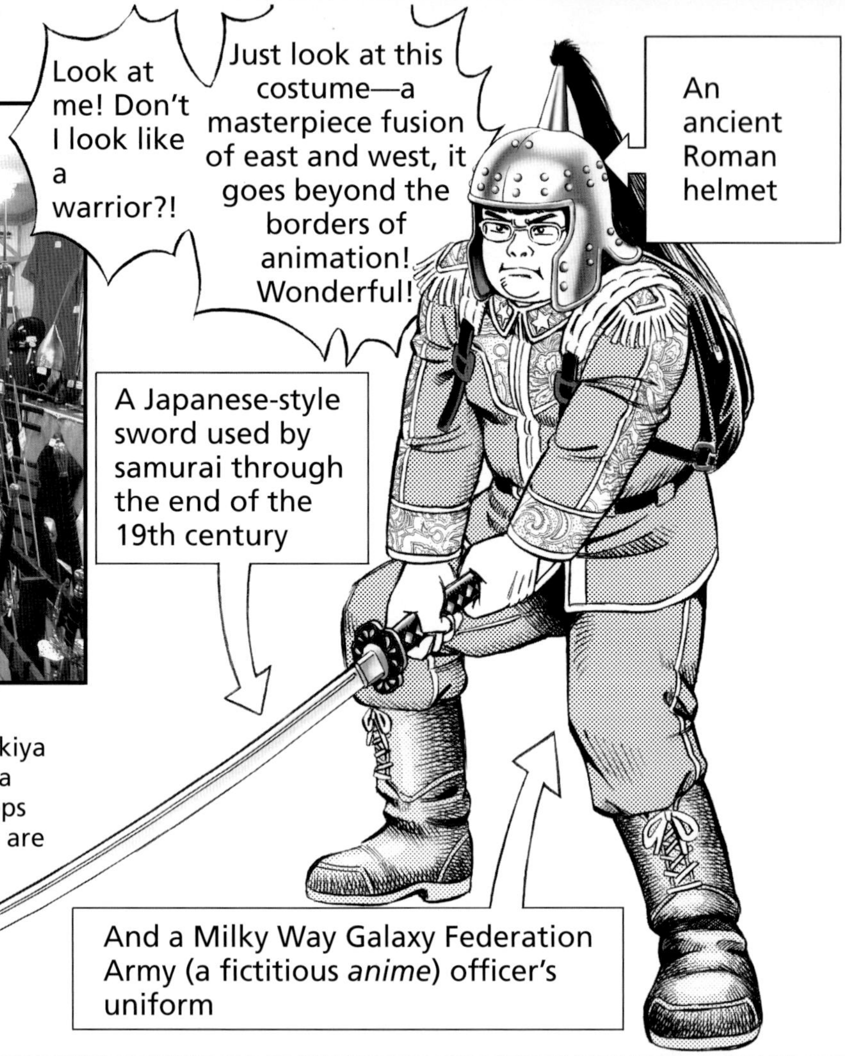

Look at me! Don't I look like a warrior?!
Just look at this costume—a masterpiece fusion of east and west, it goes beyond the borders of animation! Wonderful!
An ancient Roman helmet
A Japanese-style sword used by samurai through the end of the 19th century
And a Milky Way Galaxy Federation Army (a fictitious *anime*) officer's uniform

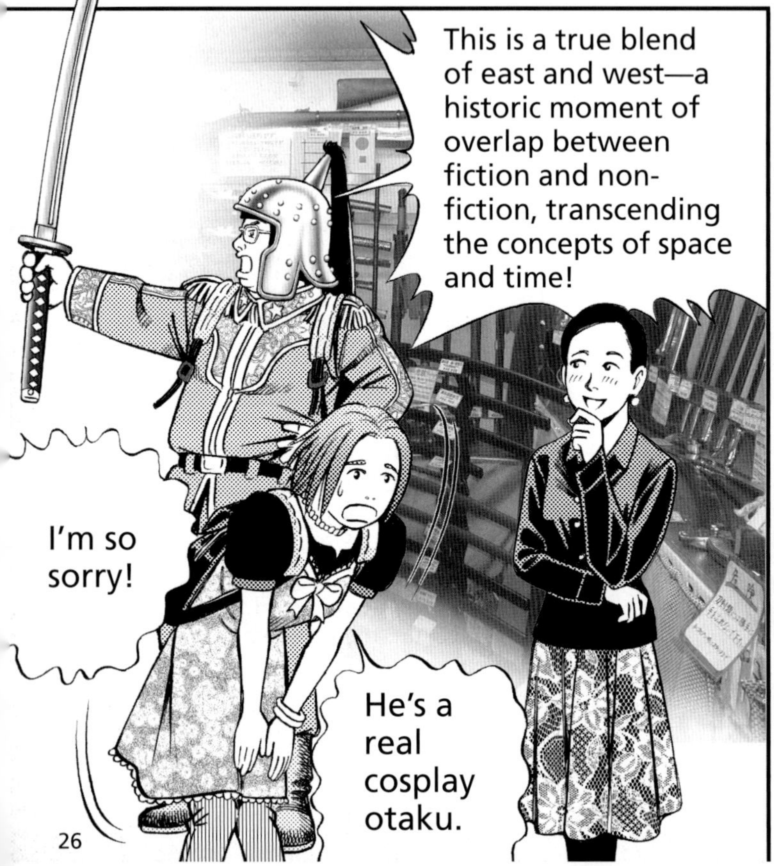

This is a true blend of east and west—a historic moment of overlap between fiction and non-fiction, transcending the concepts of space and time!
I'm so sorry!
He's a real cosplay otaku.

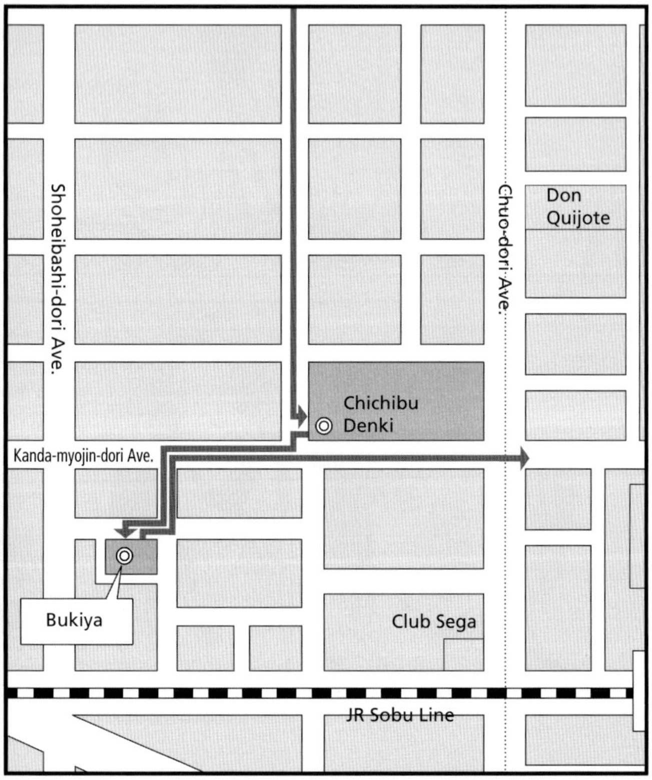

Shoheibashi-dori Ave.
Chuo-dori Ave.
Don Quijote
Chichibu Denki
Kanda-myojin-dori Ave.
Bukiya
Club Sega
JR Sobu Line

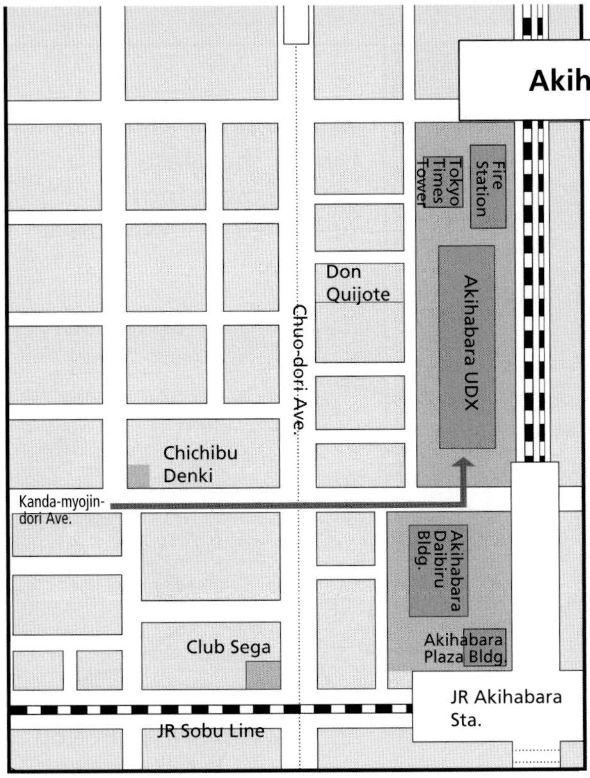
Fire Station
Tokyo Times Tower
Don Quijote
Akihabara UDX
Chuo-dori Ave.
Chichibu Denki
Kanda-myojin-dori Ave.
Akihabara Daibiru Bldg.
Club Sega
Akihabara Plaza Bldg.
JR Akihabara Sta.
JR Sobu Line

Akihabara Crossfield (as of January 2008)

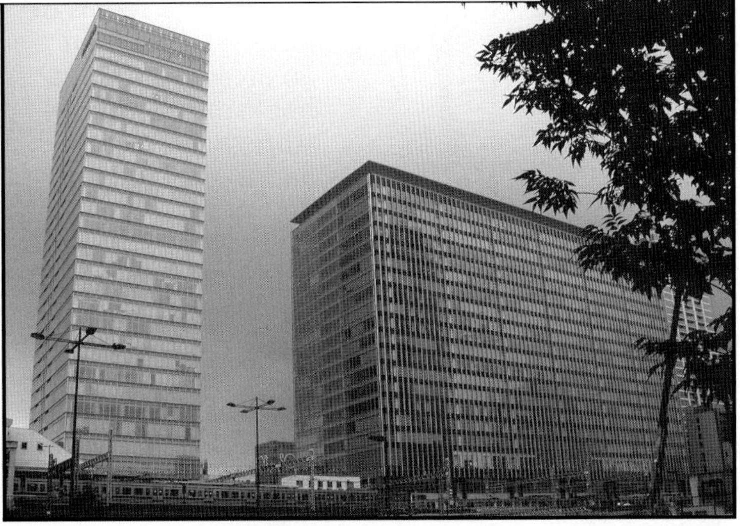

The Akihabara UDX Building

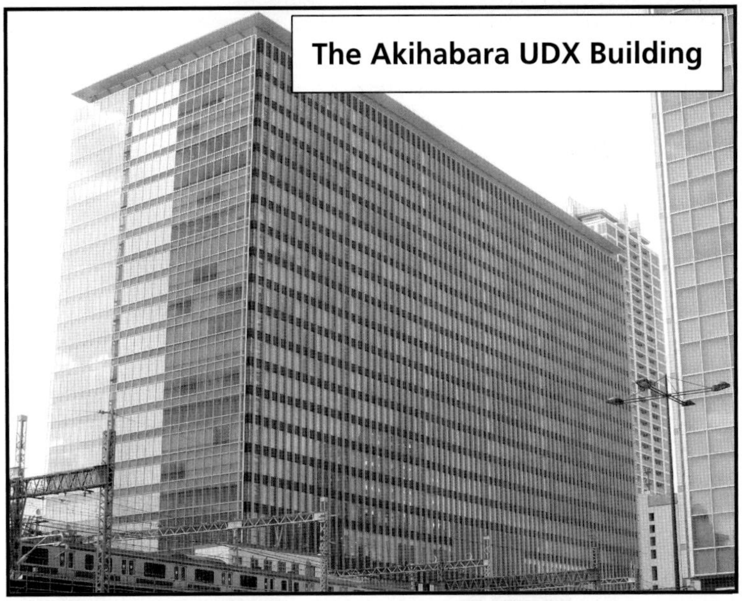

Akihabara Crossfield

This group of buildings (the Daibiru Bldg., the Akihabara UDX Bldg., the Tokyo Times Tower and the fire department) were built in accordance with Tokyo's redevelopment planning. They are comprised of offices, apartment buildings, restaurants, commercial facilities, industry-government-academia collaborative facilities, information network system facilities, showrooms, event spaces and more.

↓ A robot competition at Akihabara UDX

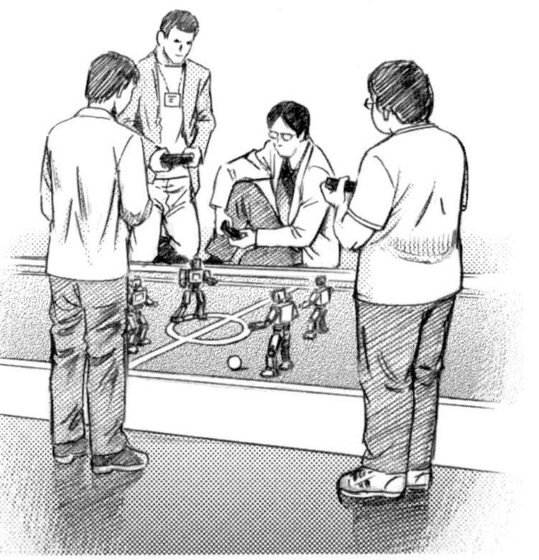

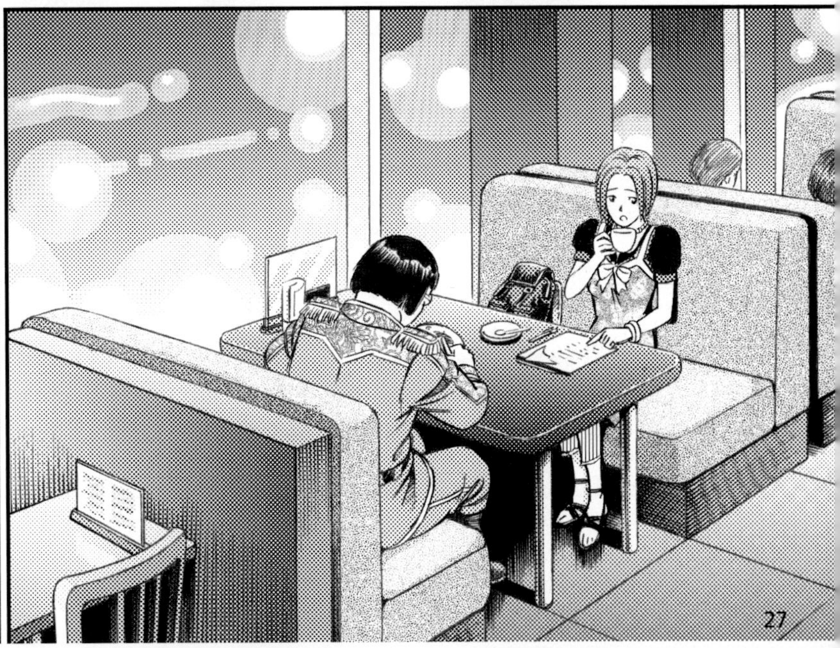

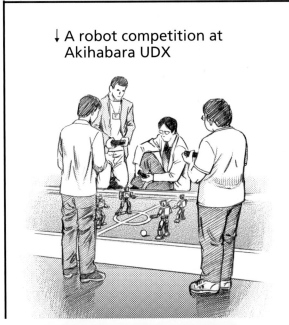

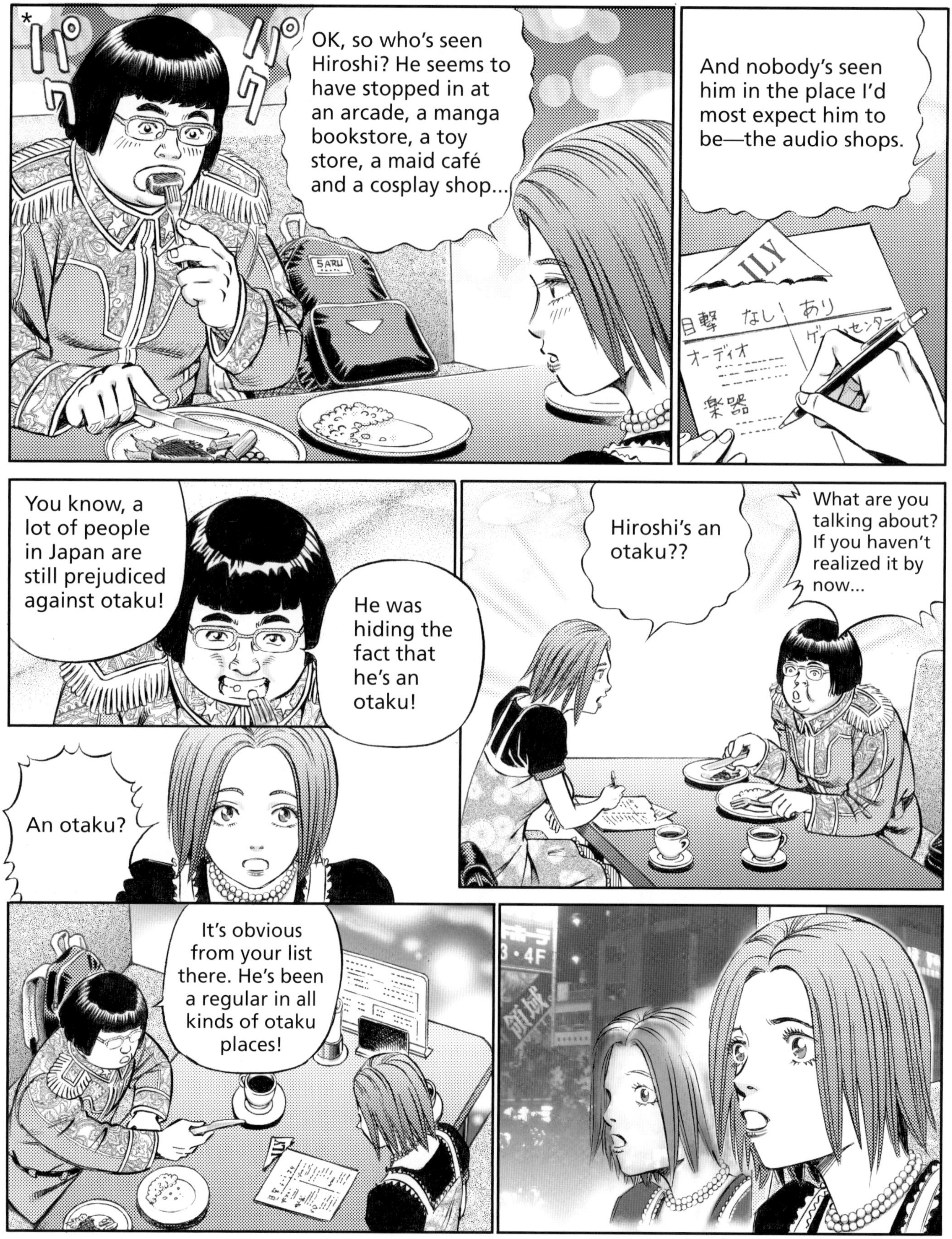
*パク パク
OK, so who's seen Hiroshi? He seems to have stopped in at an arcade, a manga bookstore, a toy store, a maid café and a cosplay shop...
And nobody's seen him in the place I'd most expect him to be—the audio shops.
ILY
目撃 なし あり
オーディオ
楽器
You know, a lot of people in Japan are still prejudiced against otaku!
He was hiding the fact that he's an otaku!
An otaku?
Hiroshi's an otaku??
What are you talking about? If you haven't realized it by now...
It's obvious from your list there. He's been a regular in all kinds of otaku places!
3・4F
領域

*Chomp, chomp

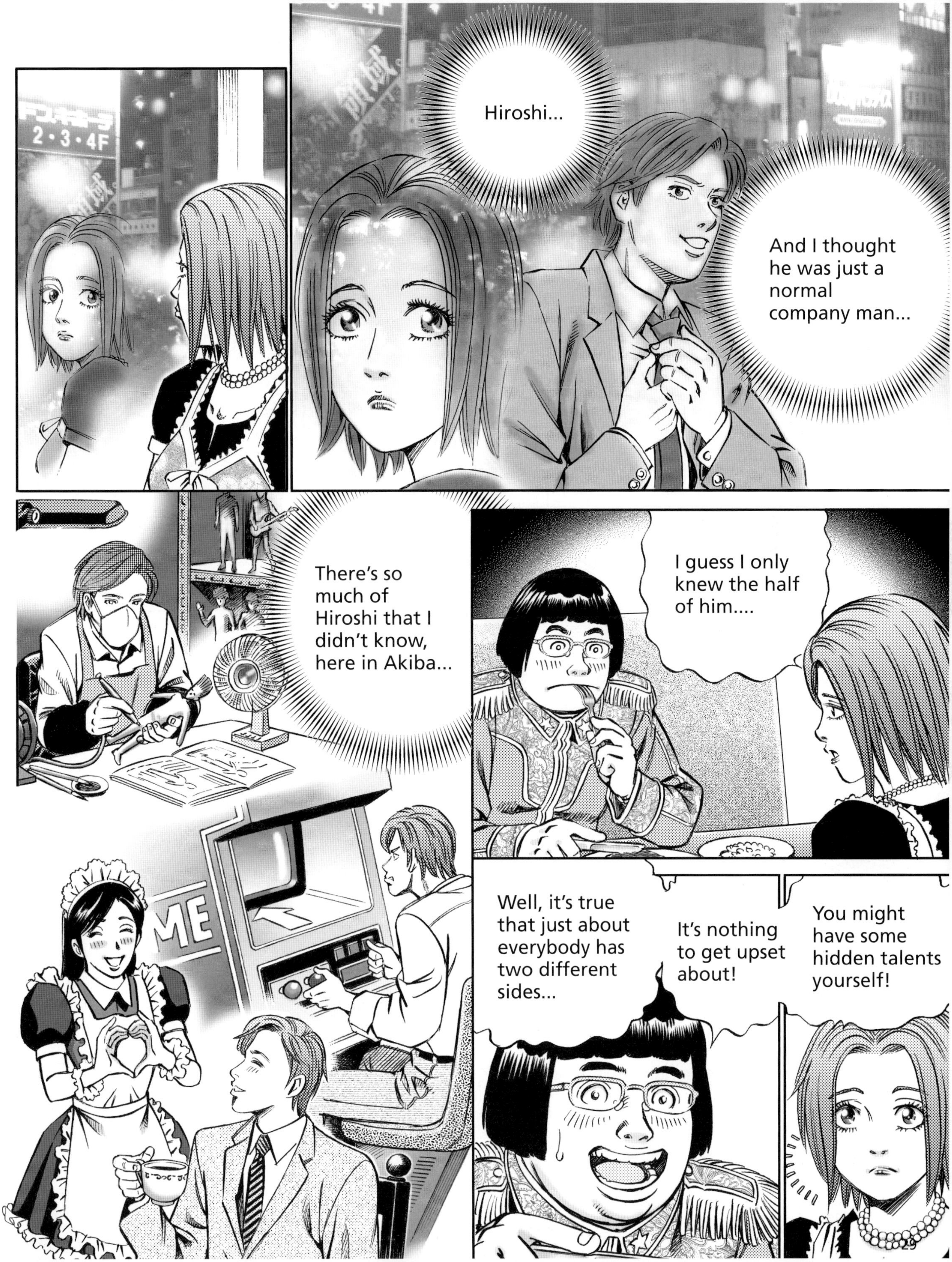
2・3・4F
Hiroshi...
And I thought he was just a normal company man...
There's so much of Hiroshi that I didn't know, here in Akiba...
ME
I guess I only knew the half of him....
Well, it's true that just about everybody has two different sides...
It's nothing to get upset about!
You might have some hidden talents yourself!

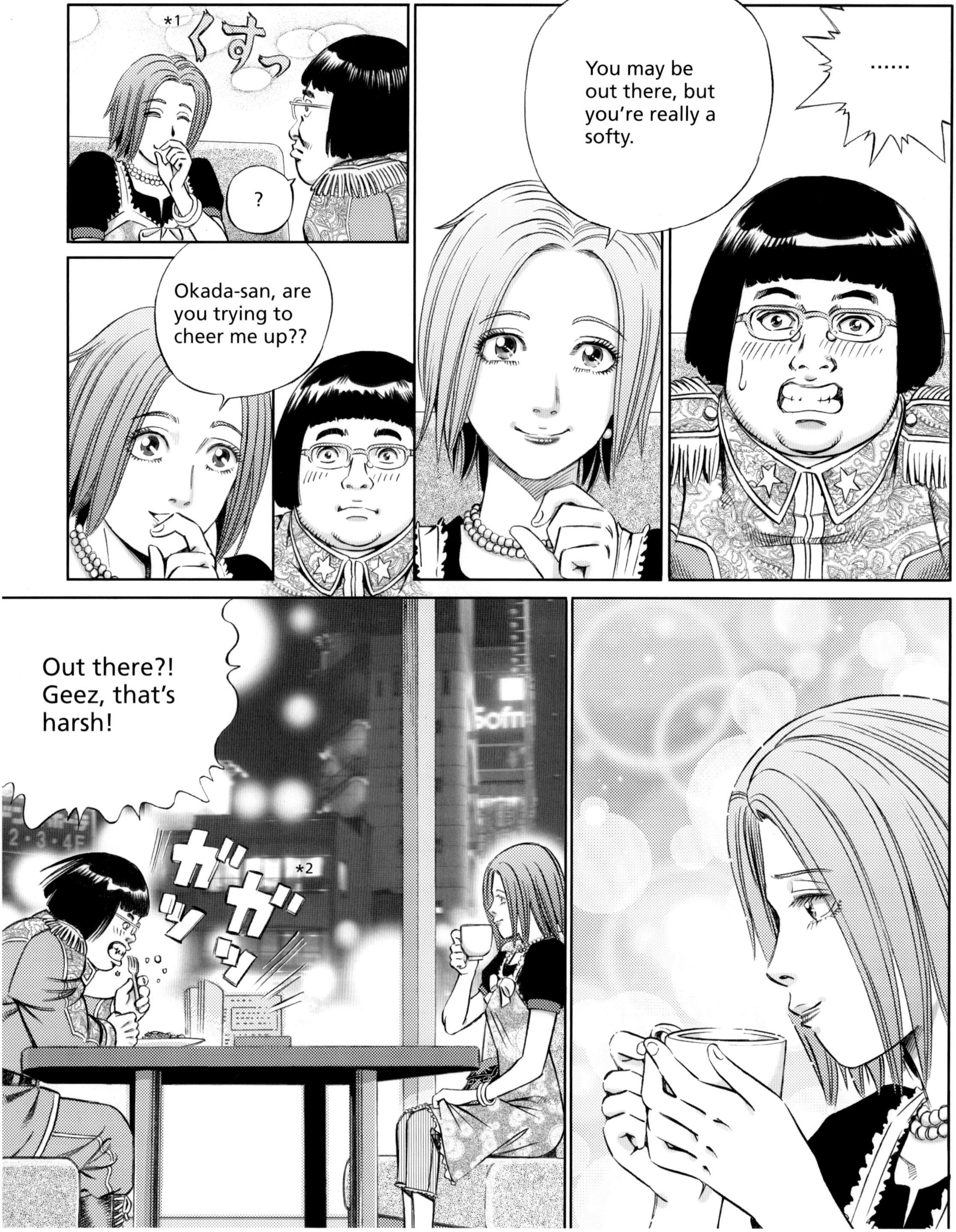
*1 くすっ
?
Okada-san, are you trying to cheer me up??
You may be out there, but you're really a softy.
......
Out there?! Geez, that's harsh!
ガツガツ *2

*1 Hee-hee! *2 Gobble, gobble

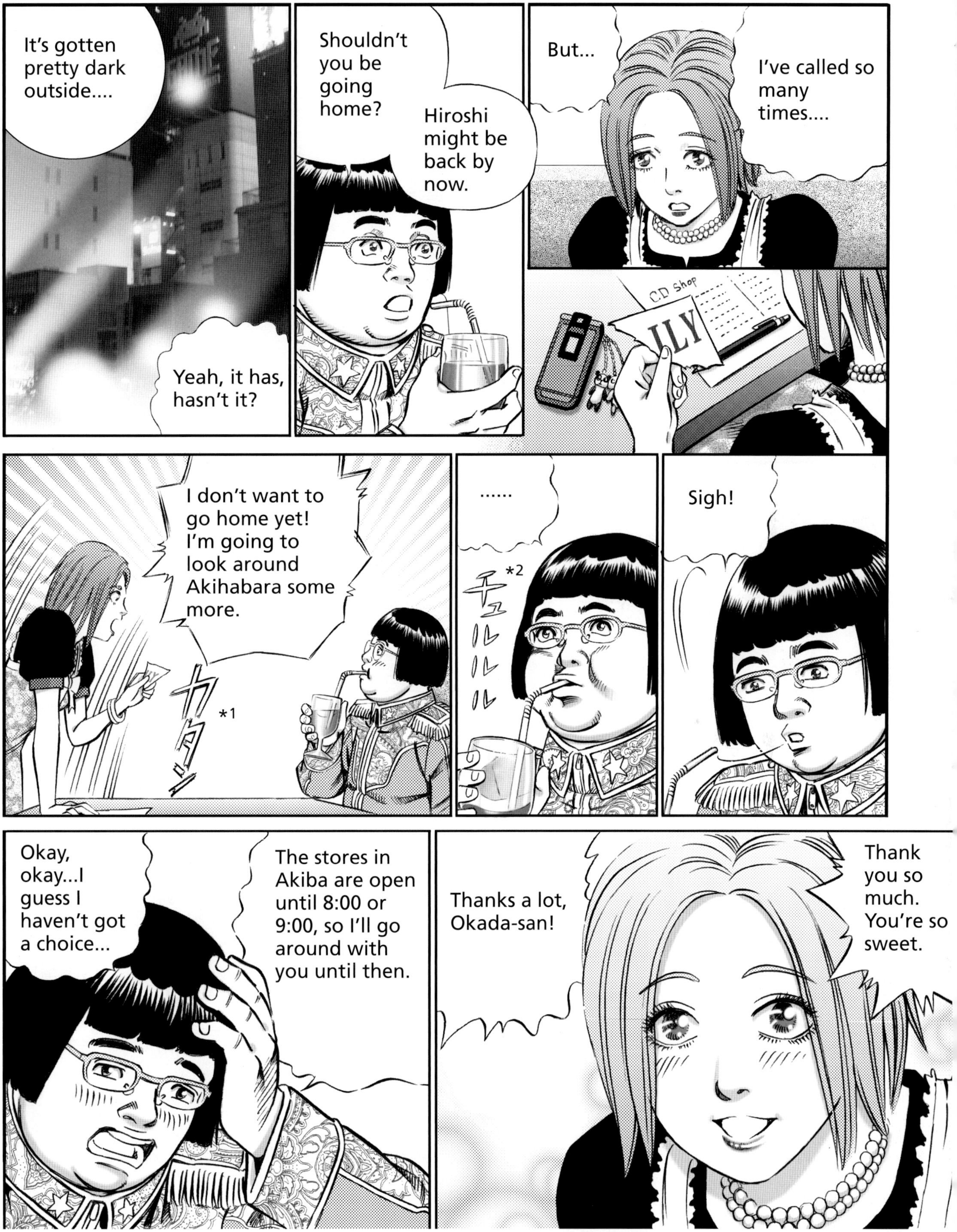
It's gotten pretty dark outside....
Yeah, it has, hasn't it?
Shouldn't you be going home?
Hiroshi might be back by now.
But...
I've called so many times....
CD Shop
ILY
I don't want to go home yet! I'm going to look around Akihabara some more.
カタッ *1
......
*2 チュルルルル
Sigh!
Okay, okay...I guess I haven't got a choice...
The stores in Akiba are open until 8:00 or 9:00, so I'll go around with you until then.
Thanks a lot, Okada-san!
Thank you so much. You're so sweet.

*1 Bam! *2 Slurp

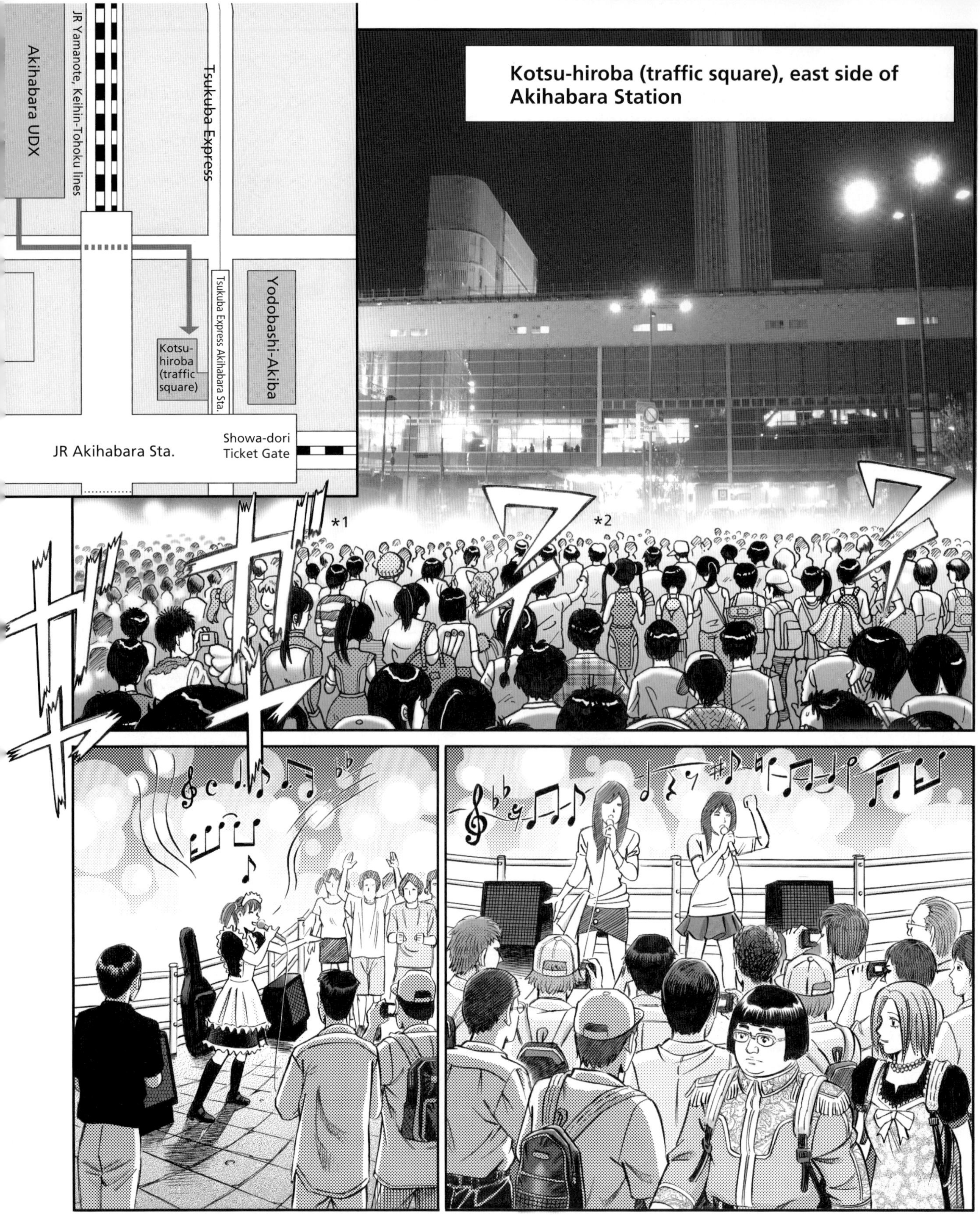
Akihabara UDX
JR Yamanote, Keihin-Tohoku lines
Tsukuba Express
Tsukuba Express Akihabara Sta.
Yodobashi-Akiba
Kotsu-hiroba (traffic square)
JR Akihabara Sta.
Showa-dori Ticket Gate
Kotsu-hiroba (traffic square), east side of Akihabara Station
*1
*2

*1 Loud cheering
*2 Yay!

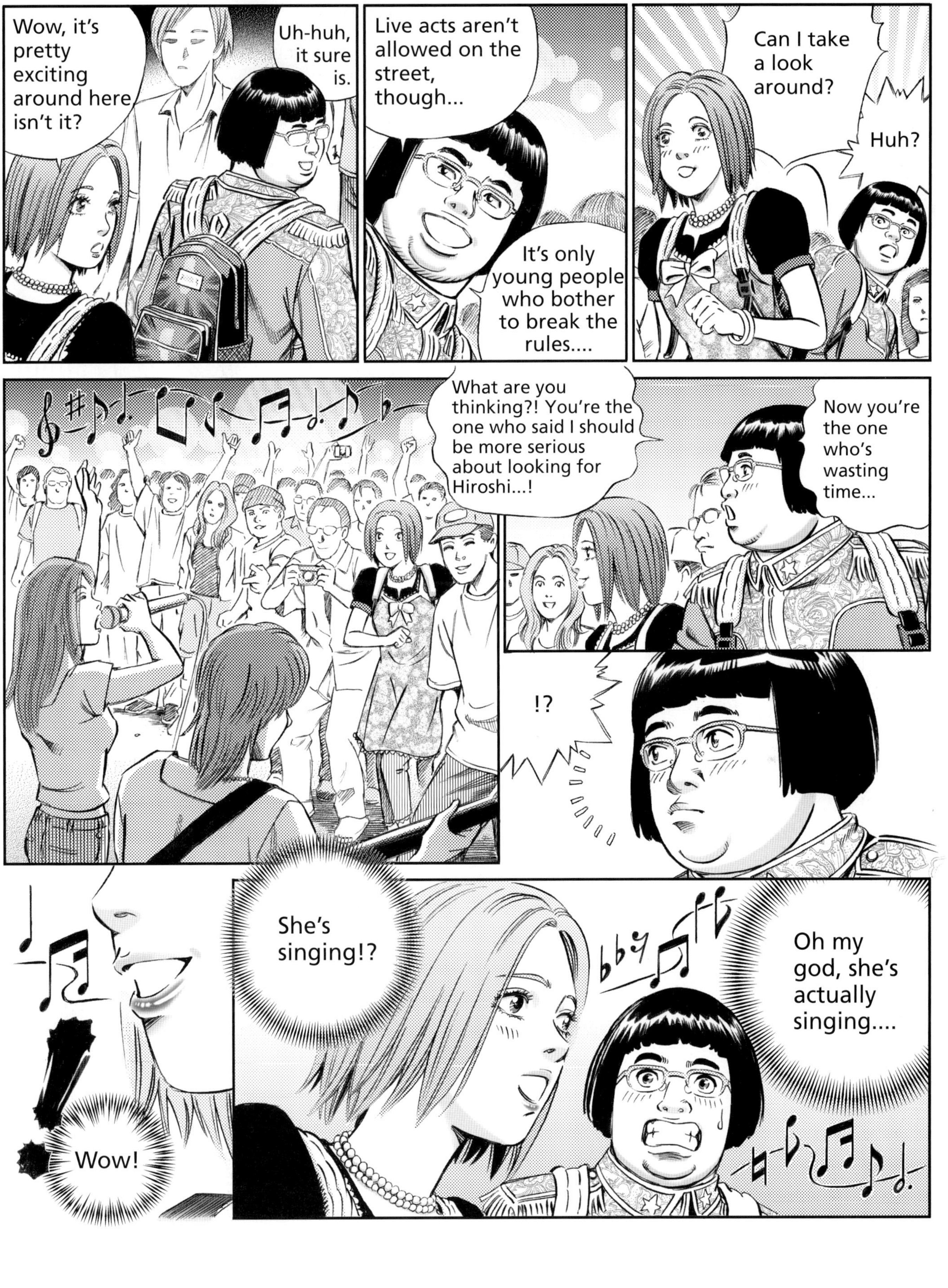

Wow, it's pretty exciting around here, isn't it?
Uh-huh, it sure is.
Live acts aren't allowed on the street, though...
It's only young people who bother to break the rules....
Can I take a look around?
Huh?
What are you thinking?! You're the one who said I should be more serious about looking for Hiroshi...!
Now you're the one who's wasting time...
!?
Wow!
She's singing!?
Oh my god, she's actually singing....

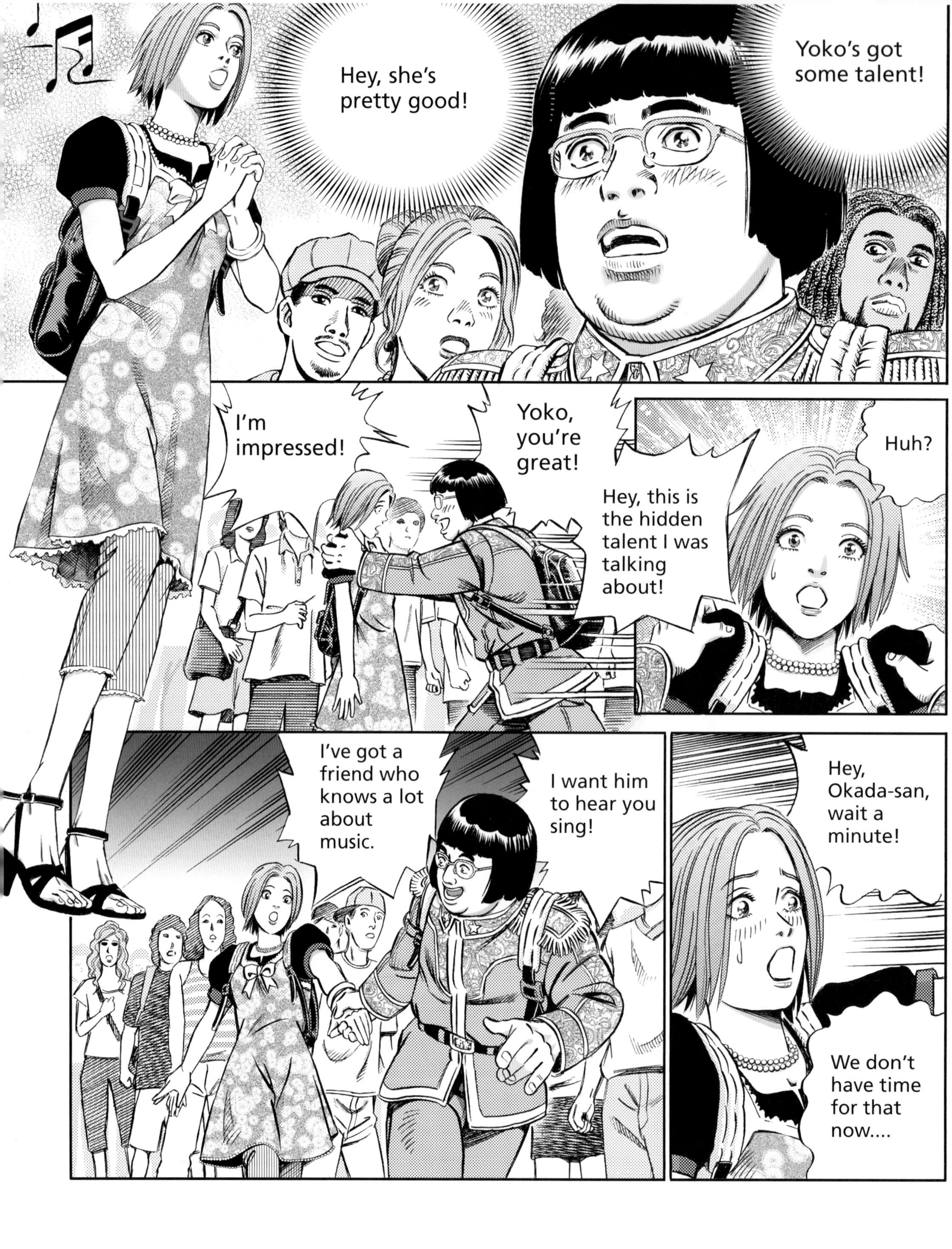
Hey, she's pretty good!
Yoko's got some talent!
I'm impressed!
Yoko, you're great!
Hey, this is the hidden talent I was talking about!
Huh?
I've got a friend who knows a lot about music.
I want him to hear you sing!
Hey, Okada-san, wait a minute!
We don't have time for that now....

No, it's okay!

And he might know something about Hiroshi!

Industrial
Light
&
Youth

明日の演奏は*
Tomorrow's show
10:00 a.m. ~

		Akihabara UDX				
		Akihabara Daibiru Bldg.	JR Akihabara Sta.	Tsukuba Express Akihabara Sta.	Yodobashi-Akiba	
				Kotsu-hiroba (traffic square)		
		Electric Town Exit			Showa-dori Ticket Gate	
JR Sobu Line						
		Rajio Kaikan				
		Mansei-bashi Police Station	Mansei Bridge			
JR Chuo Line			Kanda River			

Mansei Bridge

There he is!

There!

* Tomorrow's show starts 10:00 a.m.

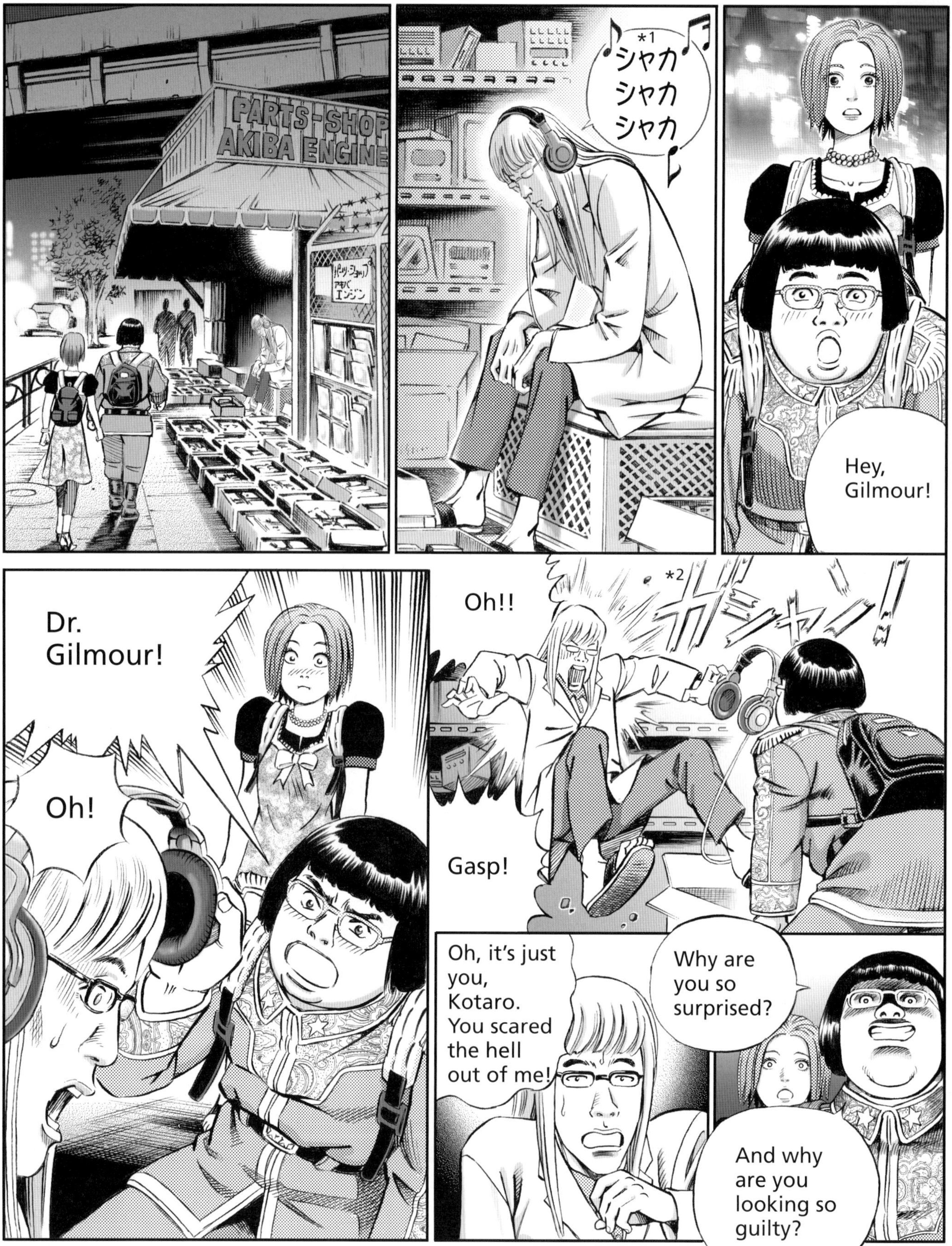
PARTS-SHOP
AKIBA ENGINE
パーツ・ショップ アキバ エンジン
*1 シャカ シャカ シャカ
Hey, Gilmour!
Dr. Gilmour!
Oh!
Oh!!
*2 ガシャン!
Gasp!
Oh, it's just you, Kotaro. You scared the hell out of me!
Why are you so surprised?
And why are you looking so guilty?

*1 Dadadada
*2 Crash!

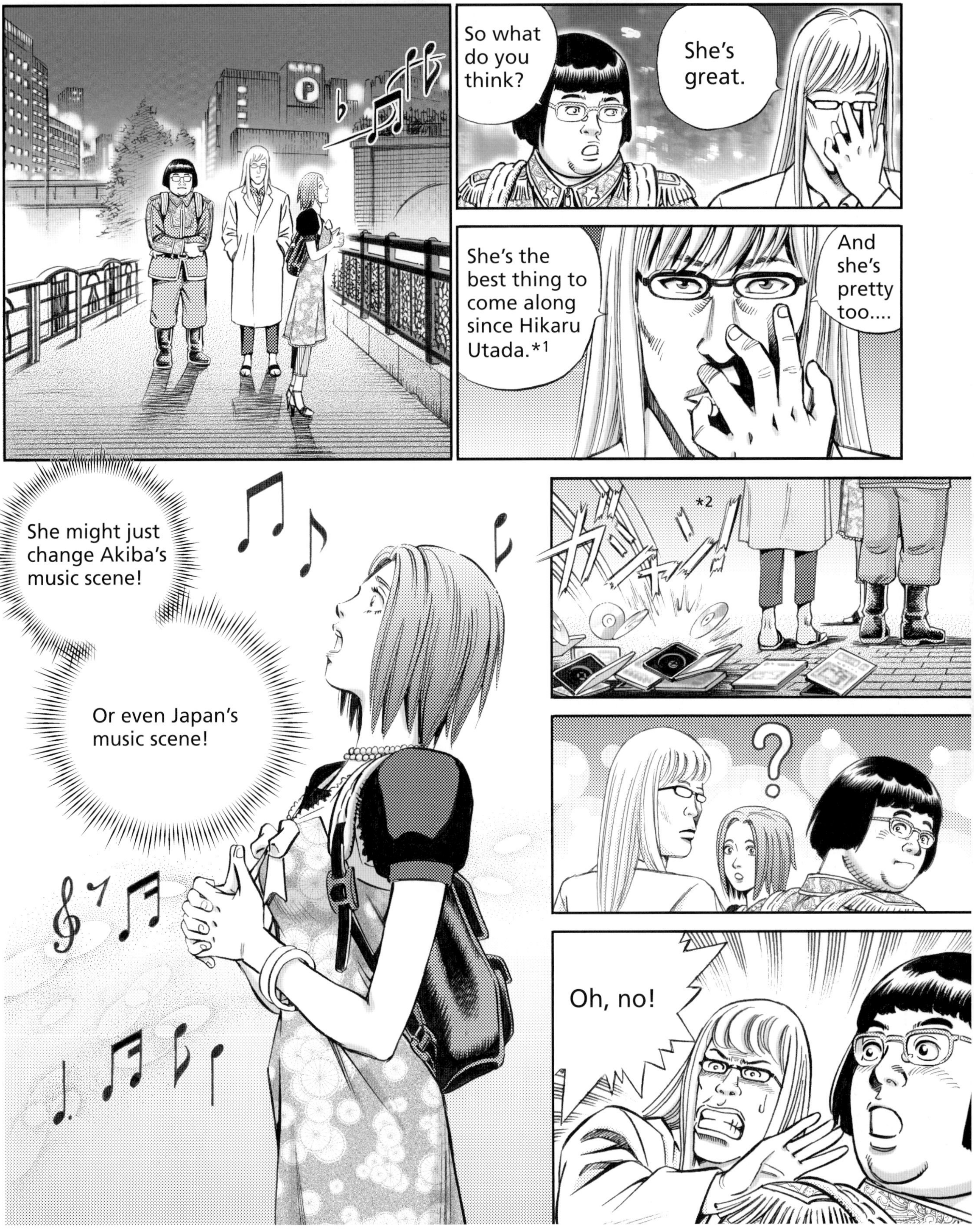

So what do you think?
She's great.
She's the best thing to come along since Hikaru Utada.*1
And she's pretty too....
She might just change Akiba's music scene!
Or even Japan's music scene!
*2
?
Oh, no!

*1 A well-known Japanese singer-songwriter. Her first album, entitled *First Love* (1999), sold more than seven million copies in Japan alone.

*2 Crash!

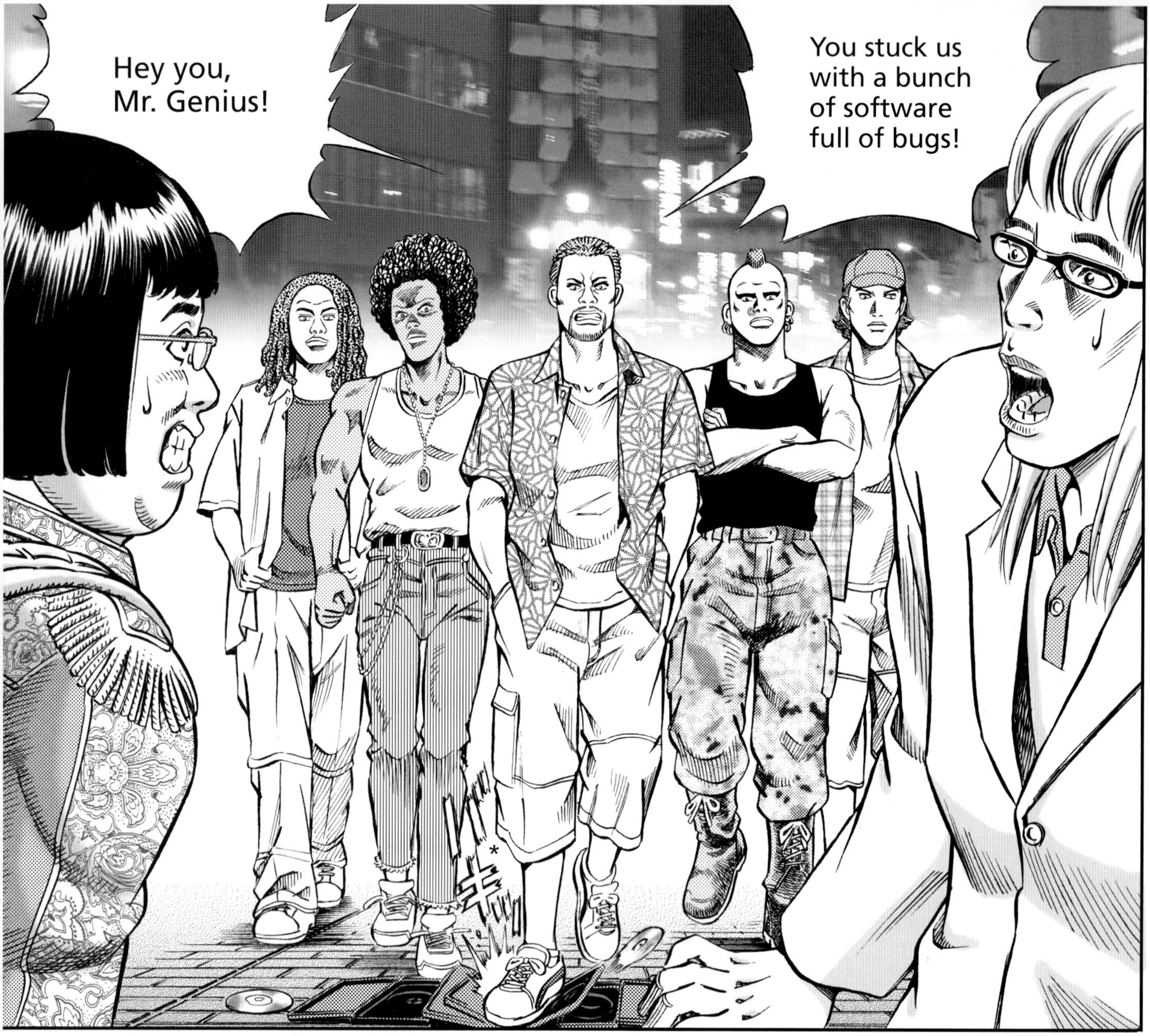
Hey you,
Mr. Genius!
You stuck us with a bunch of software full of bugs!
*

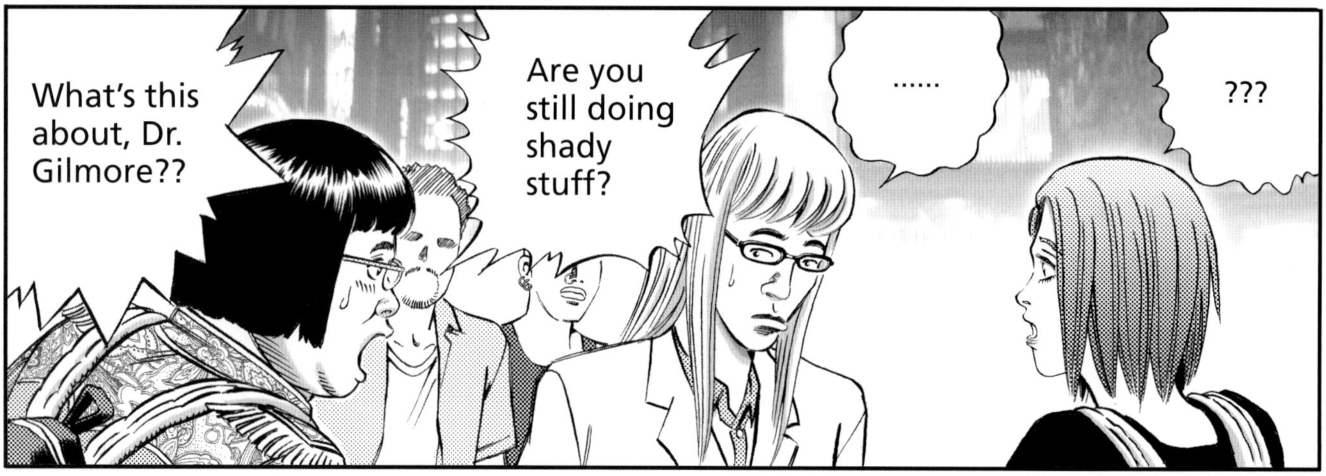
What's this about, Dr. Gilmore??
Are you still doing shady stuff?
......
???

* Snap!

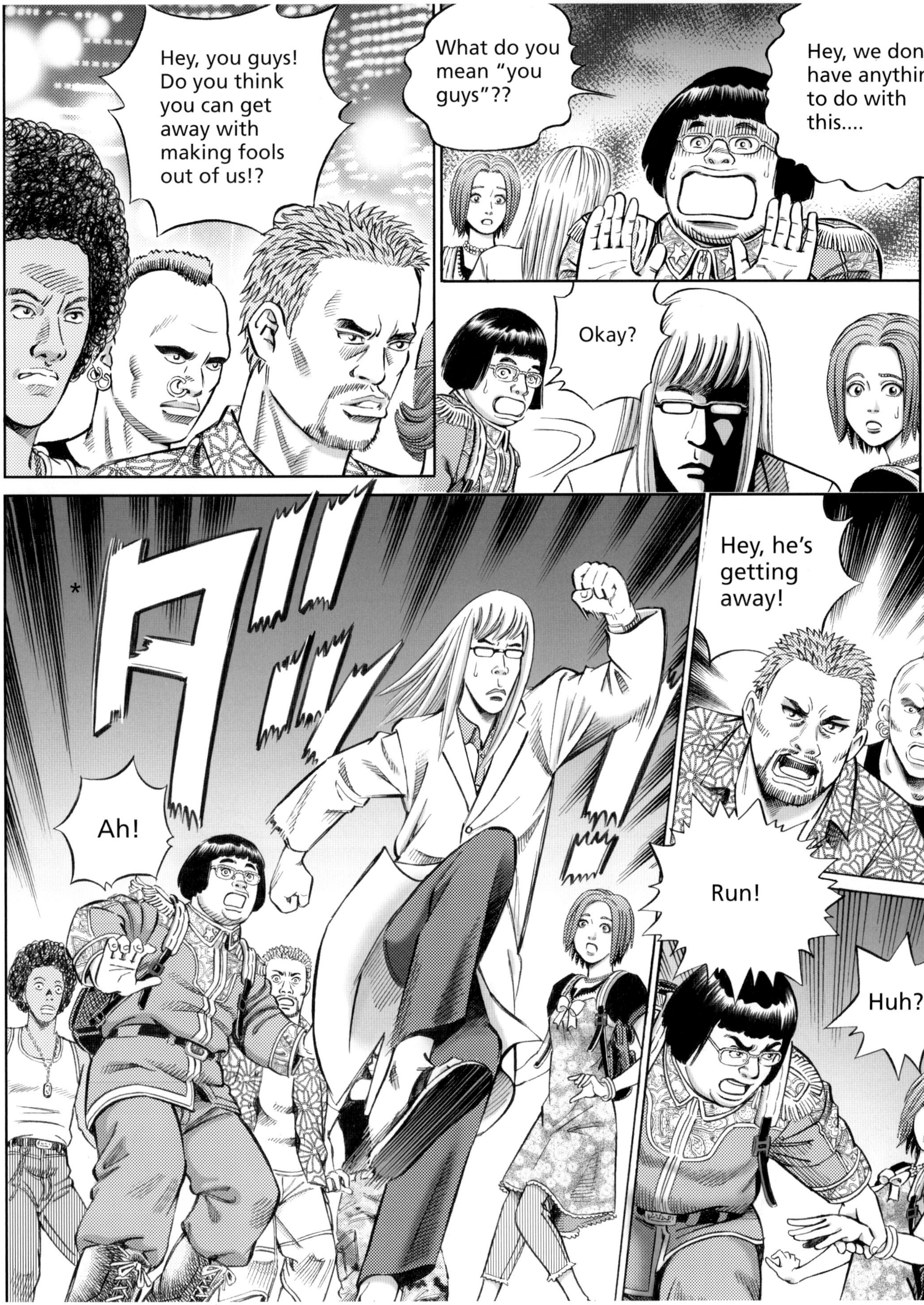
Hey, you guys! Do you think you can get away with making fools out of us!?
What do you mean "you guys"??
Hey, we don't have anything to do with this....
Okay?
*ダッ
Ah!
Hey, he's getting away!
Run!
Huh??

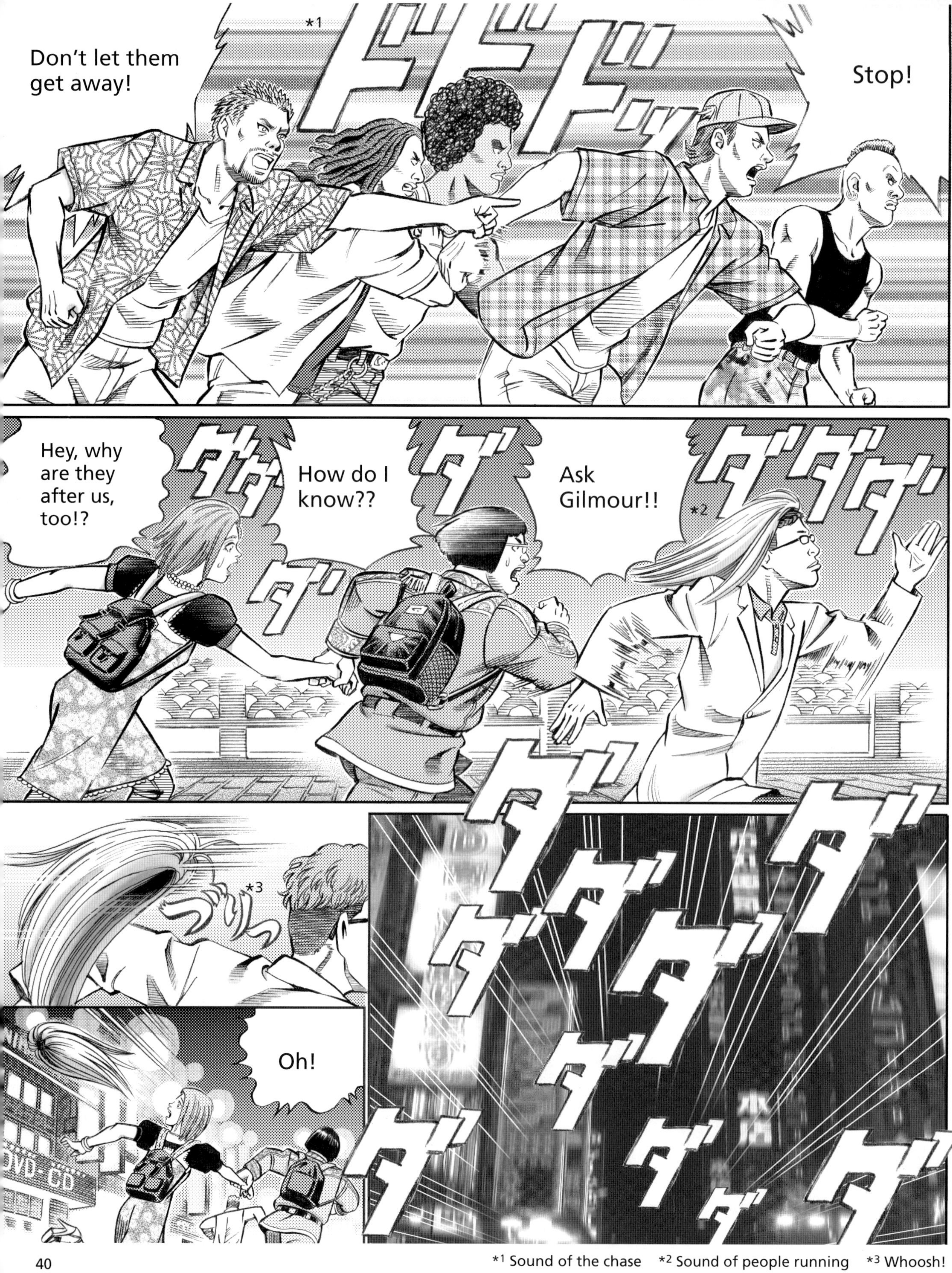
Don't let them get away!
Stop!
Hey, why are they after us, too!?
How do I know??
Ask Gilmour!!
Oh!

*1 Sound of the chase *2 Sound of people running *3 Whoosh!

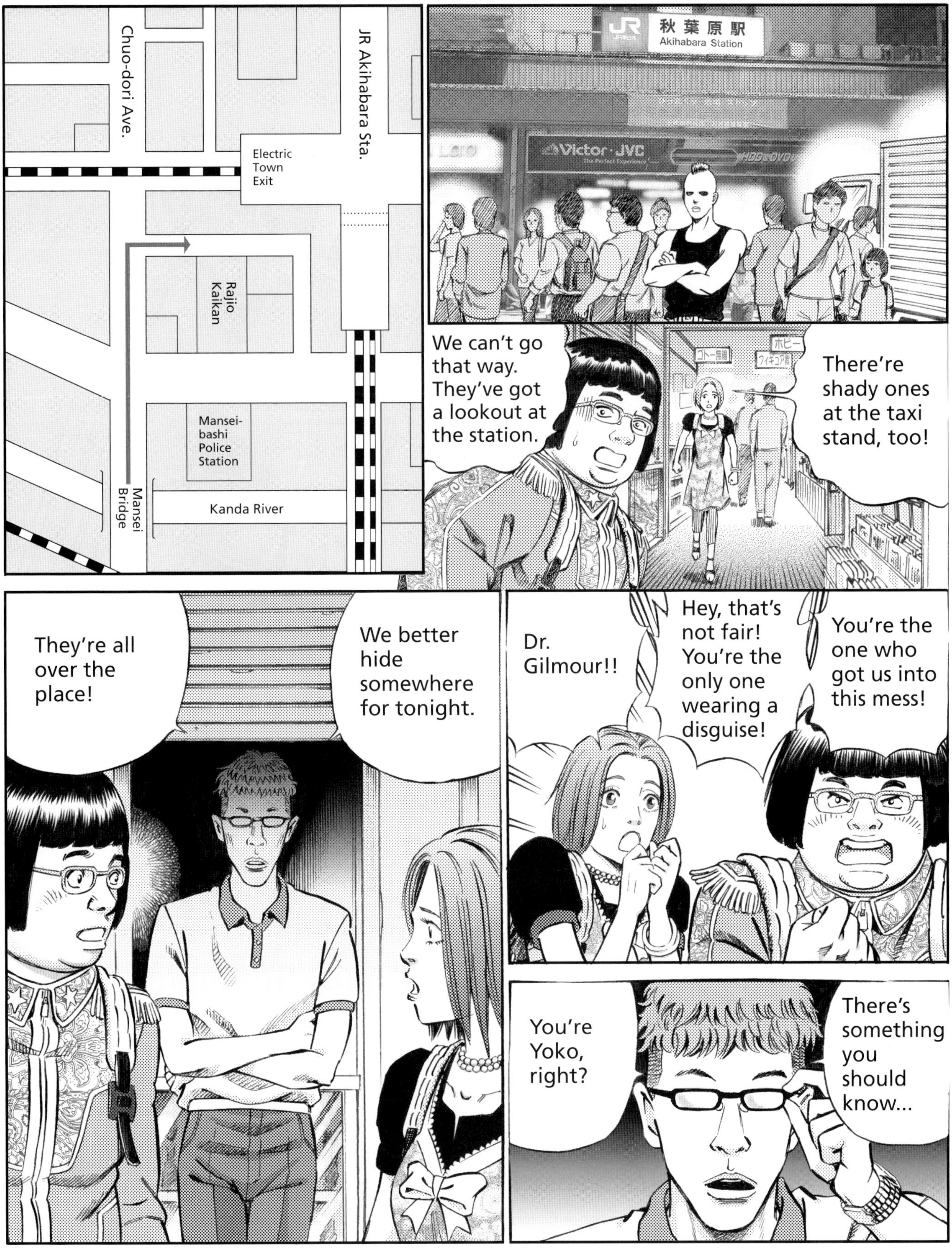
Chuo-dori Ave.
JR Akihabara Sta.
Electric Town Exit
Rajio Kaikan
Mansei-bashi Police Station
Mansei Bridge
Kanda River
秋葉原駅
Akihabara Station
Victor · JVC
We can't go that way. They've got a lookout at the station.
There're shady ones at the taxi stand, too!
They're all over the place!
We better hide somewhere for tonight.
Dr. Gilmour!!
Hey, that's not fair! You're the only one wearing a disguise!
You're the one who got us into this mess!
You're Yoko, right?
There's something you should know...

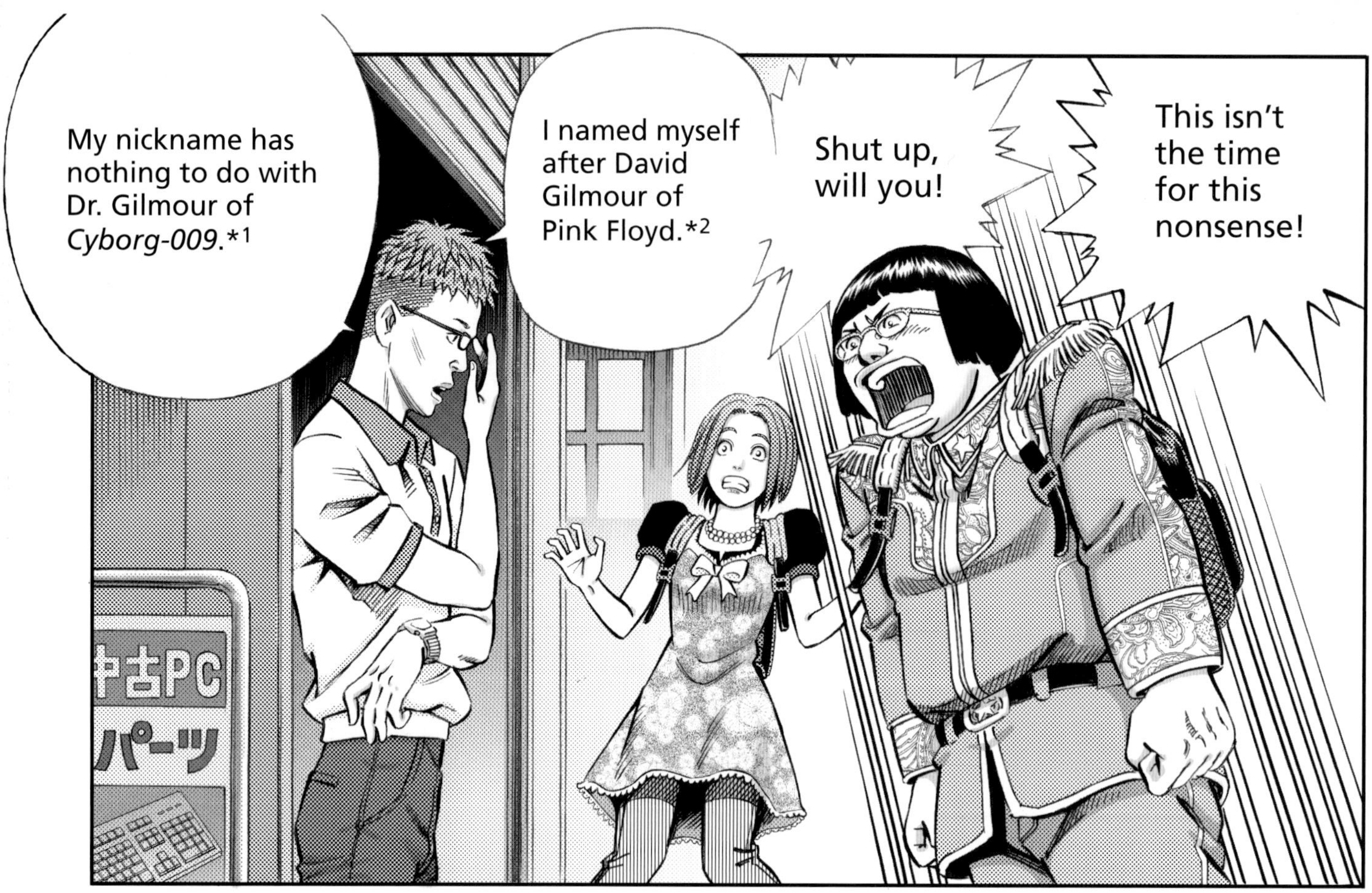
My nickname has nothing to do with Dr. Gilmour of *Cyborg-009*.*1
I named myself after David Gilmour of Pink Floyd.*2
Shut up, will you!
This isn't the time for this nonsense!
中古PC
パーツ

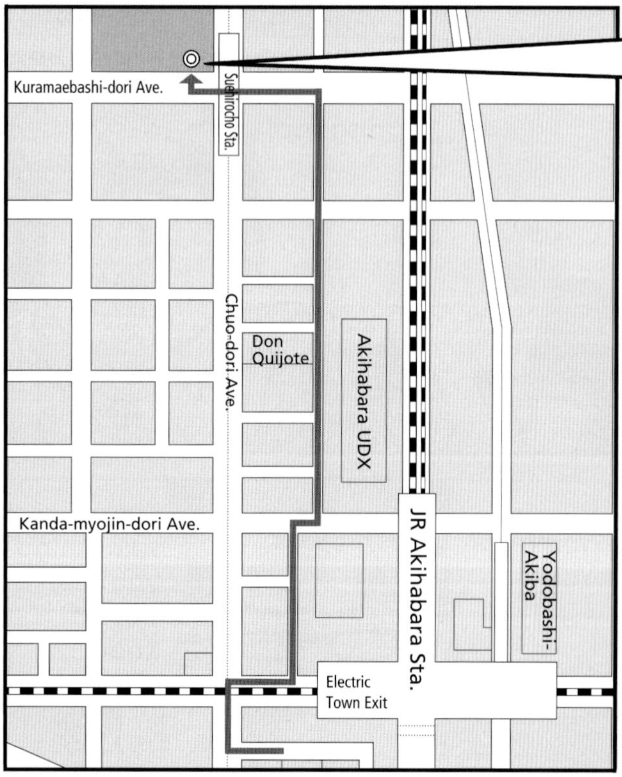
Kuramaebashi-dori Ave.
Suehirocho Sta.
Chuo-dori Ave.
Don Quijote
Akihabara UDX
Kanda-myojin-dori Ave.
JR Akihabara Sta.
Yodobashi-Akiba
Electric Town Exit

Nagomi style café
A Japanese-style Internet café, Nagomi style café features 20,000 comics, 140 magazines and 20 kinds of online games. Free drinks and ice cream served.
http://nagomi-cafe.com

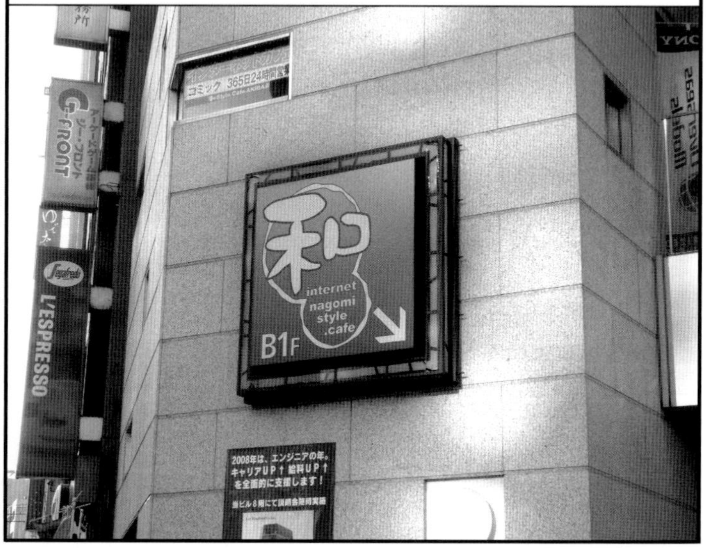
和
internet nagomi style .cafe
B1F
L'ESPRESSO

*1 A science fiction manga, this is one of the major works of manga writer Shotaro Ishinomori (1938–1998). Dr. Gilmour is one of the main characters.
*2 A progressive rock band formed in the U.K. at the end of the 1960s. Though they no longer make music, the group's albums continue to sell.

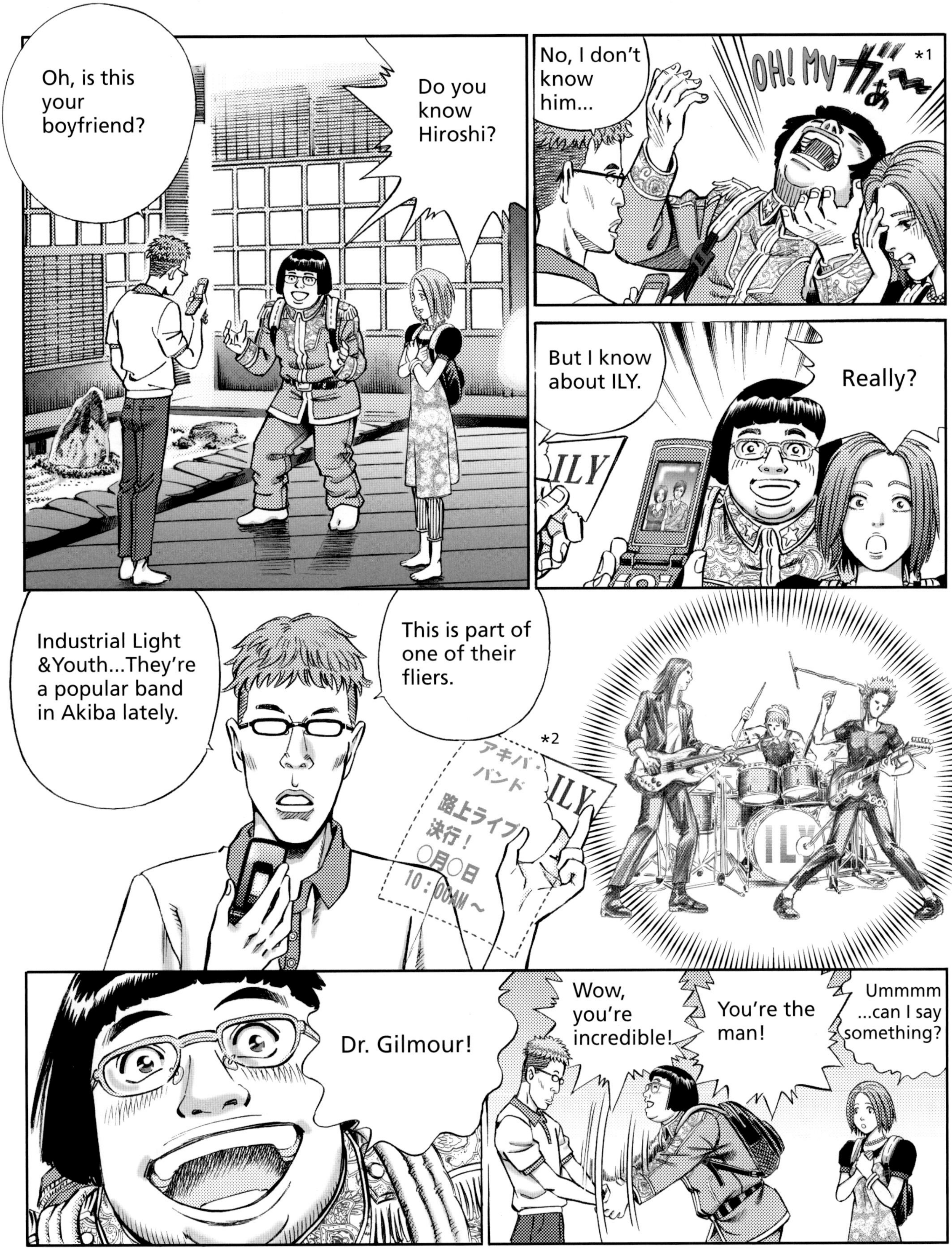
Oh, is this your boyfriend?
Do you know Hiroshi?
No, I don't know him...
OH! Myガぁ~ *1
But I know about ILY.
Really?
ILY
Industrial Light &Youth...They're a popular band in Akiba lately.
This is part of one of their fliers.
*2
アキバ・バンド
ILY
路上ライブ決行！
○月○日
10：00AM～
ILY
Dr. Gilmour!
Wow, you're incredible!
You're the man!
Ummmm ...can I say something?

*1 Oh, my god!!

*2 Akiba's own live band ILY performs (Day) (month), 10 a.m.

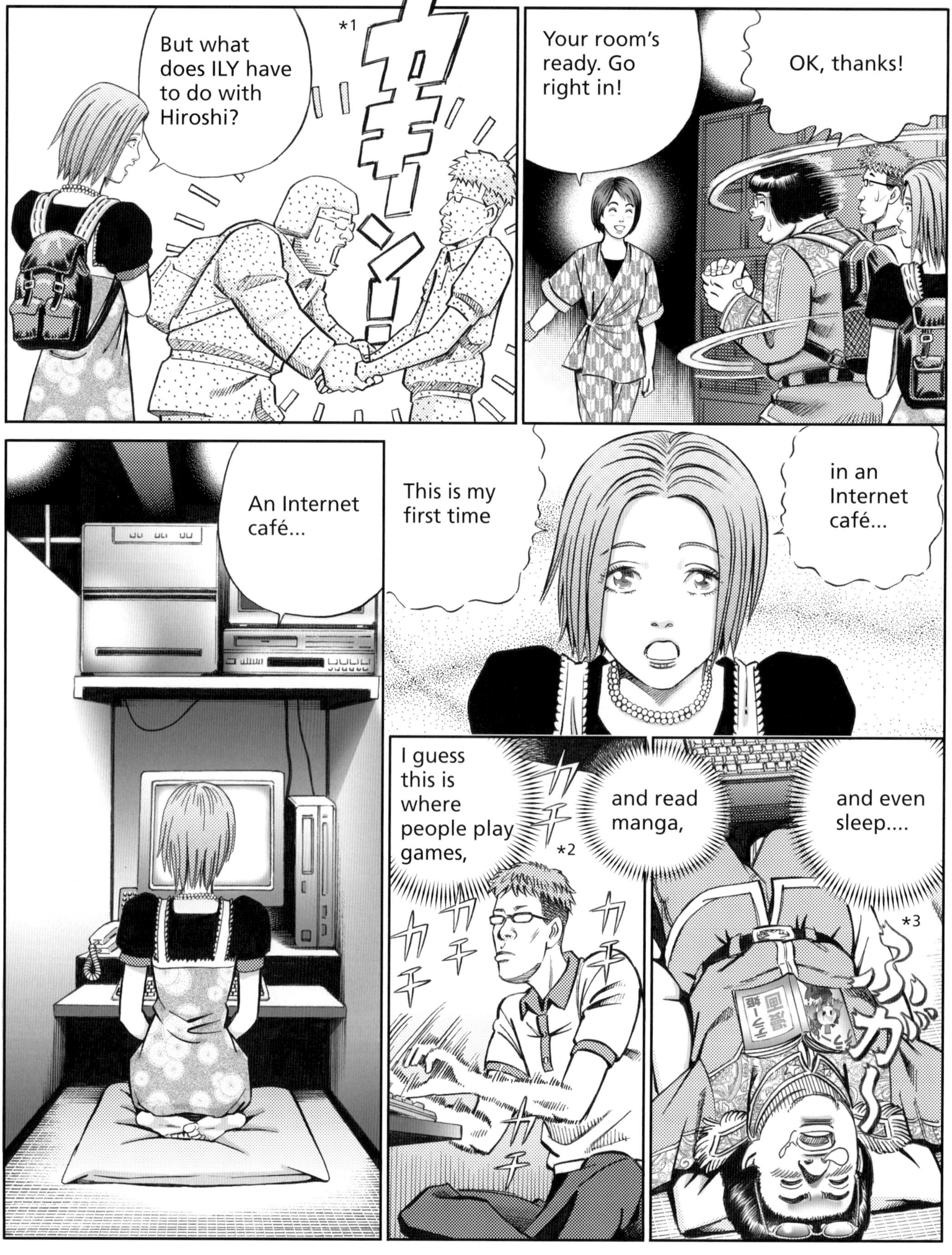

But what does ILY have to do with Hiroshi?
*1
Your room's ready. Go right in!
OK, thanks!
An Internet café...
This is my first time
in an Internet café...
I guess this is where people play games,
*2
and read manga,
and even sleep....
*3

*1 Crunch!
*2 Click, click, click
*3 The sound of snoring

I think I'll... *1

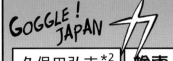

GOGGLE! JAPAN

久保田弘志*2　検索

ウェブ検索結果　83,400件

1. 弘志のお気楽Blog
大阪在住、弘志（ヒロシ）の最近のお気に入りは、何とい言
2. 「久保田」を飲むなら

GOGGLE! JAPAN

ILY　検索

ウェブ検索結果　120,000,000件

1. ily（アイエルワイ）イングリッ
…県の英会話教室。英語を身近授業は60分単位で、講師はネイ
2. 【薬天市場】ILY 薬品の

"Living the good life is doing a good search."

Who the hell said that?

Scroll! Scroll!

I'm not finding anything!

This is the story of my life, that's for sure...

GOGGLE! JAPAN

秋葉原*3　検索

ウェブ検索結果　49,100,000件

1. WEB・DE 秋葉原　…AKIBA ガイ

Scroll! Scroll!

WEB☆DE 秋葉原
WEB DE AKIBA

★NEWS＆TOPICS★　★アキバレポート★　★MAP★　★HOME★

*1 Click!
*2 Hiroshi Kubota
*3 Akihabara

History of Akihabara

ラジオ

What? What's this?
There's a rumor that a Soviet spy came to Akiba during the Cold War to buy LSI....

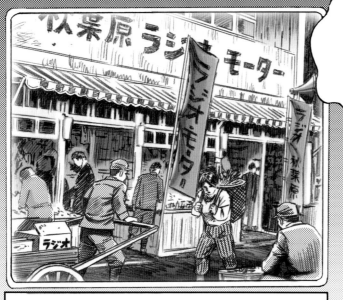

Akihabara's outdoor stands after the Pacific War (1941–45). When the vacuum tube radio became a hit product, electronics shops started opening in the area in large numbers. From then on, Akihabara continued to develop as an electronics district.

TV
PC

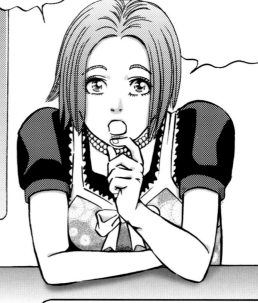

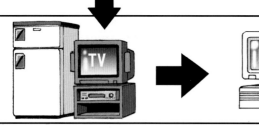

In the 1980s, electronics retailers moved to the suburbs, and Akihabara's signature product genre shifted from electronics to PCs.

In the 1990s, Akiba drew computer enthusiasts from all over Japan..

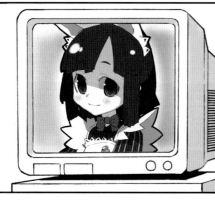

PC mania ≈

Model mania ≈

Anime mania

After the 1990s, Akiba turned into a town for otaku.*

* There are many words in Japanese for the English word "you," including *"anata"* and *"kimi."* A more informal word is *"otaku."* In the 1980s, *anime* fans began calling each other *"otaku,"* and this is the origin of the word currently meaning *anime*, figure and computer enthusiasts.

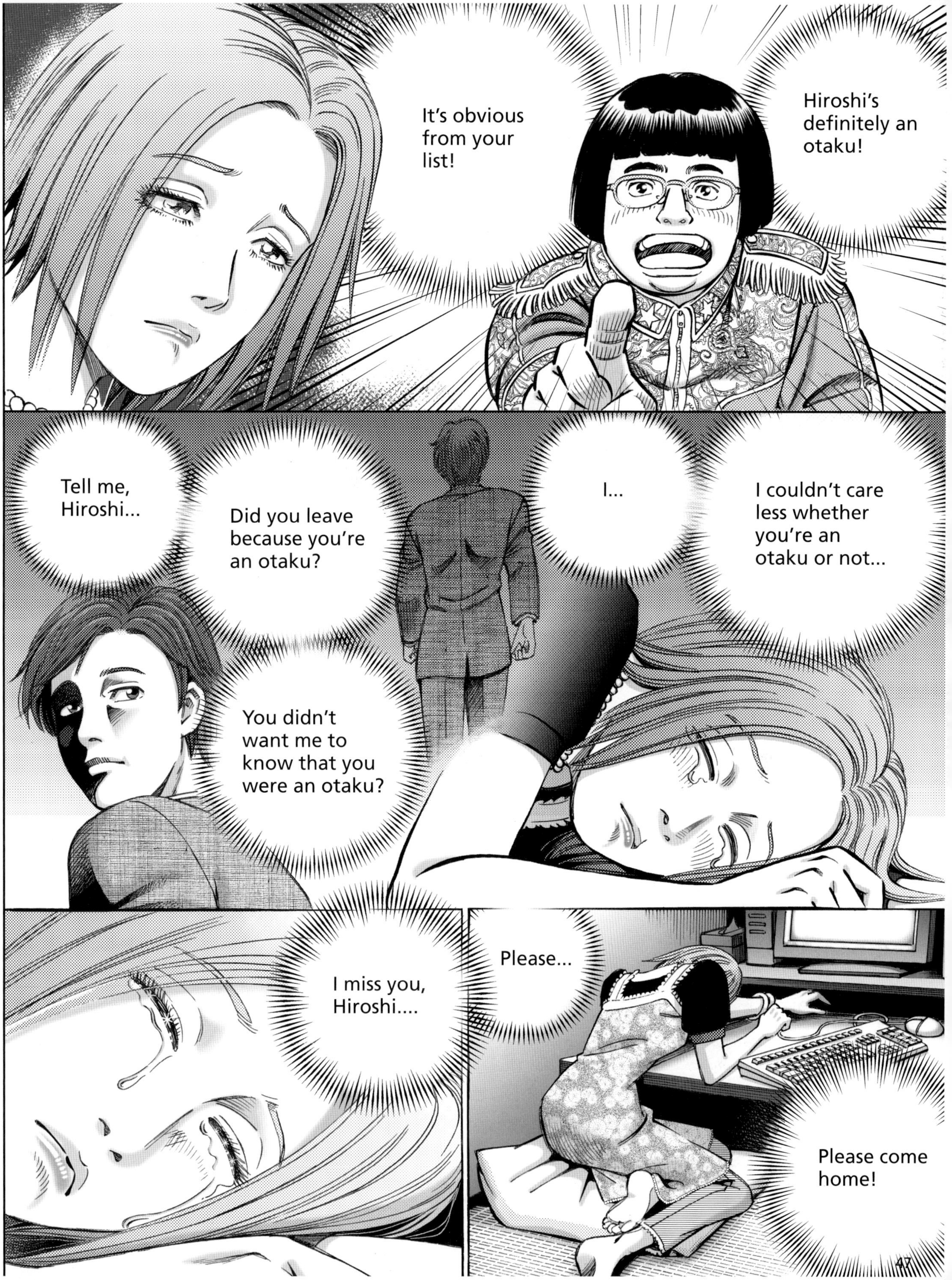
It's obvious from your list!
Hiroshi's definitely an otaku!
Tell me, Hiroshi...
Did you leave because you're an otaku?
I...
I couldn't care less whether you're an otaku or not...
You didn't want me to know that you were an otaku?
I miss you, Hiroshi....
Please...
Please come home!

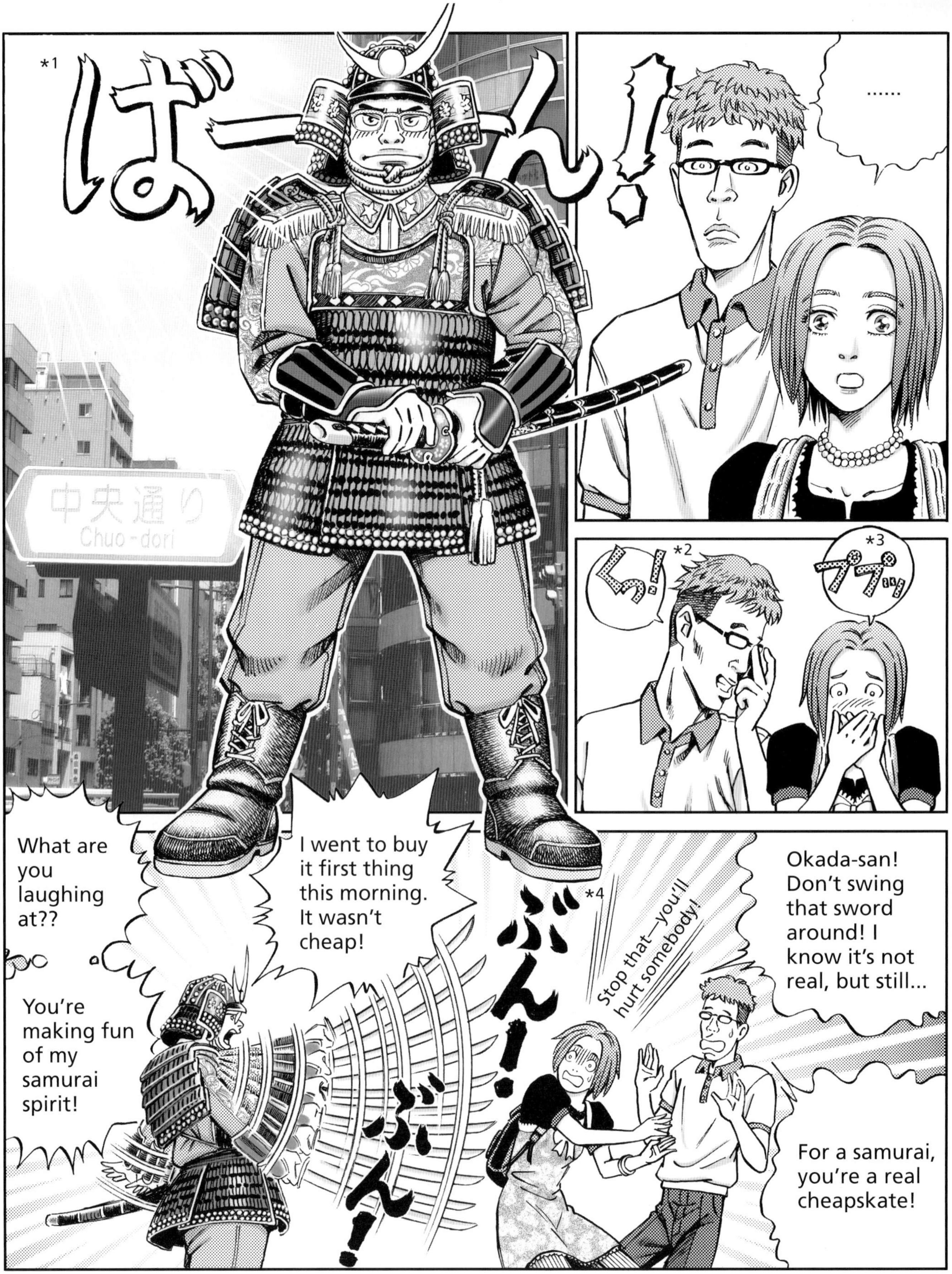
*1
ばーん!
中央通り
Chuo-dori
......
*2
くっ!
*3
ププッ
What are you laughing at??
I went to buy it first thing this morning. It wasn't cheap!
You're making fun of my samurai spirit!
*4
ぶーん!ぶん!
Stop that—you'll hurt somebody!
Okada-san! Don't swing that sword around! I know it's not real, but still...
For a samurai, you're a real cheapskate!

*1 Ta-da!!
*2 Hee-hee!
*3 Ha-ha!
*4 Vroom! Vroom!

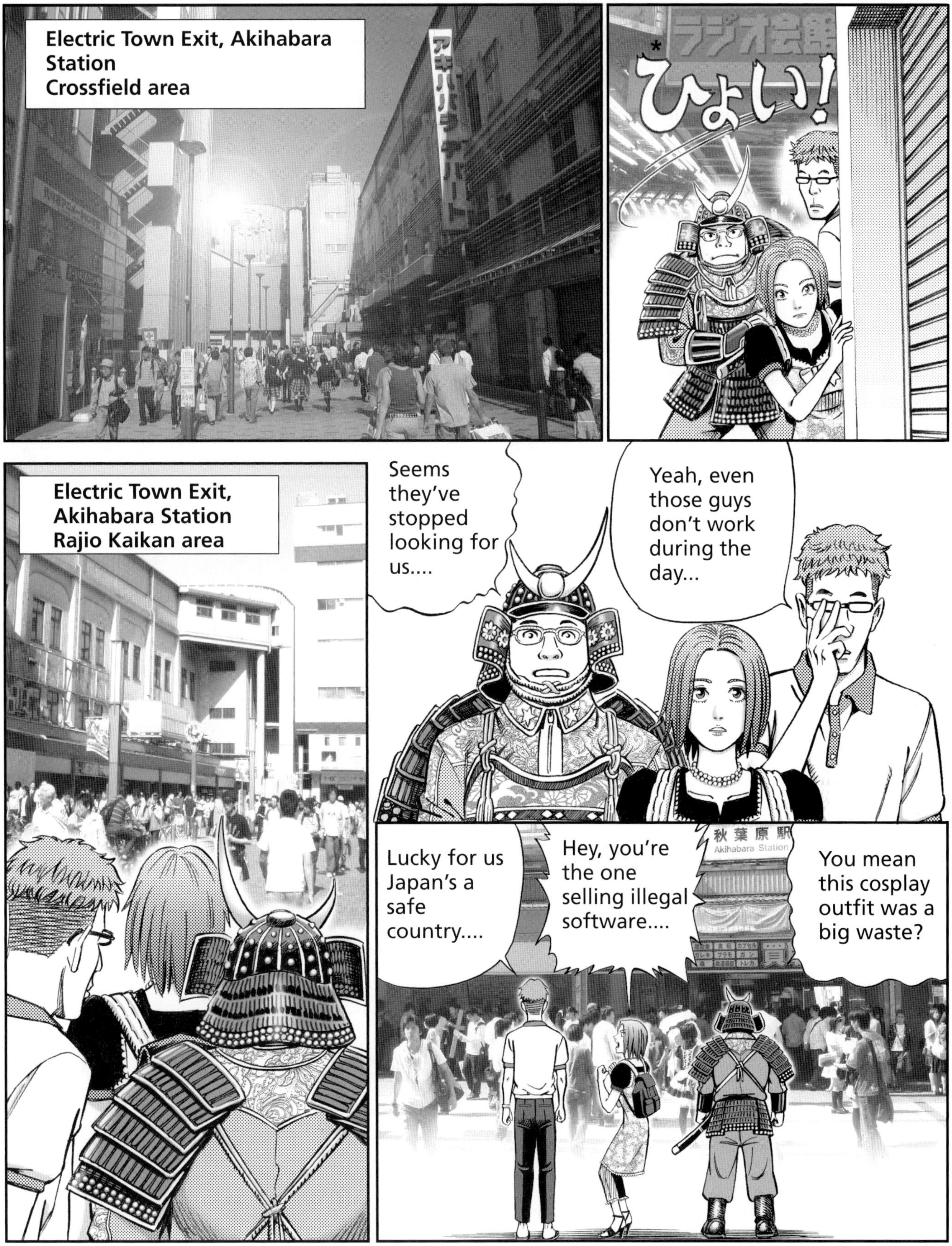
Electric Town Exit, Akihabara Station
Crossfield area
アキハバラデパート
ラジオ会館
*ひょい!
Electric Town Exit, Akihabara Station
Rajio Kaikan area
Seems they've stopped looking for us....
Yeah, even those guys don't work during the day...
Lucky for us Japan's a safe country....
Hey, you're the one selling illegal software....
秋葉原駅
Akihabara Station
You mean this cosplay outfit was a big waste?

* Look! All clear

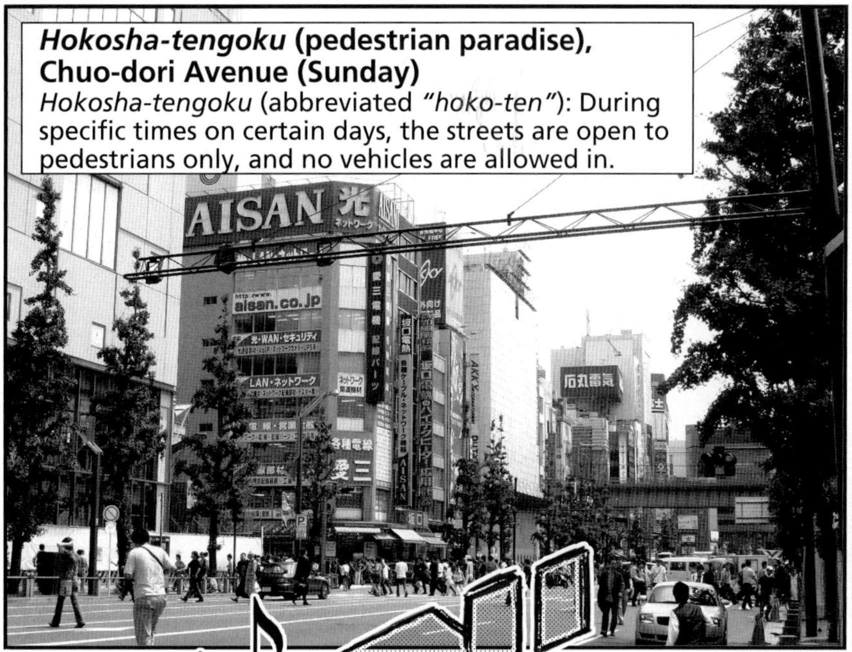
Hokosha-tengoku (pedestrian paradise), Chuo-dori Avenue (Sunday)
Hokosha-tengoku (abbreviated "_hoko-ten_"): During specific times on certain days, the streets are open to pedestrians only, and no vehicles are allowed in.
AISAN
aisan.co.jp

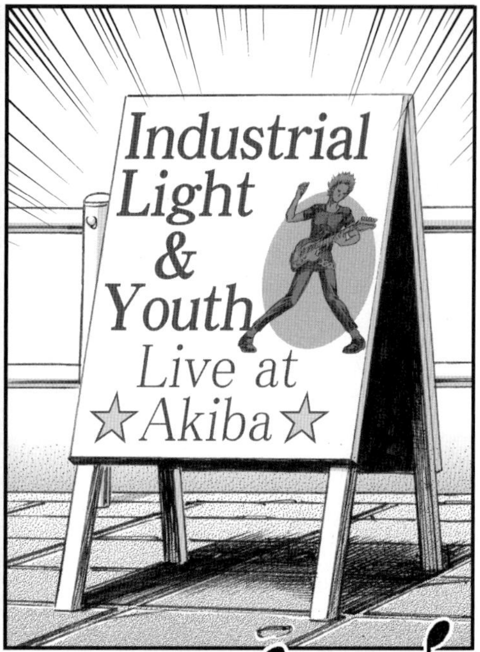
Industrial Light & Youth Live at ☆Akiba☆

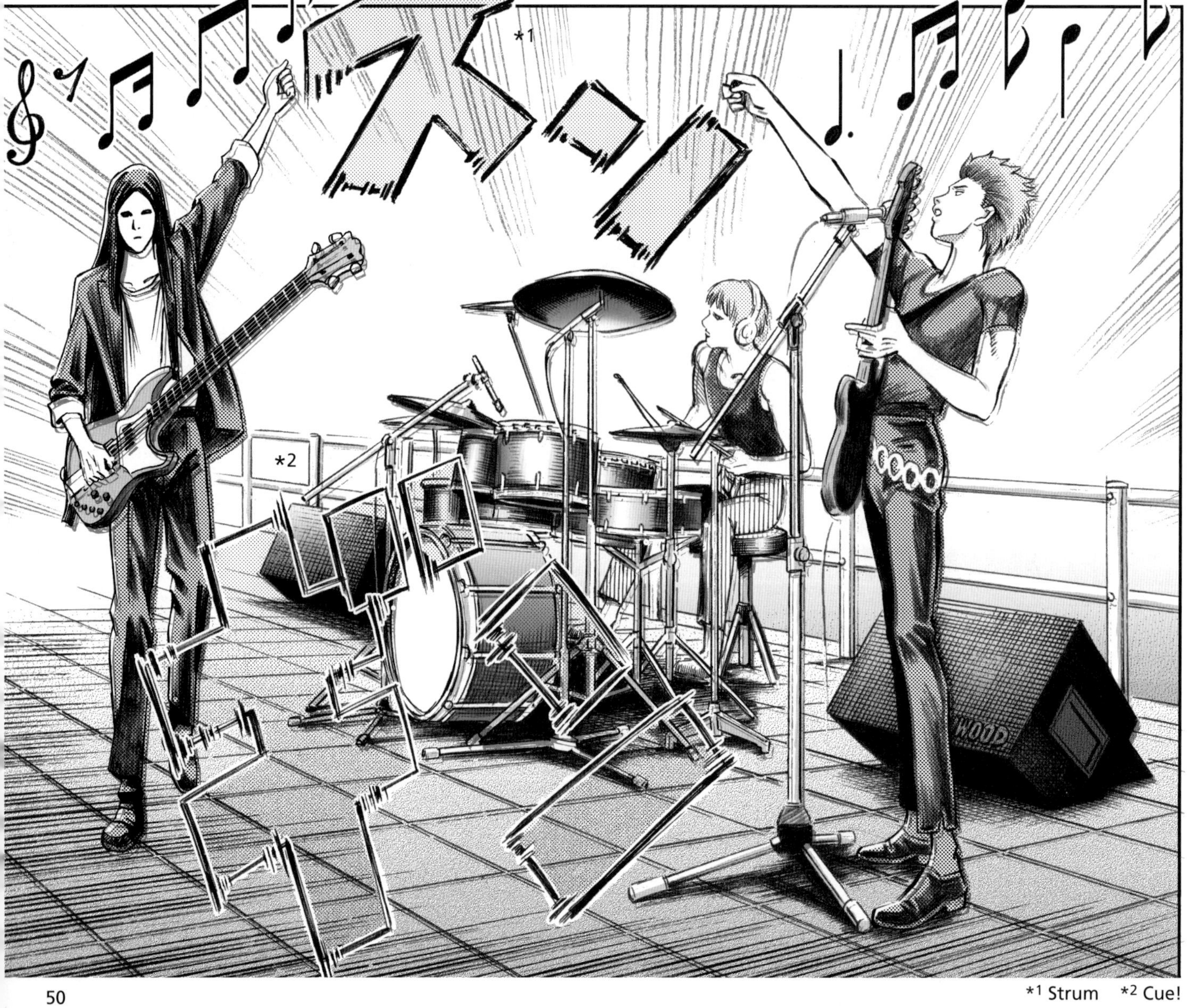
*1
*2

*1 Strum *2 Cue!

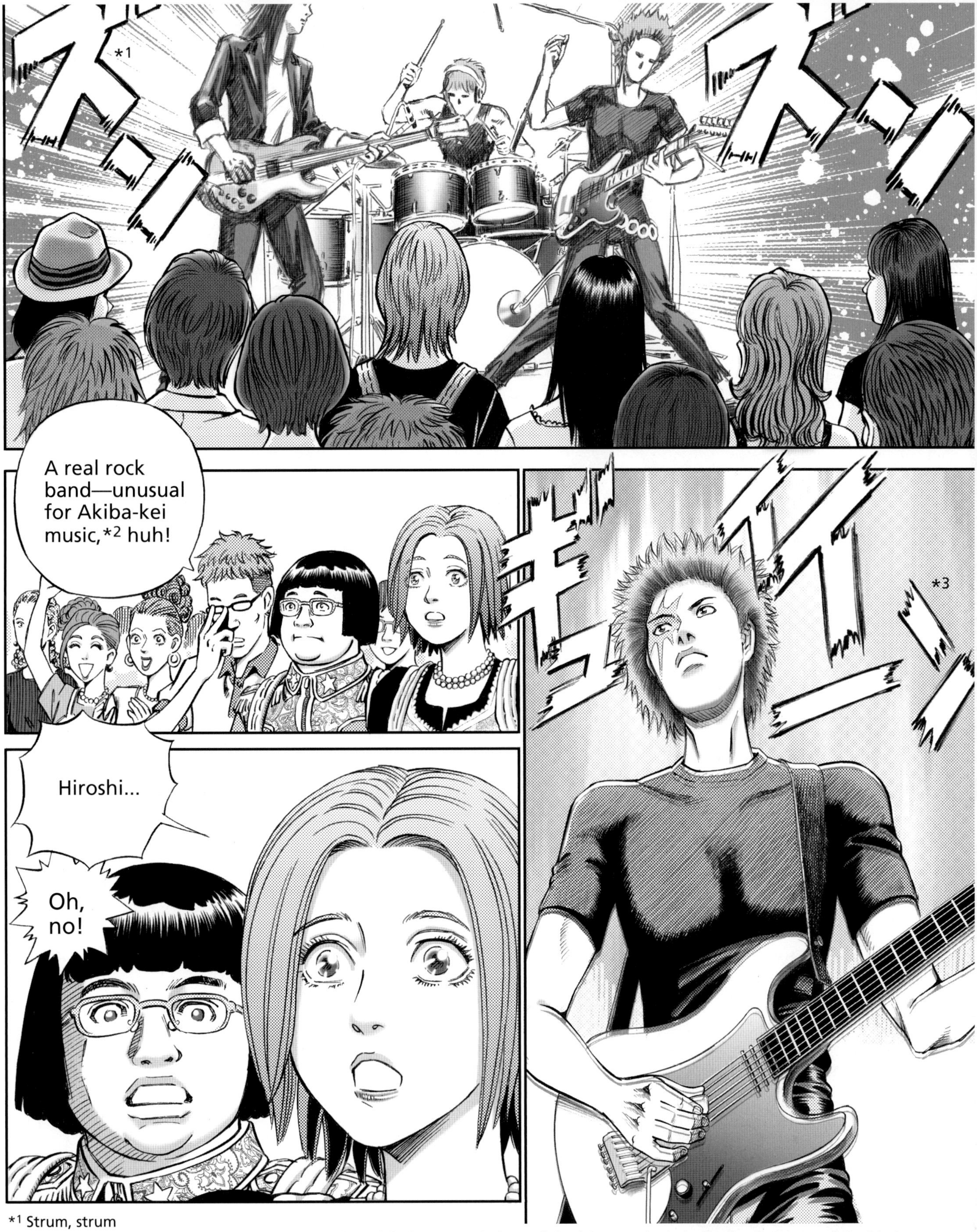
*1
A real rock band—unusual for Akiba-kei music,*2 huh!
*3
Hiroshi...
Oh, no!

*1 Strum, strum

*2 A style of music in which the artists are based in Akihabara. Musical trends in this genre include the frequent use of the kind of techno and house elements often featured in *anime* theme songs. Sometimes the popular songs sung by young *anime* voice actors are also categorized as Akiba-kei music.

*3 Cue!

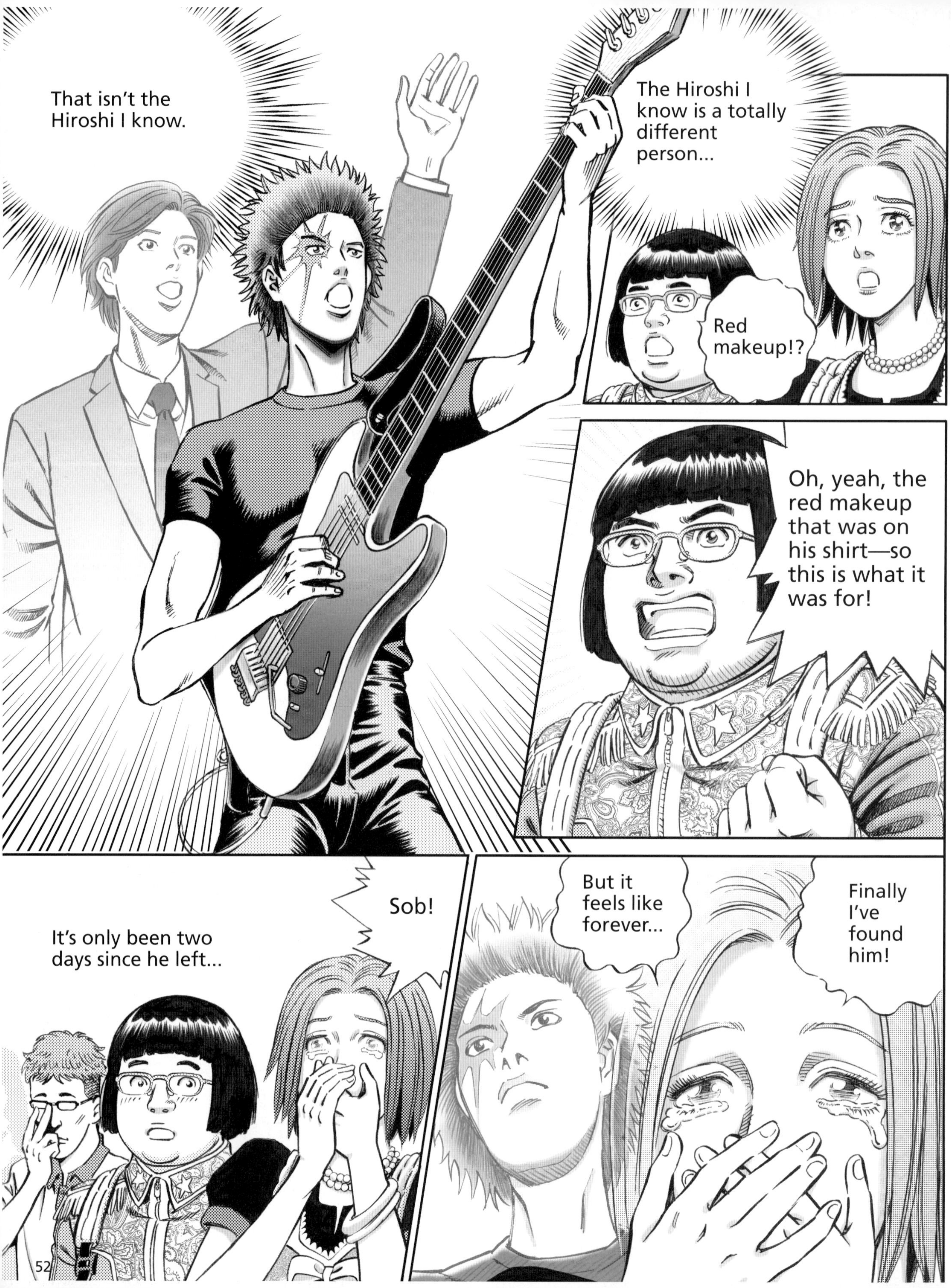

That isn't the Hiroshi I know.
The Hiroshi I know is a totally different person...
Red makeup!?
Oh, yeah, the red makeup that was on his shirt—so this is what it was for!
It's only been two days since he left...
Sob!
But it feels like forever...
Finally I've found him!

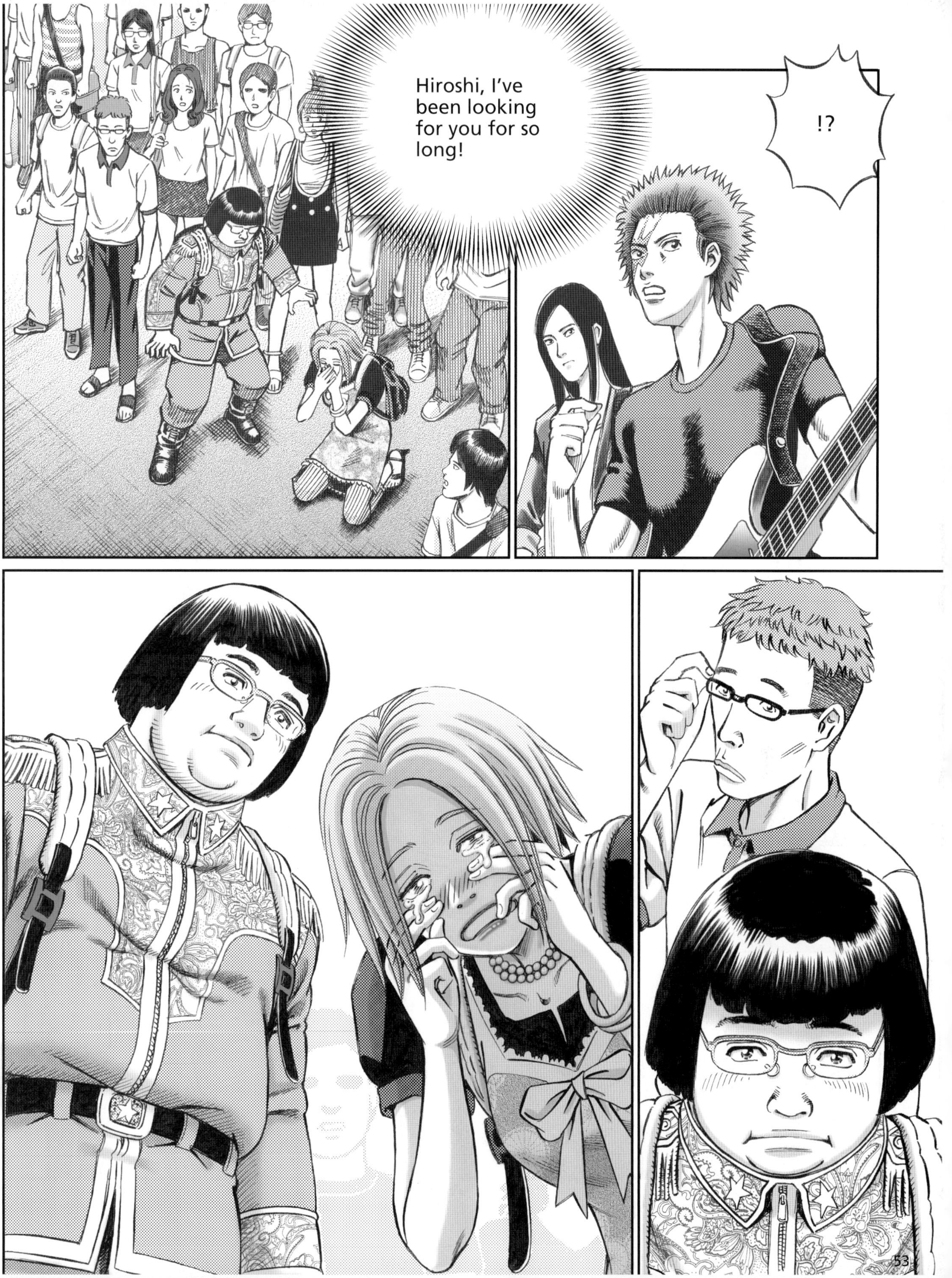
Hiroshi, I've been looking for you for so long!
!?

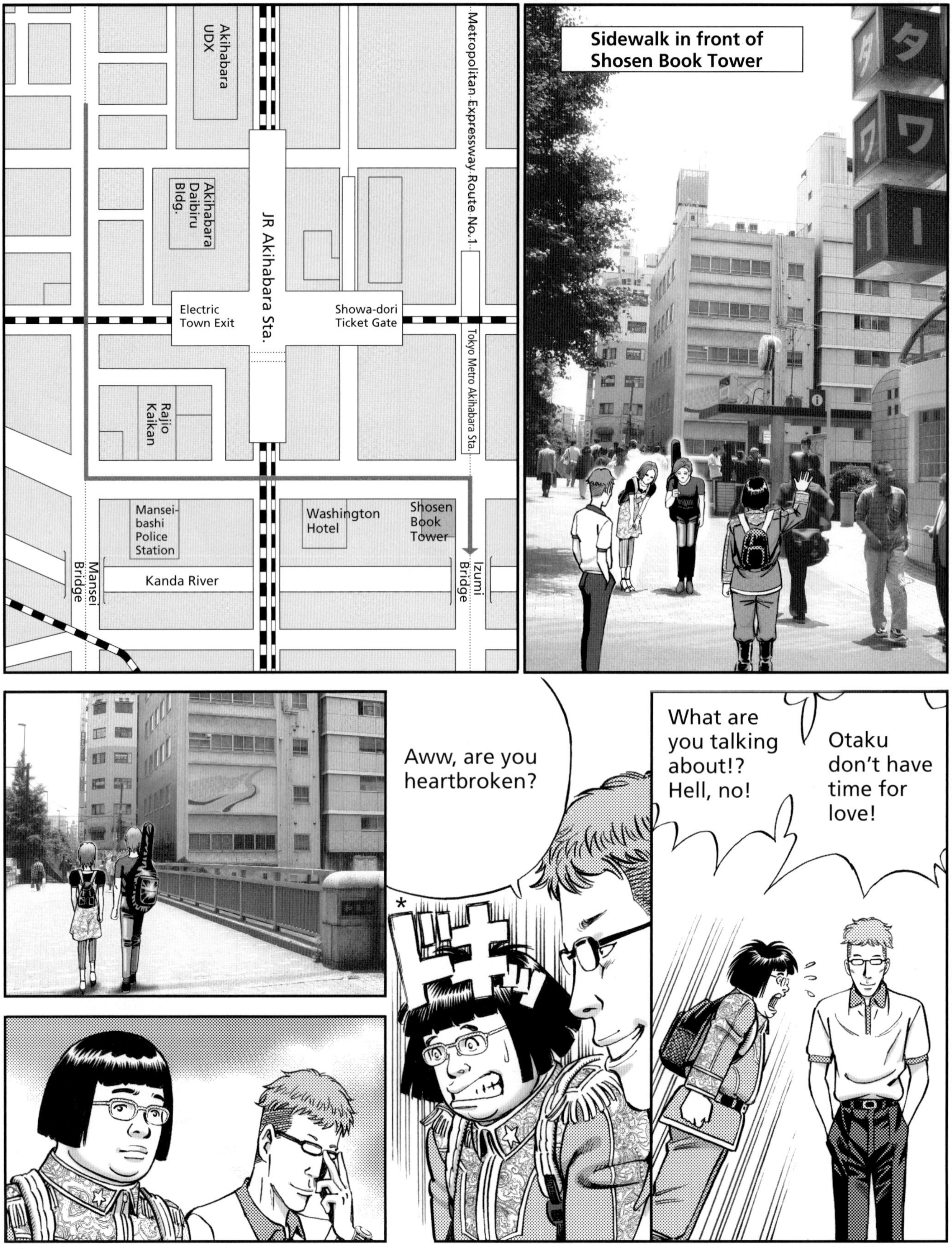
Akihabara UDX
Metropolitan Expressway Route No.1
Akihabara Daibiru Bldg.
JR Akihabara Sta.
Electric Town Exit
Showa-dori Ticket Gate
Tokyo Metro Akihabara Sta.
Rajio Kaikan
Mansei-bashi Police Station
Washington Hotel
Shosen Book Tower
Mansei Bridge
Kanda River
Izumi Bridge
Sidewalk in front of Shosen Book Tower
タワー
Aww, are you heartbroken?
*ドキッ
What are you talking about!? Hell, no!
Otaku don't have time for love!

*Shock!

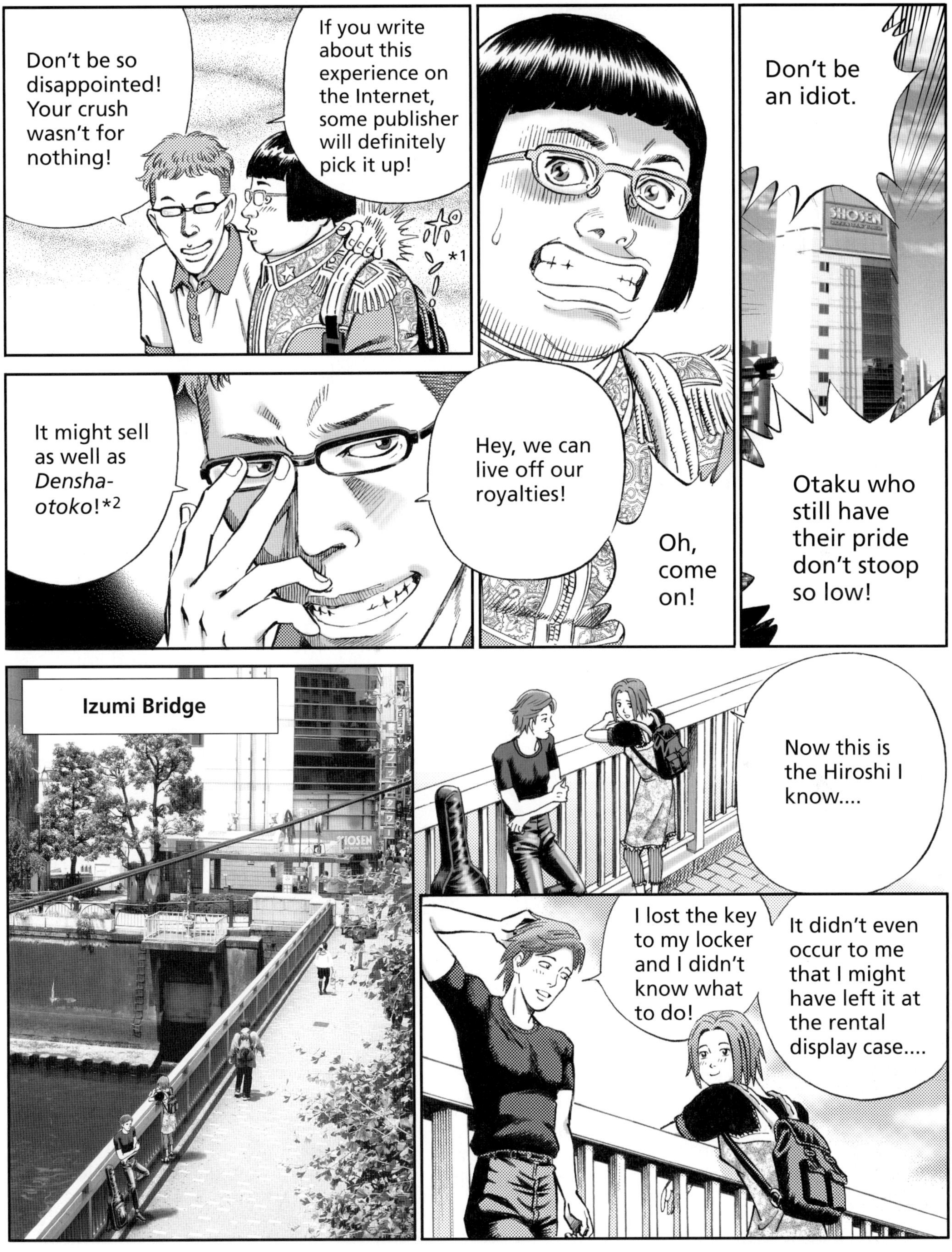
Don't be so disappointed! Your crush wasn't for nothing!
If you write about this experience on the Internet, some publisher will definitely pick it up!
*1
It might sell as well as *Densha-otoko*!*2
Hey, we can live off our royalties!
Oh, come on!
Don't be an idiot.
SHOSEN
Otaku who still have their pride don't stoop so low!
Izumi Bridge
SHOSEN
Now this is the Hiroshi I know....
I lost the key to my locker and I didn't know what to do!
It didn't even occur to me that I might have left it at the rental display case....

*1 Plonk!
*2 A love story of young otaku widely read by Japanese Internet bulletin board users became a hit novel published under the title *Densha-otoko* (2004). A movie based on the story came out in 2005.

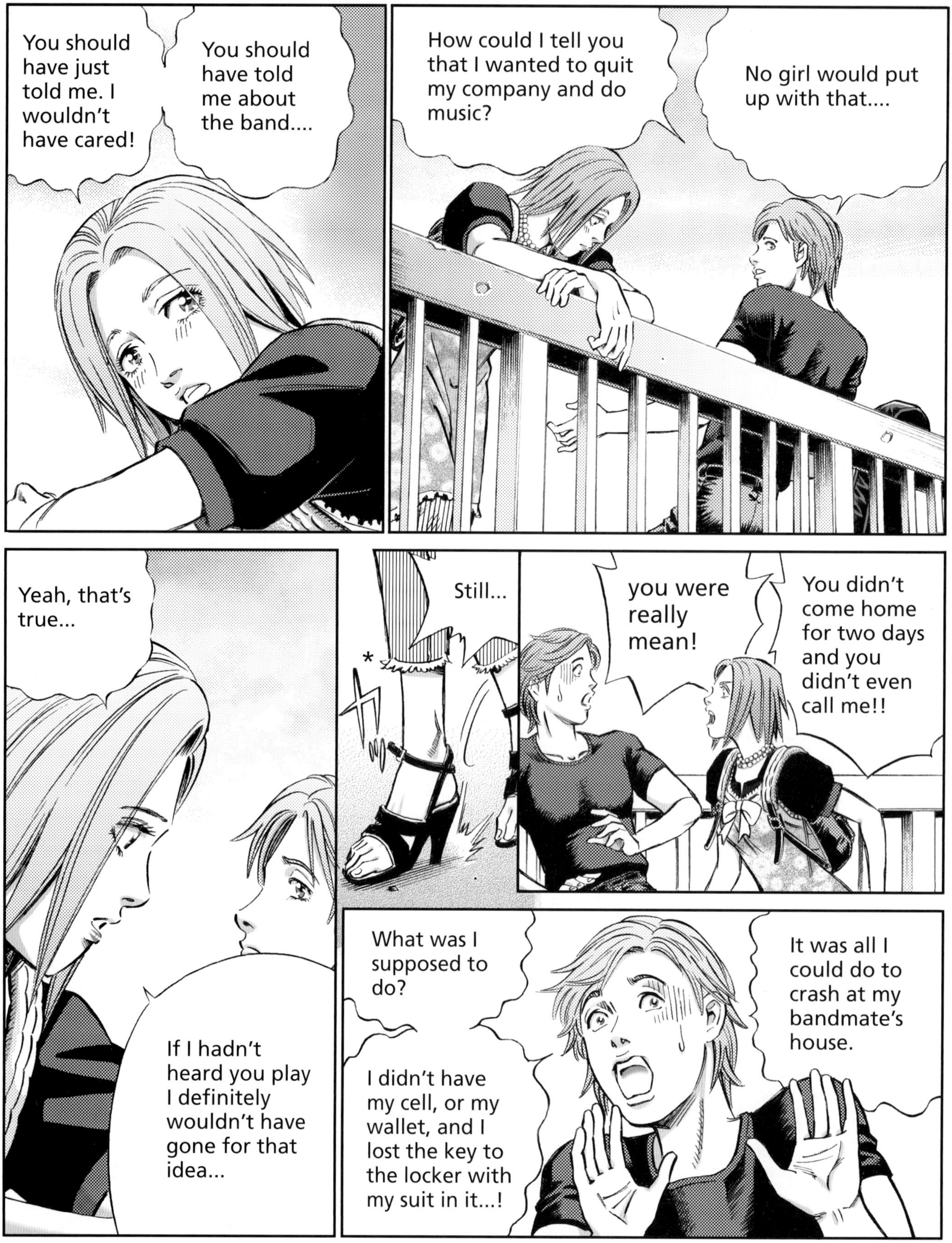

You should have just told me. I wouldn't have cared!
You should have told me about the band....
How could I tell you that I wanted to quit my company and do music?
No girl would put up with that....
Yeah, that's true...
If I hadn't heard you play I definitely wouldn't have gone for that idea...
Still...
*
you were really mean!
You didn't come home for two days and you didn't even call me!!
What was I supposed to do?
I didn't have my cell, or my wallet, and I lost the key to the locker with my suit in it...!
It was all I could do to crash at my bandmate's house.

* Stomp!

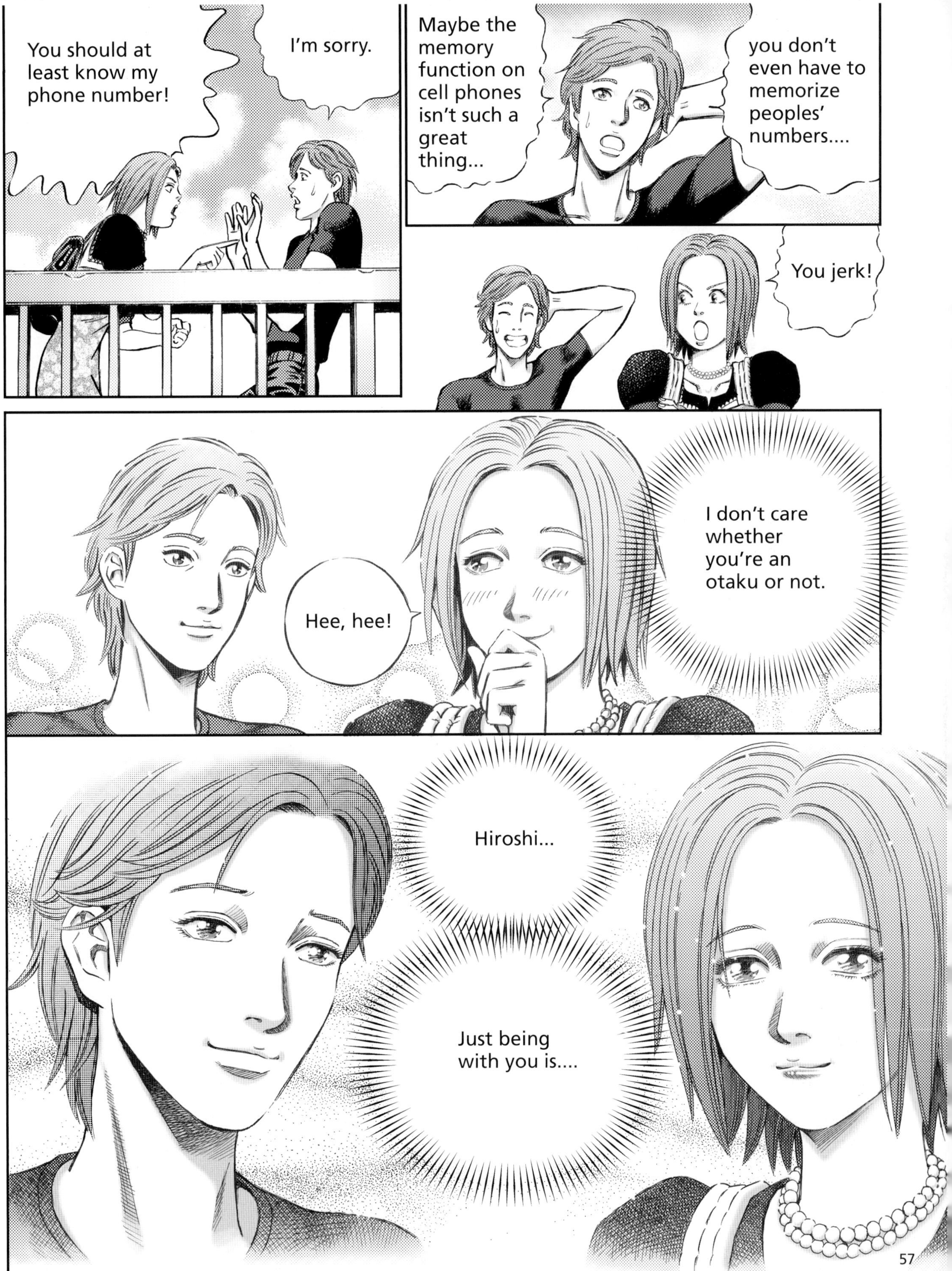
You should at least know my phone number!
I'm sorry.
Maybe the memory function on cell phones isn't such a great thing...
you don't even have to memorize peoples' numbers....
You jerk!
Hee, hee!
I don't care whether you're an otaku or not.
Hiroshi...
Just being with you is....

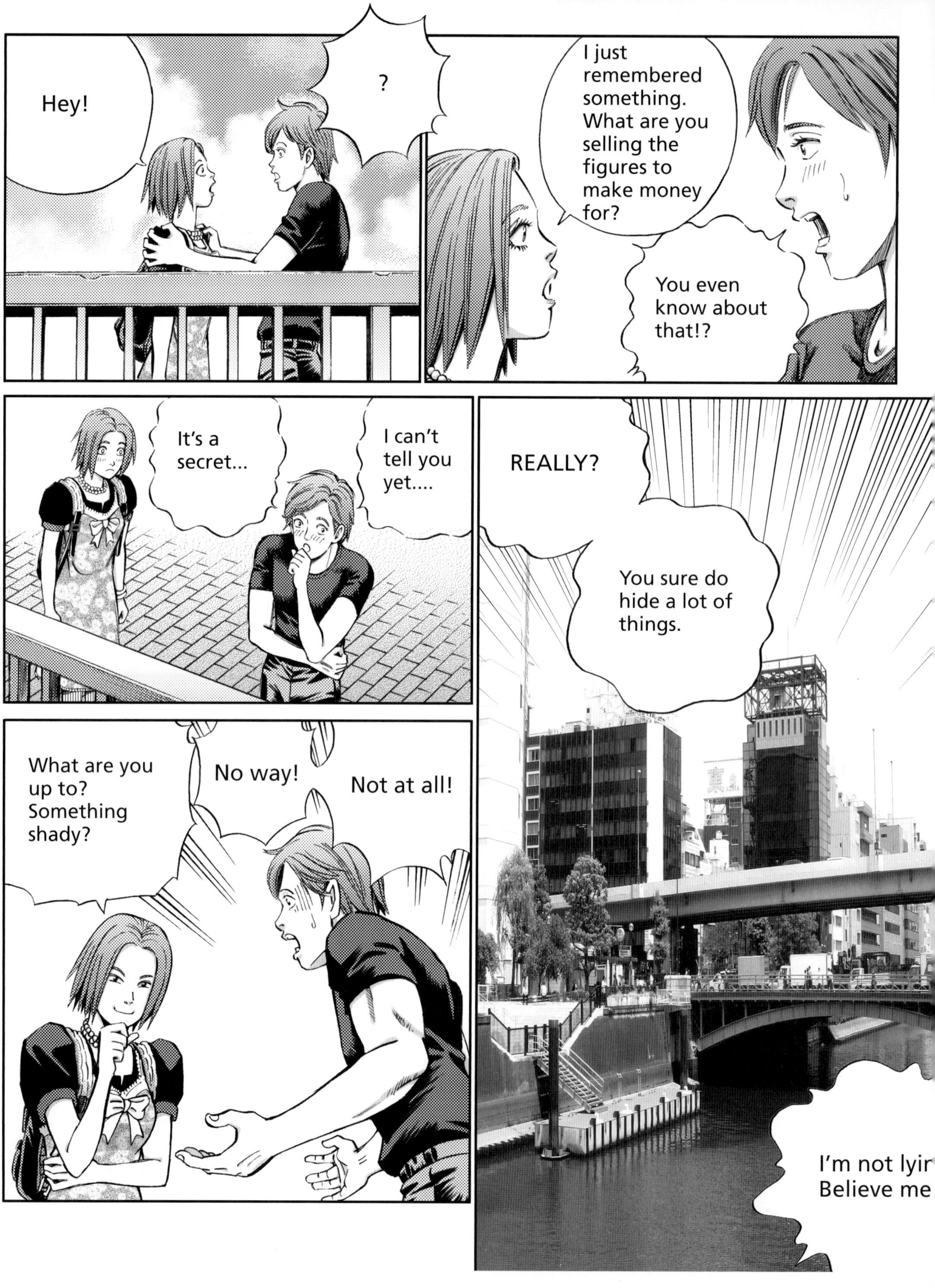
Hey!
?
I just remembered something. What are you selling the figures to make money for?
You even know about that!?
It's a secret...
I can't tell you yet....
REALLY?
You sure do hide a lot of things.
What are you up to? Something shady?
No way!
Not at all!
I'm not lyir
Believe me

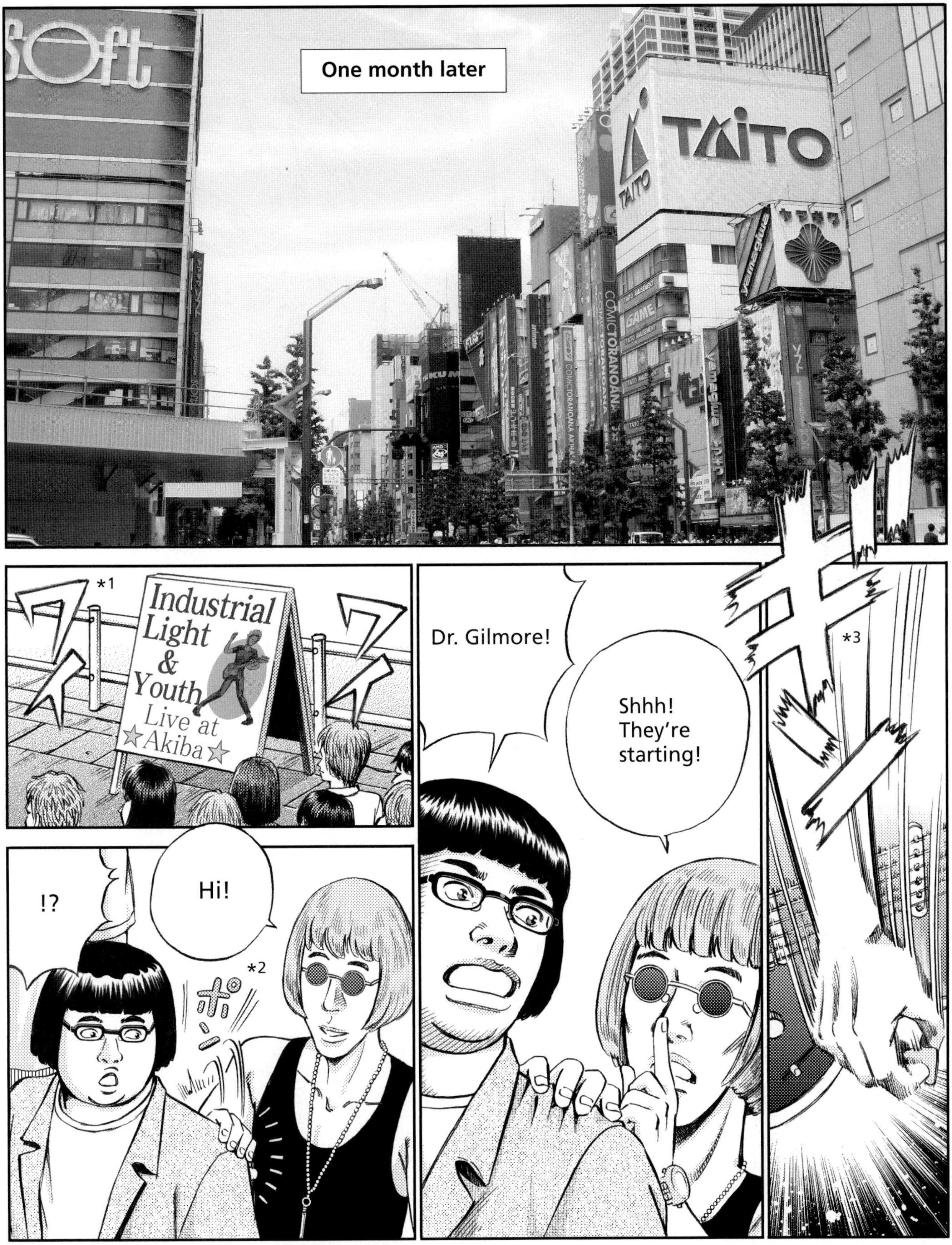
One month later
TAITO
*1
Industrial Light & Youth
Live at ☆Akiba☆
!?
Hi!
*2
Dr. Gilmore!
Shhh! They're starting!
*3

*1 Yay!
*2 Plonk!
*3 Strum, strum

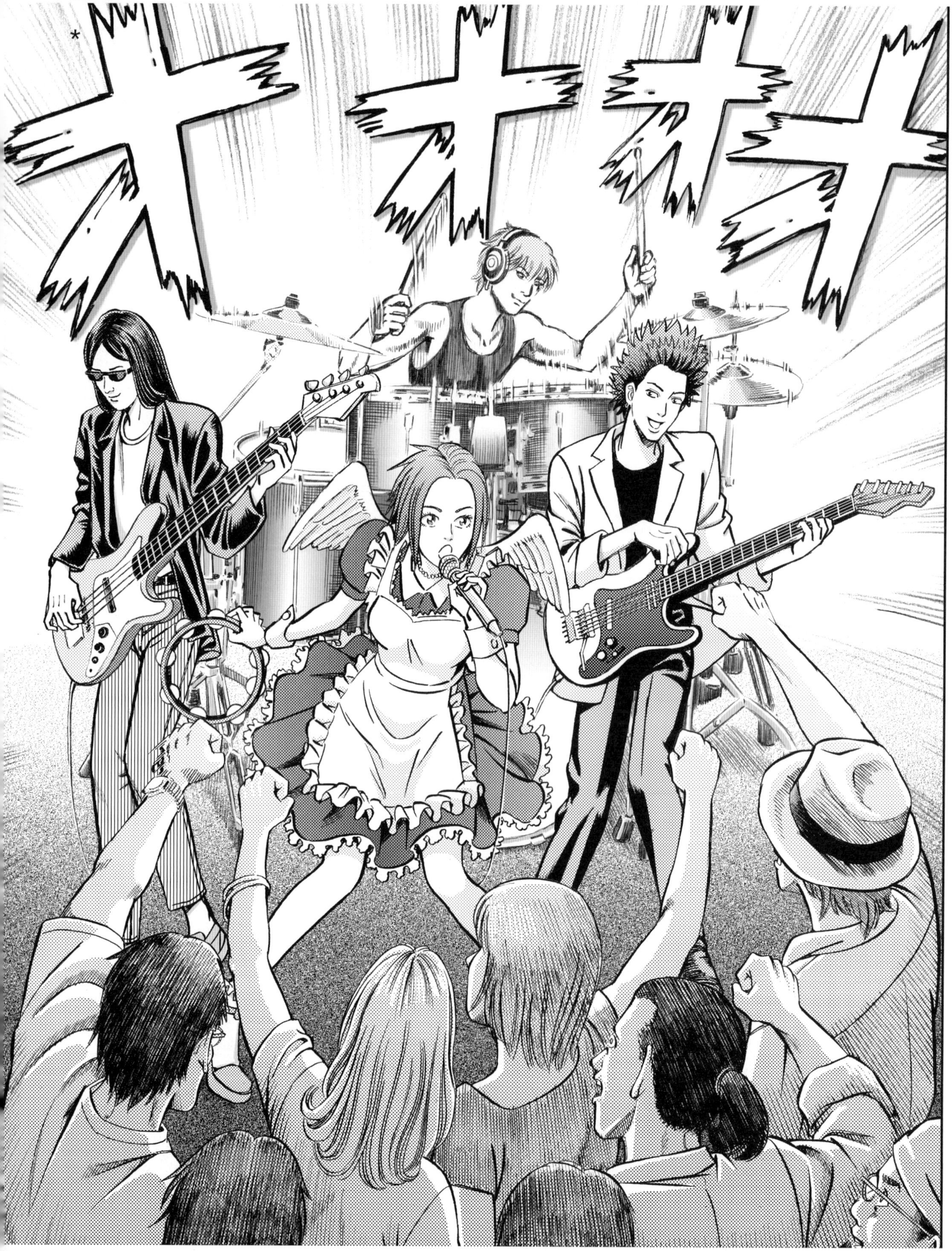
*オオオオ

*Wow!

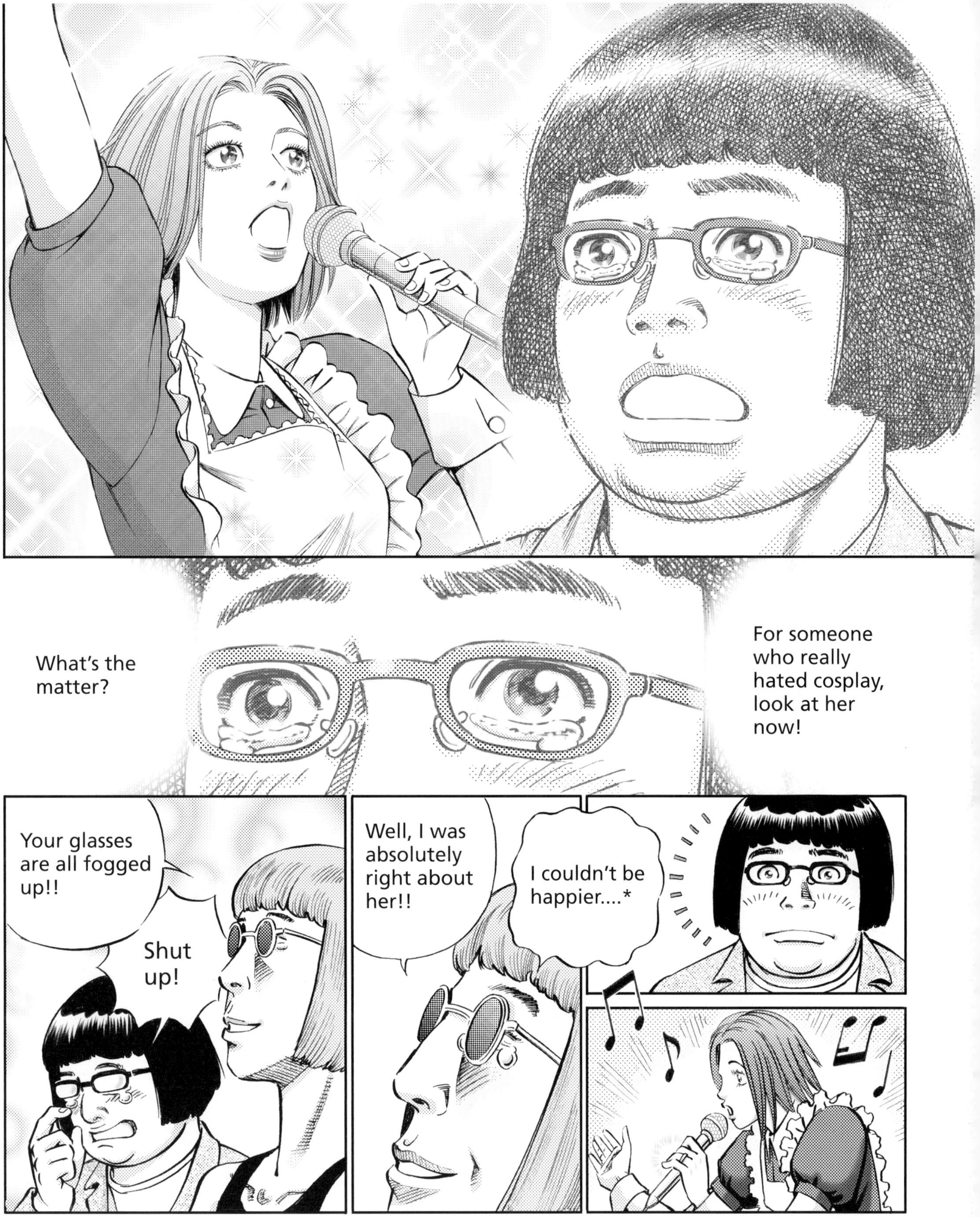
What's the matter?
For someone who really hated cosplay, look at her now!
Your glasses are all fogged up!!
Shut up!
Well, I was absolutely right about her!!
I couldn't be happier....*

* The famous last line of a certain *anime*, which every Japanese otaku knows.

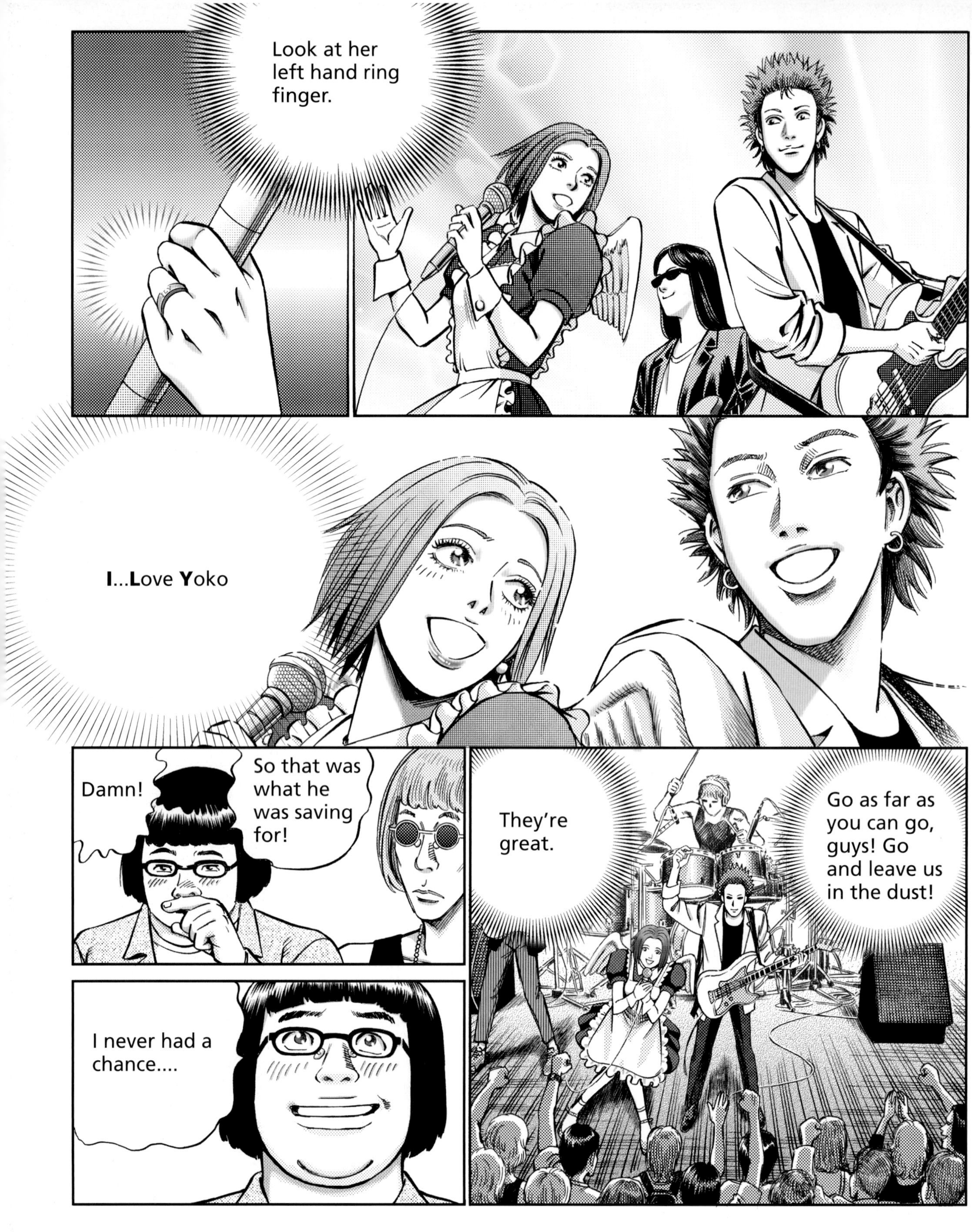
Look at her left hand ring finger.
I...Love Yoko
Damn!
So that was what he was saving for!
I never had a chance....
They're great.
Go as far as you can go, guys! Go and leave us in the dust!

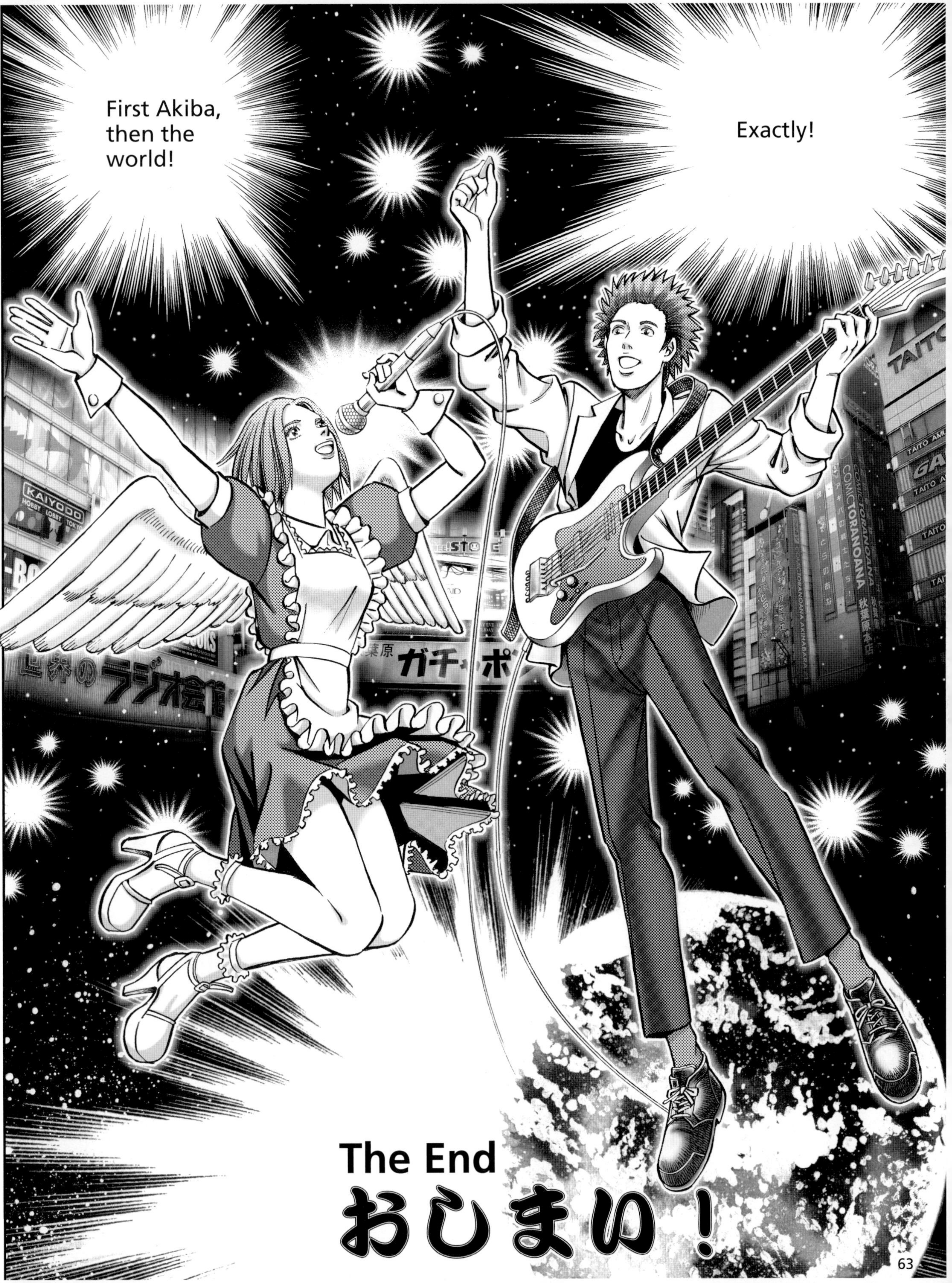
First Akiba, then the world!
Exactly!
KAIYODO
世界のラジオ会館
TAITO
The End
おしまい！

Yoko's Route through Akiba

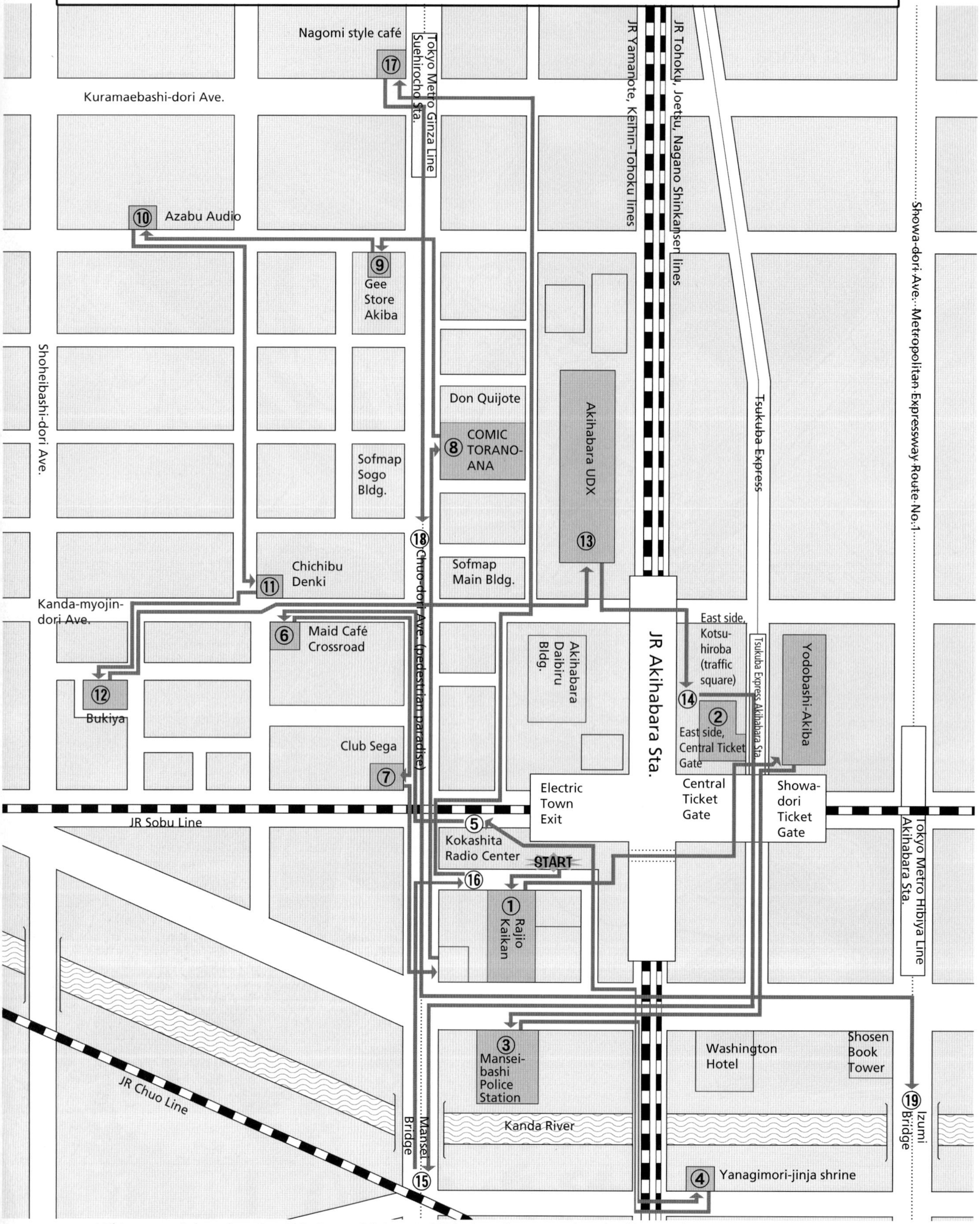

Nagomi style café
⑰
Tokyo Metro Ginza Line Suehirocho Sta.
Kuramaebashi-dori Ave.
JR Yamanote, Keihin-Tohoku lines
JR Tohoku, Joetsu, Nagano Shinkansen lines
⑩ Azabu Audio
⑨ Gee Store Akiba
Showa-dori Ave. Metropolitan Expressway Route No.1
Shoheibashi-dori Ave.
Tsukuba Express
Don Quijote
⑧ COMIC TORANO-ANA
Sofmap Sogo Bldg.
Akihabara UDX
⑬
⑱ Chuo-dori Ave. (pedestrian paradise)
Sofmap Main Bldg.
⑪ Chichibu Denki
Kanda-myojin-dori Ave.
⑥ Maid Café Crossroad
Akihabara Daibiru Bldg.
JR Akihabara Sta.
East side, Kotsu-hiroba (traffic square)
Tsukuba Express Akihabara Sta.
Yodobashi-Akiba
⑫ Bukiya
⑭
② East side, Central Ticket Gate
Club Sega
⑦
Electric Town Exit
Central Ticket Gate
Showa-dori Ticket Gate
JR Sobu Line
⑤ Kokashita Radio Center
START
⑯
Tokyo Metro Hibiya Line Akihabara Sta.
① Rajio Kaikan
③ Mansei-bashi Police Station
Washington Hotel
Shosen Book Tower
⑲ Izumi Bridge
JR Chuo Line
Kanda River
Mansei Bridge
⑮
④ Yanagimori-jinja shrine

* This manga is based on the Akihabara of February 2008, though we've taken the liberty of exaggerating just a little! But we know that all of you smart readers out there get it....

Shop & Restaurant Guide to Akiba

Akihabara's History and How It Became an Otaku Paradise

Nowadays, just about everybody knows that Akihabara—or "Akiba" for short—is an otaku paradise. But you might not have thought about how this happened, or how Akihabara became an electronics district in the first place. To answer these questions, we looked into Akihabara's history.

The name "Akihabara" derives from Chinka-sha, a shrine where people prayed for protection from fire, which once stood in the area. The shrine was dedicated to the deity Akiba-daigongen, and people began calling the shrine itself "Akiba-san." Later, it was re-named Akiba-jinja (Akiba Shrine). The area currently known as Akihabara was once the fields, or "harappa" in Japanese, surrounding Akiba-jinja. Thus it was called "Akibappara" or "Akiba-no-hara."

After World War II, the place became an electronics district, and it became home to numerous outdoor stalls. Proprietors purchased scrap items from the occupation forces to repair and sell them. At that time, many shops sold vacuum tubes or transistors, and even today a number of stores still retain the word *"musen"* (wireless, radio) in their names, a remnant of that long ago time when they carried transistors. Later, Japan underwent its super-growth period. When electric fans went on the market during this time, they sold so quickly that every single one disappeared from the shelves. When calculators appeared on the market in the late 1960s, many models sold vigorously for 100,000 yen or more each.

From that point on, Akihabara gradually turned into an otaku paradise.

The number of large electronics retailers increased, and many of the old smaller shops were forced to close, particularly after the burst of the asset-inflated "bubble" economy. Because many of the district's customers were interested in electronics, new tenants included shops offering popular games, and this drew in young people and families. When game shops began to spread around the country, Akiba's next big tenants were *anime* shops. Akiba thus made a smooth transition from electronics to games to *anime*, taking advantage of the subtle links between the three industries, and facilitating solid growth in the district by meeting the needs of the times.

The owners of Akihabara's older shops, who remember the way Akiba used to be, may feel somewhat dismayed at the area's decline as an electronics district. Though the fact that young customers visiting Akiba give the area new life may be considered a positive development, there is also a down side: complaints have arisen about the visitors failing to follow the rules of etiquette, like throwing garbage on the side of the road or blocking the way by sitting on steps.

In the end, the current otaku boom may cool down, but another genre is sure to take its place, and the specialty stores are likely to remain. Akiba is definitely a place to keep watching.

Akiba Map

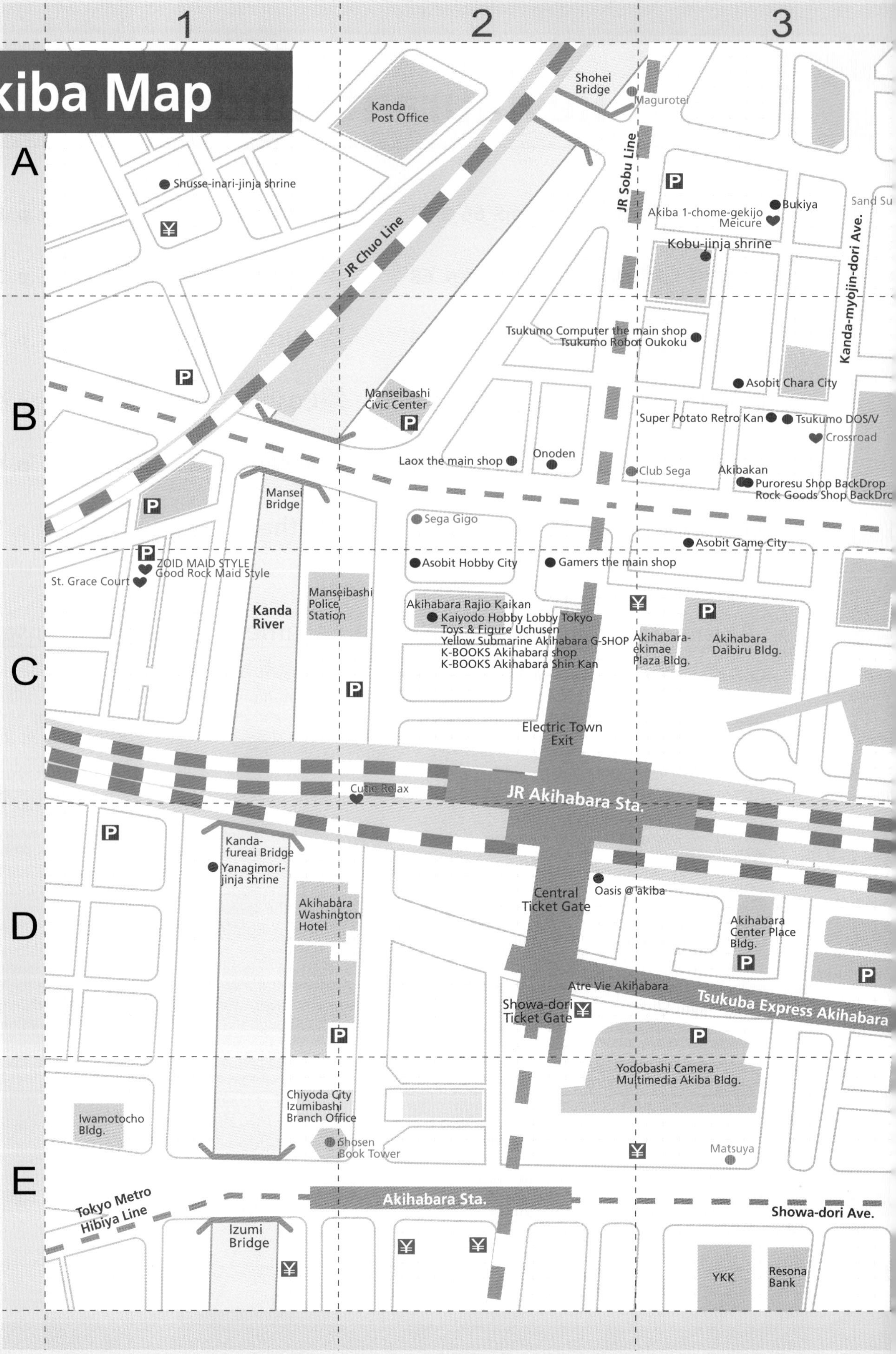
1
2
3
A
B
C
D
E
Shohei Bridge
Magurotei
Kanda Post Office
JR Sobu Line
JR Chuo Line
Shusse-inari-jinja shrine
Akiba 1-chome-gekijo Meicure
Bukiya
Sand Su
Kobu-jinja shrine
Kanda-myojin-dori Ave.
Tsukumo Computer the main shop
Tsukumo Robot Oukoku
Asobit Chara City
Manseibashi Civic Center
Super Potato Retro Kan
Tsukumo DOS/V
Crossroad
Laox the main shop
Onoden
Club Sega
Akibakan
Puroresu Shop BackDrop
Rock Goods Shop BackDrc
Mansei Bridge
Sega Gigo
Asobit Game City
ZOID MAID STYLE
Good Rock Maid Style
St. Grace Court
Asobit Hobby City
Gamers the main shop
Kanda River
Manseibashi Police Station
Akihabara Rajio Kaikan
Kaiyodo Hobby Lobby Tokyo
Toys & Figure Uchusen
Yellow Submarine Akihabara G-SHOP
K-BOOKS Akihabara shop
K-BOOKS Akihabara Shin Kan
Akihabara-ekimae Plaza Bldg.
Akihabara Daibiru Bldg.
Electric Town Exit
Cutie Relax
JR Akihabara Sta.
Kanda-fureai Bridge
Yanagimori-jinja shrine
Oasis @ akiba
Central Ticket Gate
Akihabara Washington Hotel
Akihabara Center Place Bldg.
Atre Vie Akihabara
Tsukuba Express Akihabara
Showa-dori Ticket Gate
Yodobashi Camera Multimedia Akiba Bldg.
Chiyoda City Izumibashi Branch Office
Iwamotocho Bldg.
Shosen Book Tower
Matsuya
Tokyo Metro Hibiya Line
Akihabara Sta.
Showa-dori Ave.
Izumi Bridge
YKK
Resona Bank

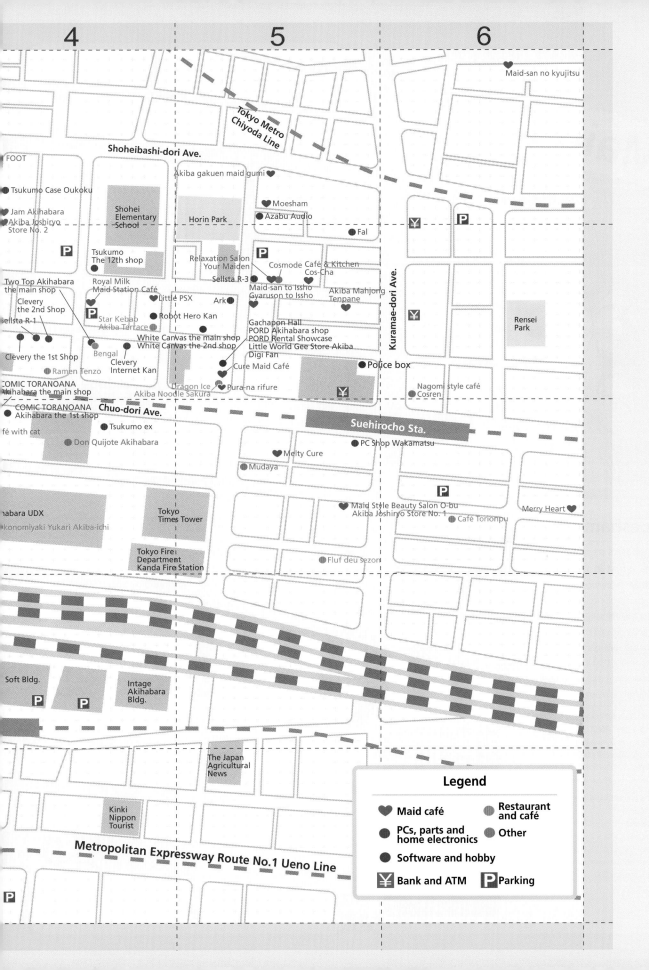

4 **5** **6**

Maid-san no kyujitsu

Tokyo Metro Chiyoda Line

Shoheibashi-dori Ave.

FOOT

Akiba gakuen maid gumi

Tsukumo Case Oukoku

Moesham

Jam Akihabara
Akiba Joshiryo
Store No. 2

Shohei
Elementary
School

Horin Park

Azabu Audio

Fal

Tsukumo
The 12th shop

Relaxation Salon
Your Maiden

Cosmode Café & Kitchen
Cos-Cha

Kuramae-dori Ave.

Two Top Akihabara
the main shop

Royal Milk
Maid Station Café

Sellsta R-3

Clevery
the 2nd Shop

Little PSX

Ark

Maid-san to Issho
Gyaruson to Issho

Akiba Mahjong
Tenpane

Rensei
Park

Sellsta R-1

Star Kebab
Akiba Terrace

Robot Hero Kan

Clevery the 1st Shop

Bengal

Clevery
Internet Kan

White Canvas the main shop
White Canvas the 2nd shop

Gachapon Hall
PORD Akihabara shop
PORD Rental Showcase
Little World Gee Store Akiba
Digi Fan

Ramen Tenzo

Cure Maid Café

Police box

COMIC TORANOANA
Akihabara the main shop

Dragon Ice

Akiba Noodle Sakura

Pura-na rifure

Nagomi style café
Cosren

COMIC TORANOANA
Akihabara the 1st shop

Chuo-dori Ave.

café with cat

Tsukumo ex

Suehirocho Sta.

Don Quijote Akihabara

Melty Cure

PC Shop Wakamatsu

Mudaya

habara UDX

konomiyaki Yukari Akiba-ichi

Tokyo
Times Tower

Maid Style Beauty Salon O-bu
Akiba Joshiryo Store No. 1

Merry Heart

Café Torionpu

Tokyo Fire
Department
Kanda Fire Station

Fluf deu sezon

Soft Bldg.

Intage
Akihabara
Bldg.

The Japan
Agricultural
News

Kinki
Nippon
Tourist

Metropolitan Expressway Route No.1 Ueno Line

Legend

♥	Maid café	◉	Restaurant and café
●	PCs, parts and home electronics	●	Other
●	Software and hobby		
¥	Bank and ATM	P	Parking

Maid Cafés

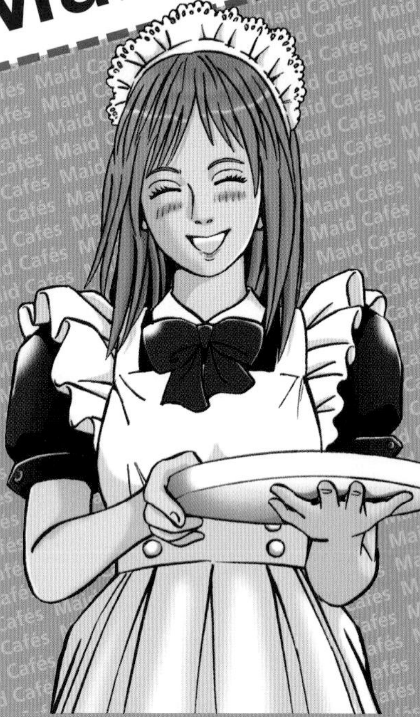

Akiba 1-chome-gekijo

Come out and have a great time with our fun-loving *meidoru*

Akiba 1-chome-gekijo is a teahouse with an extra special atmosphere: our masters and mistresses get to have lots of fun with our always-charming *meidoru*. There's tons of stuff going on every day, like spur-of-the moment game and quiz tournaments, photo sessions and much more. So come on out and join us and our *meidoru*—we think they're really something special.

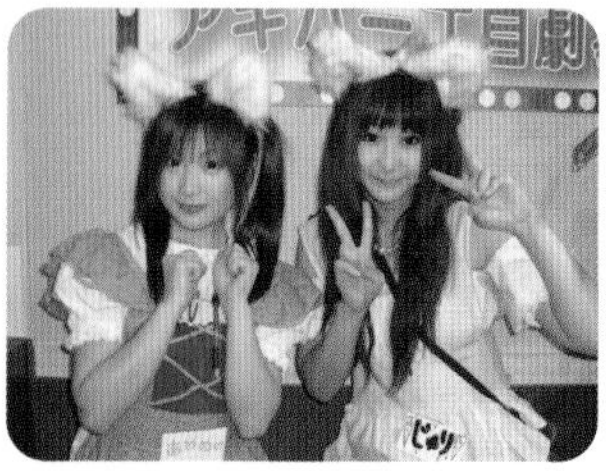

Ayame and Juri of the *meidoru* team!

Address: New Towa Bldg. 1F, 1-5-7 Soto-Kanda, Chiyoda-ku, Tokyo
Phone: 03-3254-3911
URL: http://www.maidolcafe.com/
Hours: Weekdays 12:00–21:30/Sat., Sun. & holidays 11:00–22:00; open year round

Our Recommendations
Black tea: ¥500
Kombu tea: ¥600
Omuraisu (rice-filled omelet): ¥1,200
Pancakes: ¥520
Chocolate sundae: ¥600

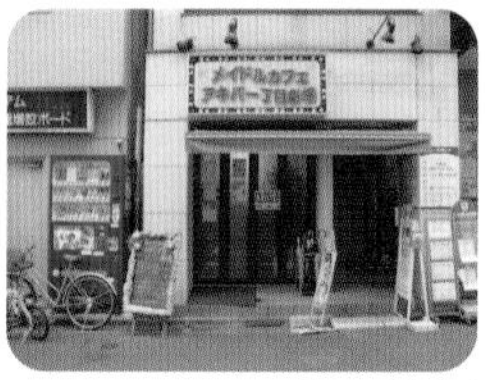

Come right in!

Moesham

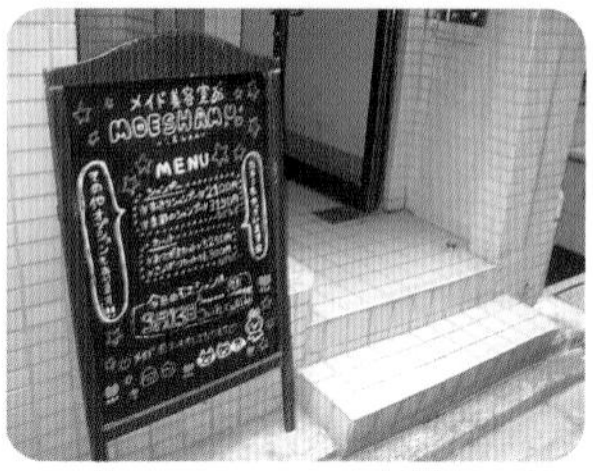

Akihabara's maid hair salon: a first in Japan!

Moesham represents Akihabara's all-new concept for the beauty salon. This is the very first hair salon in Japan where the styling's done by maids; in fact, it was such a new development that we had tons of media coverage. We've also got a special event day each week—a perfect time to check us out if you haven't already.

Address: 2F, 3-6-17 Soto-Kanda, Chiyoda-ku, Tokyo
Phone: 03-3252-8688
URL: http://www.moesham.com/
Hours: Weekdays 12:00–21:00/Sat., Sun. & holidays 11:00–20:00; closed Mon. (Tues. when Mon. falls on a national holiday)

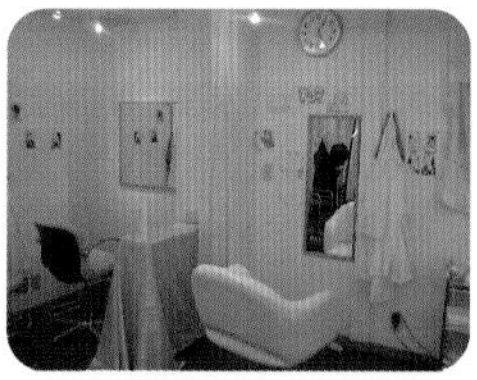

Our Recommendations
Trim: ¥5,250
Cut: ¥6,300
Shampoo: ¥2,100
Seasonal shampoo: ¥3,150
Color-enhancing shampoo: ¥5,250
"G" course: ¥10,500

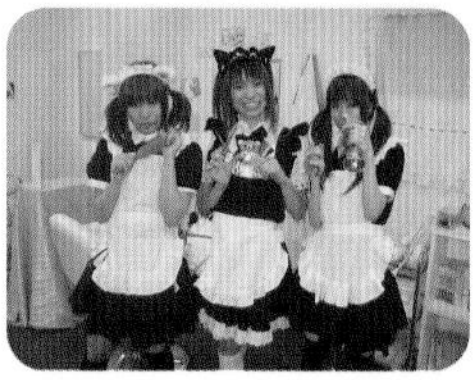

M@I FOOT

We're the ones who started the original maid reflexology: a first in the world!

It's now been four years since the concept of maid reflexology was born in Akihabara—and it's been a great four years! During this time, M@I FOOT has had more than 10,000 patrons, and we look forward to continuing to serve all of our "masters" with reflexology, hand massage, and our oxygen bar, always with a smile! So be sure to "come home" to M@I FOOT whenever you're in Akihabara!

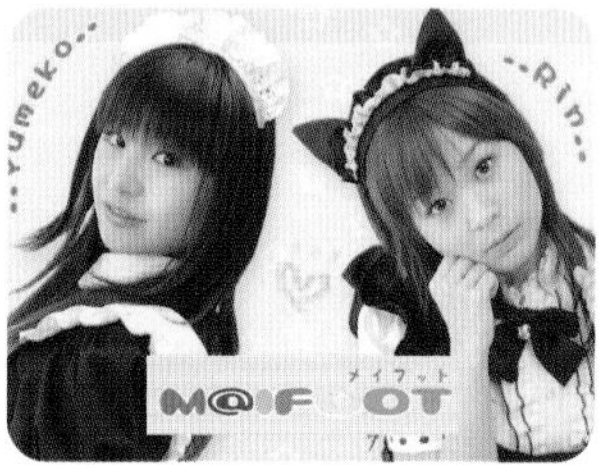
Yumeko
Rin

Yumeko and Rin

Address: Akihabara Park Bldg. 3F, 3-1-3 Soto-Kanda, Chiyoda-ku, Tokyo
Phone: 03-3253-1113
URL: http://mai-foot.com/
Hours: Weekdays 12:00–21:00/Sat., Sun. & holidays 11:00–21:00; closed for the year-end and New Year holidays

Our Recommendations
Reflexology: 20 min., ¥2,000 & up
Hand treatment: 10 min., ¥1,000 & up
Aromatherapy oxygen bar: 10 min., ¥700 & up
Eye treatment: 10 min., ¥500
Special first-visit services: ¥2,000
Maid discount: Half off on all services

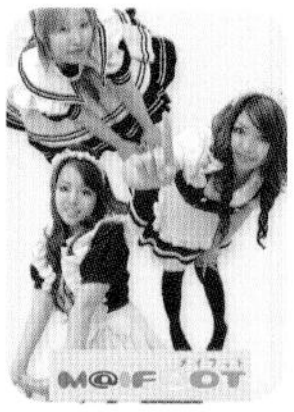

Seira, Runa and Hiyori

Merry Heart

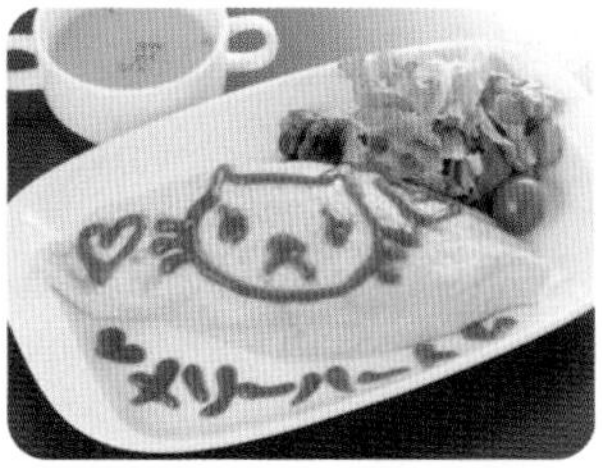

Omuraisu: our specialty

A maid café for the not-so-far future!

This maid café and bar features beautiful interior decor, plus delightful home cooking. And to make a good thing even better, our lovely maids—dressed up in our own specially-designed outfits—are here to serve you with the utmost hospitality. The menu includes our regular cocktails as well as a great choice of "maid originals." We've got lunch by day and alcohol by night, so come by whenever it suits your mood!

Address: Shimomura Bldg. B1F, 5-2-7 Soto-Kanda, Chiyoda-ku, Tokyo
Phone: 03-0835-1419
URL: http://merryheart.info/
Hours: 11:00–22:00; open year round

Our Recommendations

Heart-shaped curried rice (spicy): ¥800 (lunch)
Spaghetti with meat sauce (with lots of meat!): ¥800 (lunch)
Boo's ginger sauté: ¥800 (lunch)
Namban-style cock-a-doodle-doo chicken: ¥800 (lunch)
Dr. Takaty's favorite *omuraisu* (rice-filled omelet): ¥1,300
The usual... : ¥?00

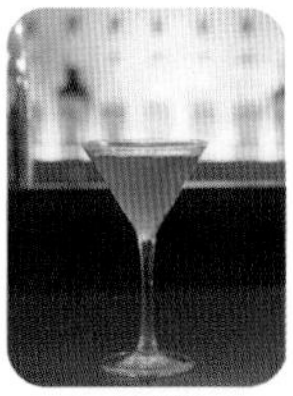

Cocktail "Lock on Your Heart"

Melty Cure

A therapeutic experience in a relaxing environment—and it's all even better with the unbeatable charm of our maids!

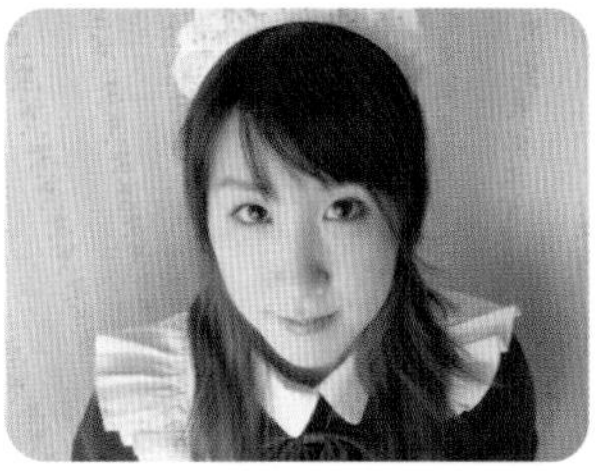

Melty Cure boasts an elegant interior designed for maximum customer comfort. Our maids, highly trained in reflexology, are ready to take all of your stress away! Their talented hands heal not just your tired body but also your heart and soul. Don't miss us—we're here to show you the best hospitality in all of Akihabara!

Address: Isuzu Bldg. 3F, 4-6-2 Soto-Kanda, Chiyoda-ku, Tokyo
Phone: 03-3254-7557
URL: http://melcure.jp
Hours: Mon.–Thurs. 12:00–21:00/Fri. & Sat. 12:00–23:00; open year round

Our Recommendations

Foot reflexology: 10 min., ¥1,000
Hand reflexology: 10 min., ¥1,000
Head reflexology: 10 min., ¥1,000
Shoulder reflexology: 10 min., ¥1,000
Extra foot reflexology with oil: 20 min., ¥2,000
Detox course: 30 min., ¥4,000

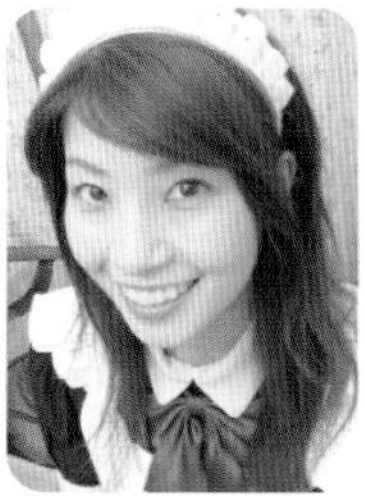

Royal Milk

Our maids are here to serve you with lots of love!

Our menu is full of delectable delights, including royal milk coffee and our never-the-same grandpa's rice—a popular lunch item. We've also got great parfaits that come with a twist—different topping depending on which of our maids makes it! In a special monthly treat one day a month, "RMA," our maids revert to their school days, with lots of games going on at night. For our masters and mistresses tired from walking Akihabara, we offer aromatherapy courses for both body and feet.

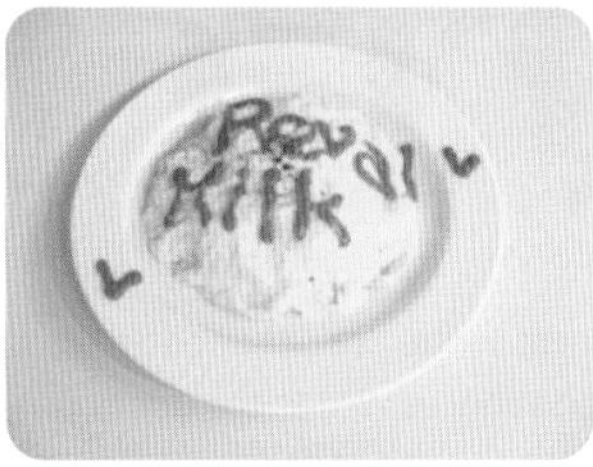

Our maids draw cute little ketchup designs on your *omuraisu* (rice-filled omelet)!

Address: Nikka Sekiyu Bldg. 2F, 3-10-12 Soto-Kanda, Chiyoda-ku, Tokyo
Phone: 03-3253-7858
URL: http://r-milk.com
Hours: 12:00–22:00; closed on the 2nd & 4th Wed. of each month

Our Recommendations

Royal milk tea/coffee: ¥700
"Order-maid" cocktails: ¥ 1,000
Home-made parfait: ¥800
Fried-egg cake: ¥700
Body care: 30 min.: ¥4,000
Foot care: 30 min.: ¥4,000

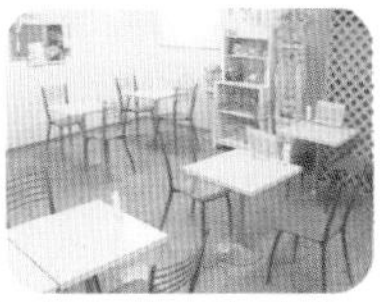

Smoking's allowed in all of our rooms—good news for all of you smokers out there!

Relaxation Salon Your Maiden

Soft *seitai*: it's completely pain-free!

At Your Maiden, we offer authentic soft-style *seitai* (Japanese-style chiropractics) that doesn't hurt a bit. Our shop features a thoroughly relaxed atmosphere complete with real antique furniture. After the treatment, enjoy a cup of tea for an even more luxurious experience. Come check us out at Your Maiden.

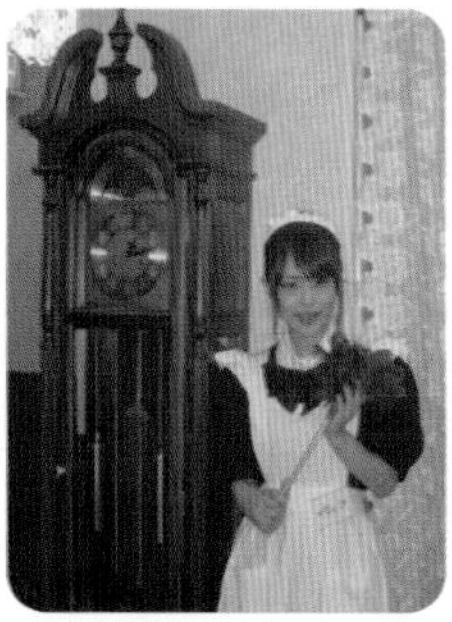

Relax in our calm atmosphere

Address: Chubu Bldg. 2F, 3-7-14 Soto-Kanda, Chiyoda-ku, Tokyo
Phone: 03-3252-2351
URL: http://www.yourmaiden.com
Hours: Weekdays 12:00–21:00/Sat., Sun. & holidays 11:00–21:00; closed Wed.

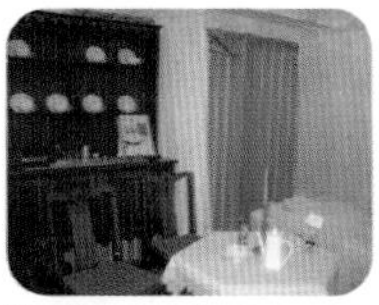

You'll love our healing space

Our Recommendations

Quick course (20 min.): ¥2,500
30 min.: ¥3.500
60 min.: ¥6,000
90 min.: ¥8.500
Eye fatigue relief: 15 min., ¥2,000
Rental change of clothes (sweatsuit top and/or bottom): ¥100 each

Café with Cat

A mysterious little place featuring magic cats!

At Café with cat, our magic cats are our trademark. Fill up a stamp card (one stamp for every ¥500 you spend), and you get a taste of their magic. Come by the shop and find out what we mean! Our menu includes everything from meals to dessert, so come join us—and our cats—for a truly unique experience.

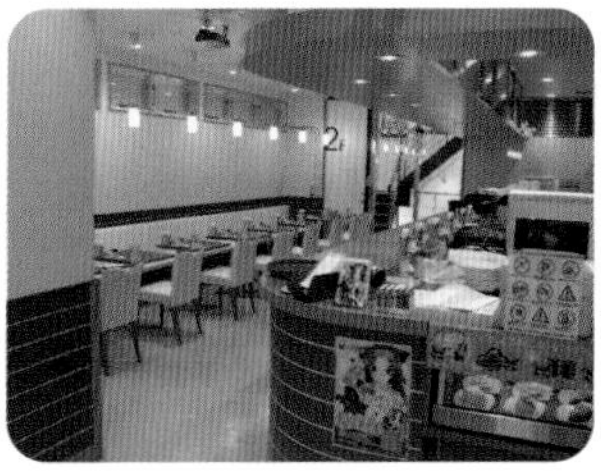
Inside Café with cat

Address: Comic Toranoana Akihabara-honten 2F, 4-3-1 Soto-Kanda, Chiyoda-ku, Tokyo
Phone: 03-3526-5330
URL: http://www.toranoana.co.jp/
Hours: 10:00–22:00; open year round

Our Recommendations

Café with cat original items
Add drink: +¥100
Breakfast: ¥400
Omuraisu (rice-filled omelet): ¥800
Beef curry: ¥700
Single-plate lunch: ¥900

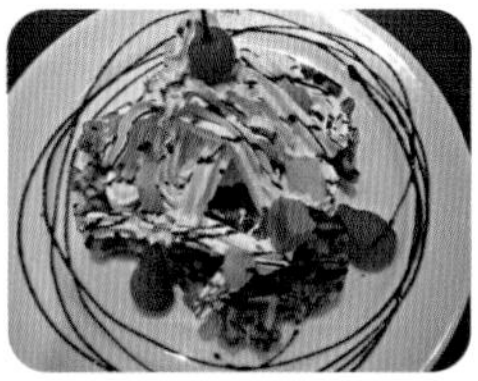
Our popular meow-meow waffle

Café & Kitchen Cos-Cha

A café and restaurant full of "angels"

Our space—and our menu—is designed for everything from tea time to mealtime to a drink. Our roomy shop is ideal for every customer, whether you're dropping in alone or with a large group. We've got nostalgic school-style seating in a reproduction of the old-fashioned classroom—for a fun flash from your past! In addition to this, we're sure you'll have a great time chatting with our angels and dining on our tasty homemade cooking. We also offer a number of special attractions. Stop in and see us—when you're here, it's just like home.

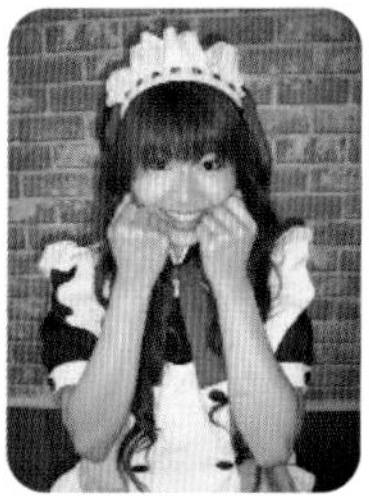
Angel Myu

Address: Isamiya Dai-hachi Bldg. 2F, 3-7-12 Soto-Kanda, Chiyoda-ku, Tokyo
Phone: 03-3253-4560
URL: http://www.cos-cha.com
Hours: Weekdays 12:00–23:00/Sat. 11:00–23:00/ holidays 11:00–22:00; open year round

Our Recommendations

Lunch: ¥500
Dinner: ¥800
Lunch-of-the-day: ¥750
Dinner-of-the-day: ¥980
Angel originals: around ¥1,000
Appetizer: ¥100

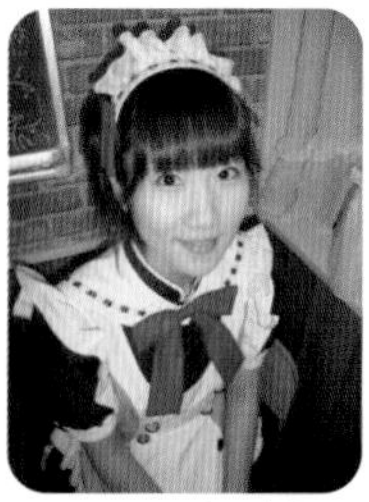
Angel Sunao

Good Rock Maid Style

Welcoming smiles from our maids, and great sake—who could ask for anything more?

This fun lounge bar is open only on weekends. Tucked away behind Niku-no-Mansei in a corner of Akihabara, we enjoy a quiet, relaxed ambiance. All of our seating is at tables, and our maids offer great conversation—always with a smile! Make us a part of your weekend entertainment.

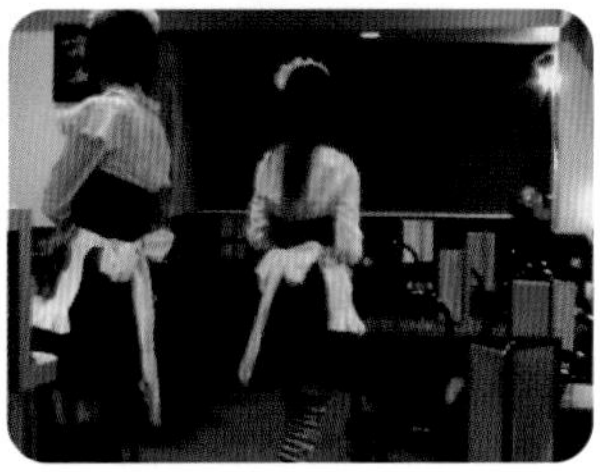
Our interior

Address: Chiyoda K2 Bldg. 1F, 2-19 Kanda-Sudacho, Chiyoda-ku, Tokyo
Phone: 03-3254-5300
URL: http://www.barzoid.com/maid/grtop.htm
Hours: Fri. 18:30–23:00/Sat. & Sun. 17:30–22:30; closed Mon.–Thurs.

Our Recommendations

Our "original-maid" cocktails: ¥1,000
Ebisu draft beer: ¥600
Shochu: ¥600 & up
Sausage combo plate: ¥800
Cesar salad: ¥800
Ice cream: ¥400

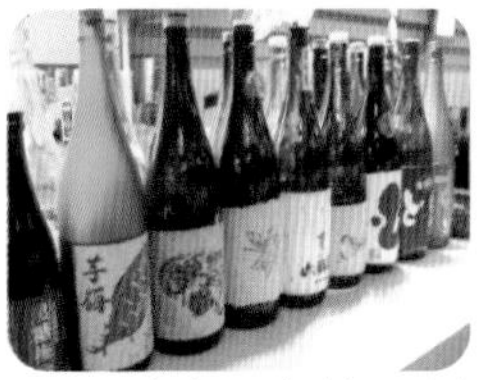
We've got both *umeshu* (plum wine) and *shochu*.

ZOID MAID STYLE

Get away from it all with our maids' smiling faces and good alcohol!

We're a regular shot bar from Tuesday through Thursday, located in a corner of Akihabara behind Niku-no-Mansei. With over 300 different kinds of alcohol and 80 cocktails to choose from, this is the place for people who love to drink. Our maids are not mere waitresses—they entertain with friendly smiles and fun conversation, as well as the drinks you love. This is the perfect getaway from the daily grind.

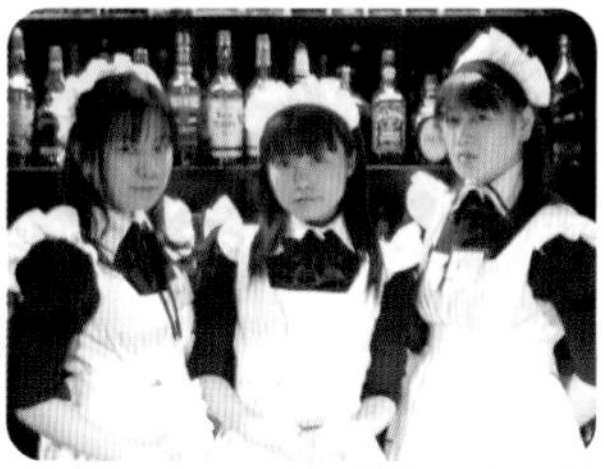
"Welcome home!"

Address: Chiyoda K2 Bldg. 2F, 2-19 Kanda-Sudacho, Chiyoda-ku, Tokyo
Phone: 03-3251-3195
URL: http://www.barzoid.com/maid/zoidtop.htm
Hours: Fri. 18:30–23:30/Sat. & Sun. 17:30–22:30; closed Mon. (Shot bar Tues.–Thurs.)

Our Recommendations

Original cocktails by our maids: ¥1,100 & up
Grasshopper: ¥800
Mohito: ¥800
Jack Rose: ¥1,000
Giant cone: ¥300
Ice cream liquor: ¥400

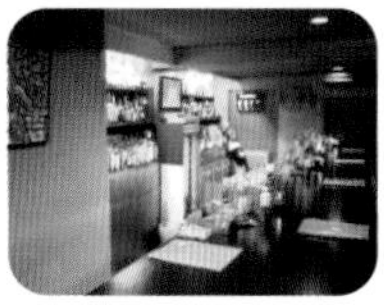
Inside our shop

Akiba Gakuen Maid Gumi

School's open in Akihabara! But there's no studying here: it's all about eating, drinking and playing games!

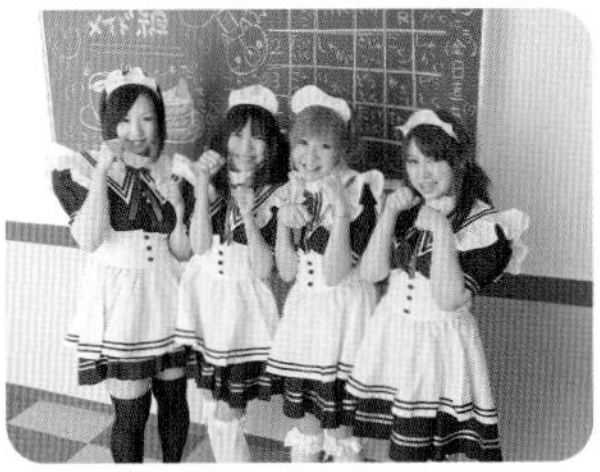
"Hi there, *sempai*!"

Akiba gakuen maid gumi is a new addition to Akihabara—and it's a fun one! Take one step inside and you're already "back at school." Cute girls in school uniforms greet you with an energetic, "Hello, *sempai* (old boy/girl)!" and a smile. By day we're a café, by night a bar, which means we're the place to go whether you want just want to relax, play fun games or drink—and much more. We might soon be on your list of your favorite places in Akiba!

Address: Maruyama Bldg. 4F, 3-6-1 Soto-Kanda, Chiyoda-ku, Tokyo
Phone: 03-3256-5960
URL: http://akbgakuen-meido.com
Hours: 12:00–5:00; open year round

Our Recommendations

School set (1 drink & 1 game): ¥1,000
Koishokudo set (1 drink + 1 dish + 1 game): ¥1,500
Hanazakari set (1 alcoholic drink + 1 appetizer + 1 game): ¥1,200
Fluffy *omuraisu* (rice-filled omelet) : ¥1,000
Neapolitan: ¥950
Eggplant in meat sauce: ¥950

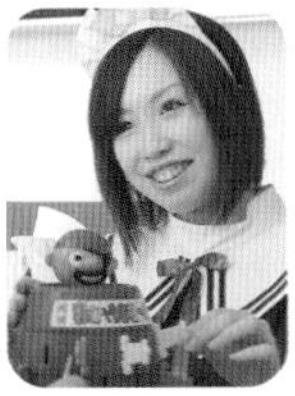
A super-fun time

Akiba Joshiryo

A truly one-of-a-kind place

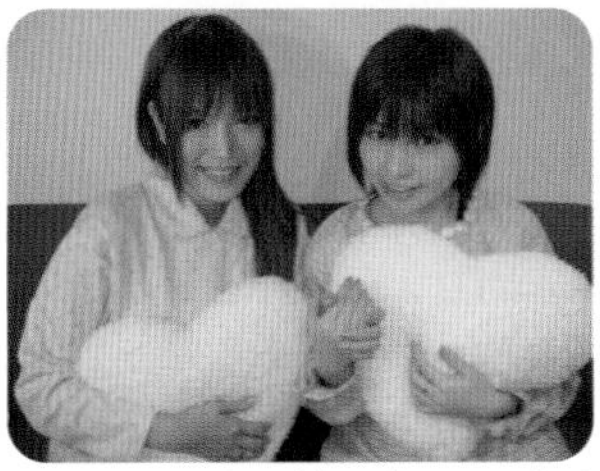
Come join us for a great time!

Akiba Joshiryo is neither merely a maid café nor a maid reflexology salon—it's in a class all by itself, offering an atmosphere like no other. The place is designed to ensure that customers can truly relax, and we have lots of games to choose from. Our maids play too, so it's even more fun! All planning and running of this unique shop is done by the girls themselves. We look forward to seeing you!

Address: Store No. 1: Saison Akihabara 3F, 4-8-3 Soto-Kanda, Chiyoda-ku, Tokyo
Store No. 2: Hashizume Bldg. 4F, 3-2-13 Soto-Kanda, Chiyoda-ku, Tokyo
Phone: 03-5294-6533
URL: http://www.planetplan.net/
Hours: Weekdays 13:00–21:30/Sat., Sun. & holidays 11:30–21:00; open year round

Our Recommendations

Regular course: 30 min., ¥1,680
Ladies' regular course: 30 min., ¥1,000
Romance *manga* de duet: ¥1,000
Costume change: ¥1,000
Reverse *moe*: try dressing as a woman: ¥1,000
Moe-tamashii-chunyu ryosei-binta: ¥1,000

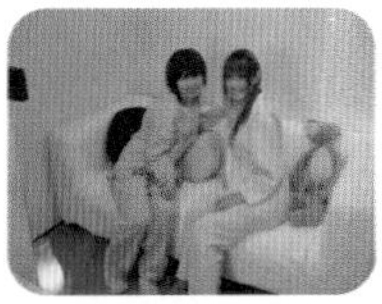
Just like home

Jam Akihabara

An ultra-stylish maid café

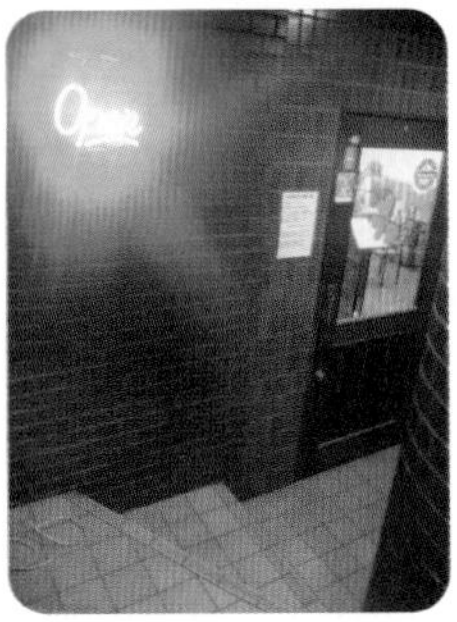
Entry & exit stairway

Jam Akihabara features a sleek, stylish atmosphere. Our reasonably-priced lunch menu (weekdays through 16:00) items start at just ¥500, and we also have an excellent choice of alcoholic beverages. Our maids wear not only the familiar uniform, but also Japanese-style outfits. When you stop in at Jam Akihabara, make it a point to try our *moe moe* "fairy" *omuraisu* (rice-filled omelet), or our surprise cake and tea set.

Address: Yamaguchi Bldg. B1F, 3-2-13 Soto-Kanda, Chiyoda-ku, Tokyo
Phone: 03-3253-1855
URL: http://jam-akiba.com/
Hours: Weekdays 11:00–23:00/Sat., Sun. & holidays 11:00–5:00; closed occasionally at irregular times

Our Recommendations

Moe moe "fairy" *omuraisu*: ¥1,200
Surprise cake and tea set: ¥650
Our *dokidoki* ("pounding heart") fairy ice cream: ¥450
Fairy tomato risotto: ¥840
Jam tea: ¥650
Heineken: ¥500

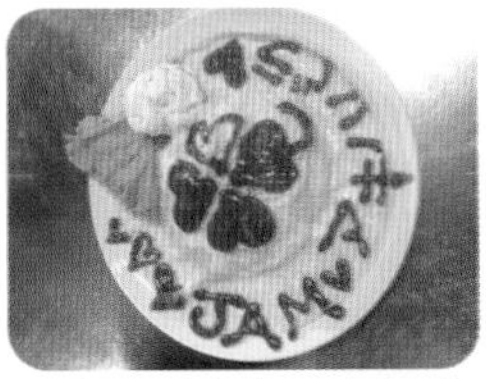
It not only looks great—it tastes terrific, too!

Akiba Mahjong Tenpane

The world's first cosplay and roll-play mah-jongg parlor

Akiba Mahjong Tenpane is no ordinary mahjong parlor. Besides the great fun of the game of mahjong, we've got lots of cute girls dressed up in cosplay outfits to chat with as you play. And since there's no betting here, even beginners at the game can relax and enjoy it. We've made mahjong even more fun with new ways of playing, such as the trading card system and the job system. Every day's a lively one here, so come on in and check us out!

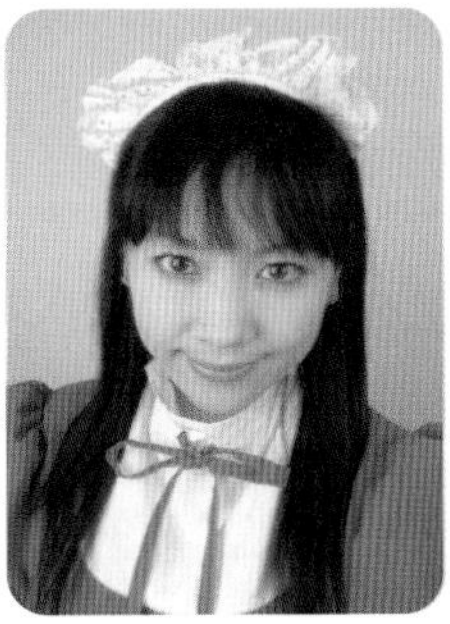
We've always got cosplay maids.

Address: Isamiya Dai-ni Bldg.3F, 3-8-5 Soto-Kanda, Chiyoda-ku, Tokyo
Phone: 03-3255-3103
URL: http://tenpa.net/
Hours: Weekdays 17:00–23:00/Fri. 17:00–1:00/Sat. 11:00–1:00/Sun. & holidays 11:00–23:00; open year round

Our Recommendations

Registration: ¥1,500 (new customer discounts available)
Single game: ¥600
One hour of mahjong: ¥500/per person
Alcoholic beverages: ¥500
Meals: ¥300 & up
New entry mode: ¥1,000

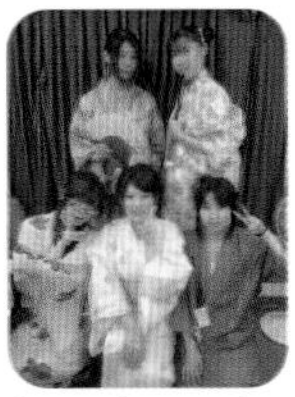
A scene from a *yukata* (casual summer *kimono*) event

Crossroad

Come to the Crossroads for a taste of luxury in a thoroughly relaxed atmosphere.

Our clients are treated to our luxurious and therapeutic reflexology, as well as *seitai* (Japanese-style chiropractics) with a focus on foot therapy, shoulders and lower back, all in high-end reclining chairs from northern Europe. At our café, we offer an extensive menu including seven kinds of coffee, six kinds of tea, a food and sweets menu, alcoholic beverages, special daily offerings and more. No table charges.

A lusciously sweet tower: definitely for anyone with a sweet tooth!

Address: Mitsuwa Bldg. 4F, 1-11-4 Soto-Kanda, Chiyoda-ku, Tokyo
Phone: 03-3252-9601
URL: http://www.cross-road.cc/
Hours: 12:00–21:30; closed occasionally at irregular times

Our Recommendations

Foot therapy: 30 min. ¥3,500
Hand therapy: 30 min. ¥3,000
Seitai: 30 min. ¥3,500
Tea (choice of 6 varieties): ¥600 & up
Afternoon tea set: ¥1,700
Parfaits hand-made by our maids: ¥900

Try our foot therapy: it's healing for your whole body, and for your soul, too!

Maid-san to Issho

Get 100 times more fun out of a trip to Akihabara: tour the town with our seasoned guides!

At Maid-san to Issho, we're old professionals at guiding our "masters and mistresses" around Akihabara. Our master Akihabara guides take you around Akiba like you're on a fun date, visiting local Akiba attractions including maid cafés, karaoke spots, restaurants, video arcades and more. The more you get to know about Akiba from Maid-san to Issho, the more you'll love the place!

Group photo at our karaoke event

Address: Watanabe Bldg. 5F, 3-8-17 Soto-Kanda, Chiyoda-ku, Tokyo
Phone: 03-3253-0681
URL: http://www.maidsan-i.com/
Hours: 10:00–23:00; closed Mon.

Our Recommendations

Trial: 45 min., ¥3,000
60 min. & up: ¥3,000/30 min.
Additional 30 min.: ¥3,000
180 min. & up: 2 maids accompany the client; you can also visit places outside Akihabara
Additional options: ¥1,000

Popular "Maid-san to Issho" parade along the Pedestrian Paradise

Gyaruson to Issho

Girl cosplayers dressed as men: Try us for a tour "date" around Akiba

Group photo at our "Road Night III" event

Our charming garcons (handsome girls dressed as men!) are ready to take their masters and mistresses around Akiba, and we think the experience is 100 times more fun this way! When you spend a little time with these cosplayers, you'll come to understand their great appeal. And it's not just for girls—guys are welcome, too!

Address: Watanabe Bldg. 5F, 3-8-17 Soto-Kanda, Chiyoda-ku, Tokyo
Phone: 03-3253-5270
URL: http://www.maidsan-i.com/garcon/index.html
Hours: 10:00–23:00; closed Mon. (Tues. when Mon. falls on a national holiday)

Our Recommendations

Trial: 40 min. ¥2,000 (Men: 45 min., ¥3,000)
60 min. & up: ¥2,000, 30 min. (Men: 30 min., ¥3,000)
Additional 30 min.: ¥2,000 (Men: 30 min., ¥3,000)
Clients can visit places outside of Akihabara for long courses of 180 min. or more.
Photos (no limit) ¥1,000
Purikura photos free for women only! (developing paid for by clients)

Chuo-dori Pedestrian Paradise

Cure Maid Café

We're the best spot for healing magic in all of Akihabara

With decor done in nostalgic warm early Victorian style, our shop is the perfect getaway from the hustle-and-bustle of the big city. We've even got a little garden for scenic views of the changing seasons, as well as specially-selected background music, making our range of therapeutic services even better. Whether you're by yourself or with a friend, this is the ultimate experience in relaxation.

Home-made pound cake by our maids—yum!

Address: Gee Store Akiba 6F, 3-15-5 Soto-Kanda, Chiyoda-ku, Tokyo
Phone: 03-3258-3161
URL: http://www.curemaid.jp
Hours: Mon.–Thurs. 11:00–20:00 (Last call 19:30)/Fri. & Sat. 11:00–22:00 (Last call 21:30)/Sun. & holidays 11:00–19:00 (Last call 18:30)/ Day before holidays 11:00–22:00 (Last call 21:30); open year round (closed during the year-end & New Year holidays)

Our Recommendations

Champion pork cutlet curry: ¥800
Home-made pound cake: ¥400
Cure trifle (Berry Mary or Apple Bee): ¥550
Our special spaghetti & meat sauce, the "Yama": ¥3,000
Tea (Darjeeling, Assam or Earl Gray): ¥450
Cure Maid Café original herb tea: ¥450

Professional live performances every Saturday

Cutie Relax

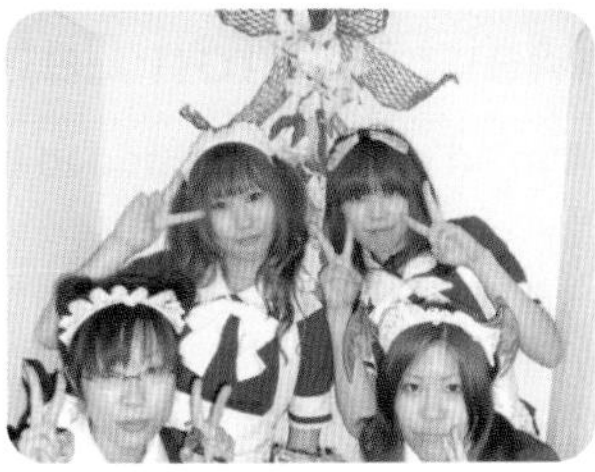

Come see our adorable maids.

Reflexology made fun with our charming maids

This is the maid reflexology shop closest to Akihabara Sta. Electric Town Exit. If you like reflexology, you'll love this, because it's even better when it's done by maids! We highly recommend our detox service. A mild electrical current run through your arms and legs releases toxins through the soles of your feet, and you'll wake up the next morning feeling clean and refreshed (results may vary depending on the individual). We offer a range of services that our clients love—we know because they keep coming back! Come home to Cutie Relax whenever you're in Akihabara.

Address: New Akihabara Center 2F, 1-16-10 Soto-Kanda, Chiyoda-ku, Tokyo
Phone: 03-5296-8030
URL: http://www.cutierelax.com/
Hours: 12:00–22:00; open year round

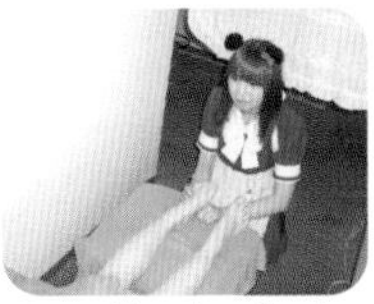

Our maids make reflexology even more fun.

Our Recommendations

Foot therapy: 20 min. ¥2,500 & up
Hand therapy: 20 min. ¥2.500 & up
Double therapy: 40 min. ¥4,500 & up
Full-body therapy: 70 min. ¥7,000 & up
Detox foot bath (25 min.) plus something extra: ¥5,000
Back therapy: 30 min. ¥5,000 & up

St. Grace Court

Happy nuns and priests-in-training come out to greet you!

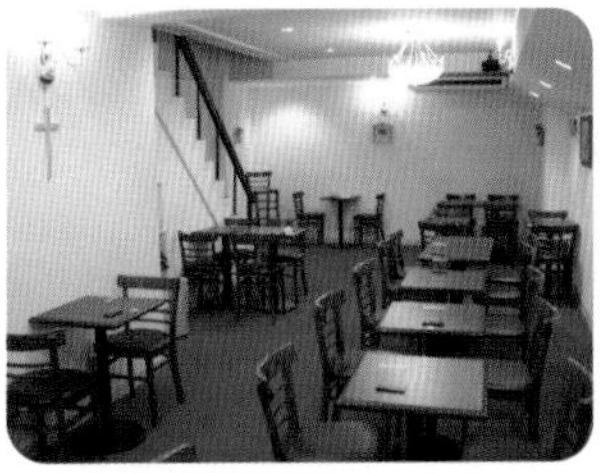

Our church-motif interior

Stray sheep, come to St. Grace Court! Our happy nuns and priests-in-training are here to take you back into the flock! Whether you're lost in Akiba or confused about life, St. Grace Court is great fun, even for those of you new to cosplay. We're open till dawn on Friday, Saturday, and days before holidays. So let's spend the night out together!

Address: Chiyoda K1 Bldg. 1F&B1F, 2-19-33 Kanda-Sudacho, Chiyoda-ku, Tokyo
Phone: 03-5298-5947
URL: http://www.st-gracecourt.com
Hours: 12:00–23:00/Fri. & Sat., day before holidays 12:00–5:00; closed occasionally (once a month)

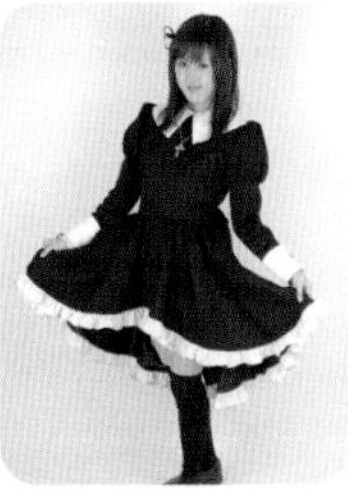

Our happy nuns can't wait for you to come in!

Our Recommendations

Stewed pork cubes on rice: ¥1,000
Nun curry: ¥930
Priest-in-training curry: ¥930
Japanese-style hamburger¥ 1,200
Eggplant and *miso* hamburger: ¥1,200
Thai-style spicy minced pork on rice: ¥1,000

Pura-na Rifure

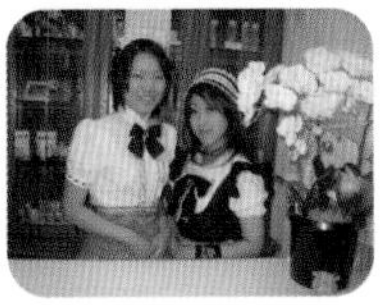

"Welcome home, master and mistress!"

Authentic Chinese-style foot pressure point massage: better still when it's done by maids!

Located just one minute from Suehirocho Station on the Tokyo Metro Ginza Line, Pura-na rifure is easily accessible. Come in and let our maids help you release all of your stress with time-tested Chinese-style therapeutic techniques. We recommend our detox footbath and reflexology. A first in Akihabara, the footbath works using sodium ions to draw out toxins. Our most popular services are our special reflexology and facial/lymphatic massage—both done in our VIP room is an added bonus!

Address: Sumiyoshi Bldg. 5F, 3-16-17 Soto-Kanda, Chiyoda-ku, Tokyo
Phone: 03-3252-1558
URL: http://plarna.jpn.org/akiba/index.html
Hours: Mon.–Fri. 12.00–22:00/Sat. 11:30–22:30/Sun. & holidays 11:30–21:00; open year round

Our Recommendations

Reflexology: 35 min. ¥3,800
Detox (25 min.) and reflexology (25 min.): ¥4,900 (total of 50 min.)
Special foot and full-body reflexology course (in the VIP room!): 85 min., ¥8,500 + ¥500 (preferred therapist request fee)
Men's facial lymphatic massage (in the VIP room!): 45 min., ¥6,500 + ¥500 (preferred therapist request fee)
Men's facial lymphatic massage & Lifting C (in the VIP room!): 90 min., ¥15,000 + ¥500 (preferred therapist request fee)
Facial pressure point therapy: 25 min., ¥2,500

Meicure

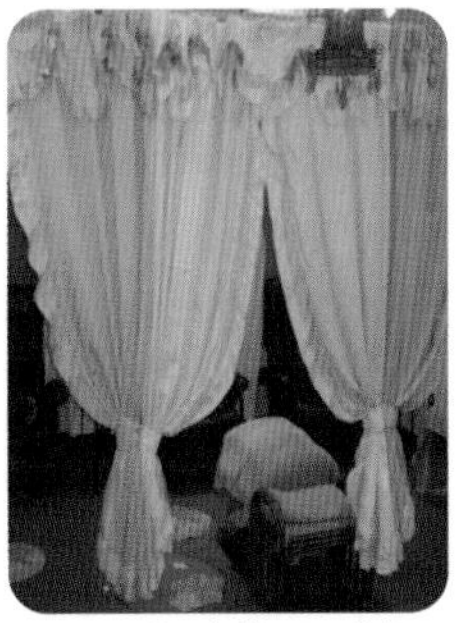

Our "girl's room" decor

Foot & body therapy

At Meicure, we offer full-body therapy by our charming maids. Thoroughly trained in reflexology, we provide healing for both body and mind for all of our masters and mistresses! But that's not all we've got: check out our fun events and special privileges as well. We can't wait to see our masters and mistresses, so hurry in to see us!

Address: New Towa Bldg. 2F, 1-5-7 Soto-Kanda, Chiyoda-ku, Tokyo
Phone: 03-3251-0977
URL: http://www.maicure.com
Hours: 11:00–22:00 (Reception closed: 21:00); open year round (with some exceptions)

Our Recommendations:

Foot therapy: 20 min., ¥2,100 & up
Arm therapy: 10 min., ¥1,050 & up
Shoulder massage: 10 min., ¥1,260 & up
Stretching & body therapy: 10 min., ¥1,260 & up
Ear care: 20 min., ¥2,520 & up
Head massage: 20 min., ¥2,520 & up

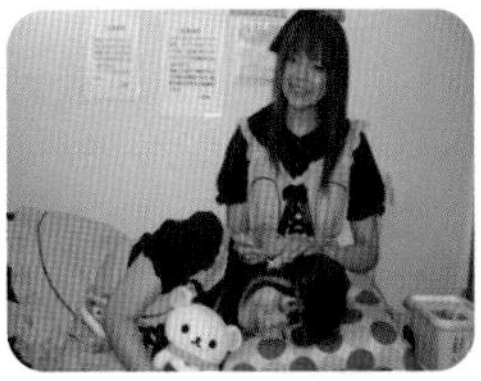

Ear cleaning time

Maid-san no Kyujitsu

When you're in Akihabara, stop in at Maid-san no kyujitsu

Monthly *moe* events

When they're not working at their masters' mansions, our maids are free to show you around Akihabara and surrounding areas, including maid cafés, karaoke rooms, game parlors, restaurants and more! It's like a date and a tour all in one. For our masters and mistresses who can't come to Akihabara, we offer a chat service where you can talk to our maids live.

Address: Yamanaga Bldg., 3-6-9 Yushima, Bunkyo-ku, Tokyo
Phone: 03-6410-8835
URL: http://www.maid-kyu.com/
Hours: 12:00–23:00; open year round

Our Recommendations
Trial: 30 min., ¥2,000 & up
Photos: ¥1,000 (unlimited)
Cheki: ¥500 each
Preferred guide request: ¥1,000
Extra time: 10 min., ¥1,000
Consultation with a maid: 20 min., ¥3,000

How about some shopping together?

Maid Station Café

A maid café with an added bonus: great food!

Maid Station Café boasts a terrific menu full of home-made delights and great drinks. One of our favorites is our chicken cutlet on rice with pork-flavored soup (¥800). It not only tastes great, it's pleasing to the eye as well! Customers can also play old-fashioned computer games on the big-screen TV. We've got lots of other fun options too, so come and check us out!

A spacious, relaxing atmosphere done in white

Address: 3-10-12 Soto-Kanda, Chiyoda-ku, Tokyo
Phone: 03-3253-0033
URL: http://maid-station.com/
Hours: Weekdays 12:00–22:00; closed Mon. (Tues. when Mon. falls on a national holiday)

Our Recommendations
Chicken cutlet on rice: ¥800
Chef's choice pasta: ¥800
Tonjiru ramen noodles: ¥800
Eggs made by our maids: ¥500
Cocktails: ¥700

Most of the dishes on our extensive menu are home-made.

Little PSX

A maid bar where you can even play darts!

Hot off the grill

Starting at 17:00, we're a maid bar complete with dart games. Have fun with our Internet dart game machines and 170 different kinds of cocktails—our maids await with a smile! And for the uninitiated, our maids will be happy to give you lessons, so why not try darts and see how much fun it can be? We're open on Saturdays, Sundays and holidays during lunch as a maid café instead of a bar—but we've still got the darts!

Address: Isamiya Dai-san Bldg. 3F, 3-10-5 Soto-Kanda, Chiyoda-ku, Tokyo
Phone: 03-5297-5475
URL: http://littlepsx.com/
Hours: Weekdays 17:00–23:00/Fri. 17:00–5:00/Sat. 12:00–5:00/Sun. & holidays 12:00–23:00; open year round

Our Recommendations
Draft beer: ¥600
"Amber time": ¥700
Little PSX (cocktail): ¥1,000
Moe omuraisu (rice-filled omelet): ¥1,000
Junk snack-of-the-day: ¥450
Sausage-sentai: ¥800

Our huge drink menu has over 170 choices.

Maid Style Beauty Salon O-bu

An all-new concept in the beauty salon—complete with maid stylists

With maids serving our clients, O-bu is an altogether new idea for the beauty salon. They're dressed as maids, but don't worry: all of our staff, from those providing counseling to follow-up service, have experience in hair styling. We've also got lots of other great options besides haircuts, so drop in when you're in Akihabara—even if you don't need a cut just yet!

"Welcome back!"

Address: Saison Akihabara 1F, 4-8-3 Soto-Kanda, Chiyoda-ku, Tokyo
Phone: 03-5296-2006
URL: http://www.o-bu.jp/
Hours: Weekdays 12:00–20:00/Sat. 12:00–21:00/holidays 11:00–20:00; closed on Thurs.

Our Recommendations
Cut: ¥5,500
Color: ¥8,000 & up
Cut & perm: ¥13,000 & up
Head massage: ¥2,000 & up
Other massages: ¥1,000 & up
Preferred stylist request fee: ¥500

Our team of maids

Large Retail Stores

Don Quijote Akihabara

Don Quijote—discount oasis

Our familiar exterior

Everybody knows that Don Quijote is the place to go for discounts, but amongst all the Don Quijote stores around Japan, the Akihabara store is special. The "Cosplay Kan" section offers the biggest selection in the country with over 1,400 outfits to choose from—all the time! But it doesn't end there: the Akihabara store offers the kind of variety and low prices you've come to expect from Don Quijote, including everyday items, food items, variety goods, and much more. And when you're done shopping, sample the entertainment typical of Akiba—a maid café, an "idol playhouse" and more, all in the same building!

Address: 4-3-3 Soto-Kanda, Chiyoda-ku, Tokyo
Phone: 03-5298-5411
URL: http://www.donki.com/index.php
Hours: 10:00–5:00; open year round

Everything goes for low prices.

Laox the Main Shop

With tons of product choices, Laox is popular with foreign visitors and Japanese alike

The Laox chain has more than 10 stores in Akihabara, and amongst these the main shop boasts the only full range of electronics. Home electronics for use in Japan can be found up to the third floor, while the fourth floor and up offer electronics and other products for use in other countries, as well as souvenirs including traditional Japanese items such as weapons, kimono and more. From B1 through the seventh floor, you'll find incredible selection—it's no exaggeration to say that Laox offers the greatest variety in all of Akihabara.

Address: 1-2-9 Soto-Kanda, Chiyoda-ku, Tokyo
Phone: 03-3253-7111
URL: http://www.laox.co.jp/
Hours: 10:00–21:00; open year round

Floor Guide

B1F: Domestic Models Floor (Single-item audio equipment, home theater systems)

1F: Domestic Models Floor (Televisions, DVD recorders, digital cameras, movie cameras, mobile phones)

2F: Domestic Models Floor (PCs, printers, PC peripherals)

3F: Domestic Models Floor (Air conditioners, refrigerators, washing machines, microwaves, kitchen items, beauty aids)

4F: Overseas Floor (Televisions, DVD recorders, digital cameras and movie cameras designed for use in countries other than Japan)

5F: Overseas Floor (PCs, games, digital audio equipment and headphones designed for use in countries other than Japan)

6F: Oversees Floor (watches, cosmetics, beauty aids, health products, electronics for use in countries other than Japan and transformers)

7F: Overseas Floor (Souvenirs, toys, writing materials, suitcases)

Tons of electronics for use in other countries

Traditional Japanese-style decor

A souvenir of your trip to Japan

Onoden

An electronics store with friendly service

Onoden is extremely well-known as one of Akihabara's large electronics stores, and you might recognize us by our "Onoden-boya" mascot. If you're looking for electronics, our massive selection will not disappoint. The B1 through fourth floors feature mainly home electronics, while the fifth floor offers electronics for use overseas as well as traditional Japanese craft items. Onoden has long been a prominent part of the Akihabara scene, so if you've never been in, pop by when you're there and see what we're about.

Address: 1-2-7 Soto-Kanda, Chiyoda-ku, Tokyo
Phone: 03-3253-3911
URL: http://www.onoden.co.jp/oos/
Hours: Mon.–Sat. 10:00–20:00/Sun. 9:40–19:40/holidays 10:00–20:00; open year round

Floor Guide

B1F: Vacuum cleaners, electronic cooking devices, beauty aids, calculators, washlet toilet seats
1F: Digital cameras, camcorders, PCs, PC supplies, mobile phones, telephones, digital audio equipment, electronic dictionaries
2F: Refrigerators, washing machines, air conditioners, air purification systems, massage chairs, seasonal items
3F: Audio equipment, TVs, HDDs, BD recorders, projectors, AM/FM radios
4F: All types of lighting/lighting planning services
5F: Duty free shop, electronics for use in countries other than Japan (digital cameras, PCs, TVs, DVD players and more), watches, traditional craft items, Shiseido cosmetics, game machines

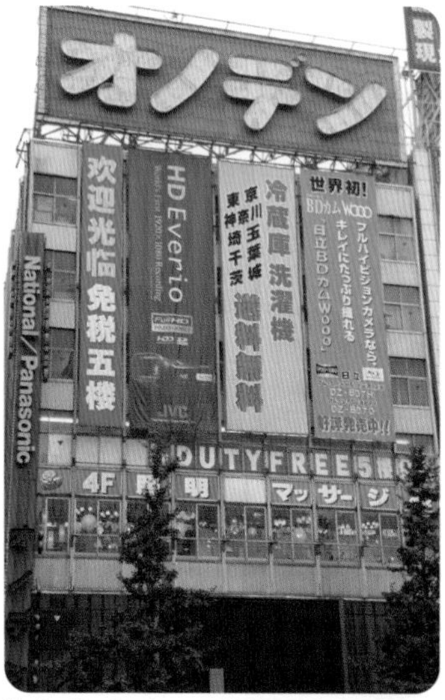
オノデン
HD Everio
National/Panasonic
DUTYFREE
The familiar view from outside!

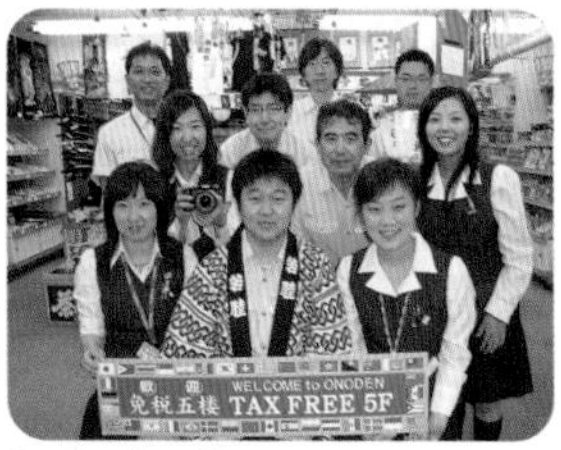
TAX FREE 5F
Our friendly staff greet customers.

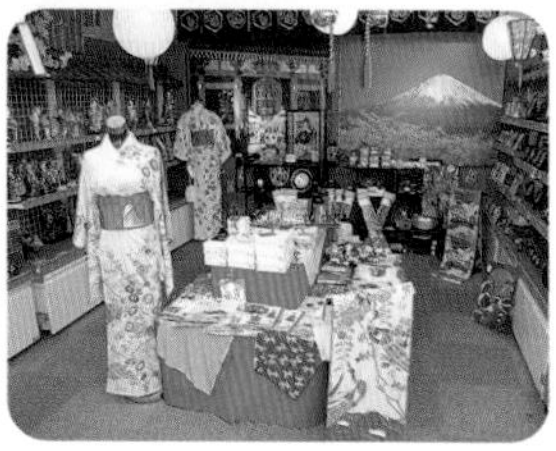
Traditional Japanese items

Tsukumo Computer the Main Shop

The total PC shop

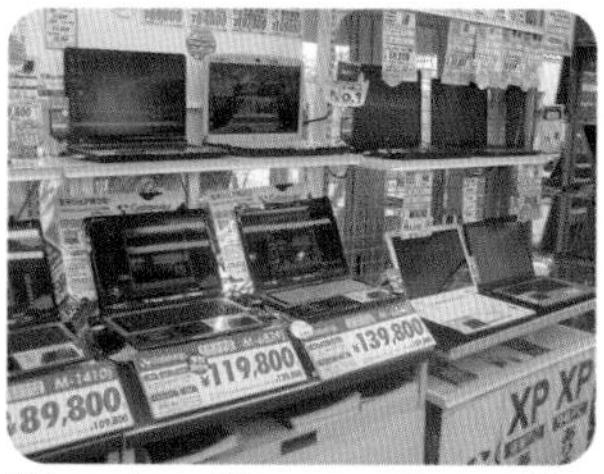
¥119,800
89,800
XP
We've got everything you want for your PC.

Tsukumo Computer the main shop is Tsukumo's key presence in Akihabara. Together with main shop II and main shop III, we've got a staggering total of 12 floors all in one place. Offering not only not only Windows PCs and Mac, but also peripherals, software, PC parts and more, this is the ultimate in computer-related selection.

Address: 1-9-7 Soto-Kanda, Chiyoda-ku, Tokyo
Phone: 03-3253-5599
URL: http://shop.tsukumo.co.jp/
Hours: Mon.–Sat. 10:30–20:00/Sun. & holidays 10:30–19:30; open year round

Floor Guide

Main Shop
B1F: Consultation desk (advice on building customized personal computers and LC monitors)
1F: eX.computers and notebook computers
2F: Printers and networks
3F: Robots
4F: PC cases

Main Shop II
B1F: Motherboards
1F: Parts
2F: Drives
3F: Special event floor
4F: Capture equipment

PC Main Shop III (eMachines, mobile phones and monitors)

Tsukumo ex

Come to the PC parts specialist for the best selection in the industry

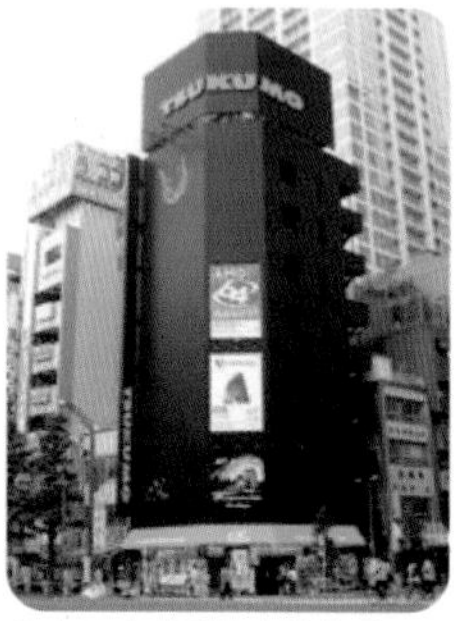
Tsukumo's "PC Tower" dominates the Akiba skyline.

Tsukumo ex's beautiful black building stands out on Akihabara's main street, Chuo-dori Avenue. The store lives up to the image of its stunning exterior with the largest selection of PC parts in the industry. With an amazing variety of products and huge inventory, Tsukumo ex meets the needs of everyone from PC-building newbies to professionals. And it's lots of fun!

Address: 4-4-1 Soto-Kanda, Chiyoda-ku, Tokyo
Phone: 03-5207-5599
URL: http://shop.tsukumo.co.jp/
Hours: Mon.–Thurs. 11:00–20:30/Fri. 11:00–21:00/Sat. 10:30–20:30/Sun. & holidays 10:30–19:30; open year round

Floor Guide

1F: CPUs, HDDs, memory items
2F: Peripherals, network equipment
3F: Motherboards, monitors
4F: PC cases, accessories
5F: Customized PCs
6F: Support

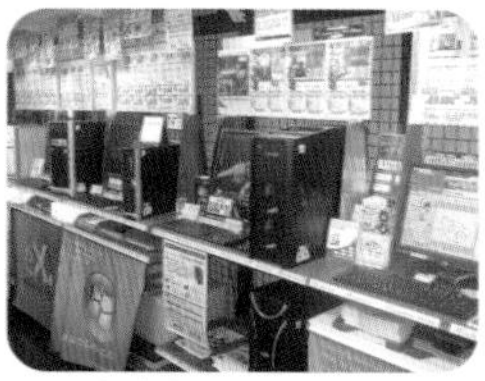
Unrivalled selection and inventory

Tsukumo DOS/V

We're one of Akihabara's giants, and we've got the selection to prove it!

The big PC store with the green trim

This superstore rivals Tsukumo Computer the main shop in size, offering terrific product selection and sample displays of excellent cost-performance items, including pre-owned products, outlet products and cut-price merchandise. We've also got loads of pre-owned upgrade peripherals unavailable new, pre-owned parts and even some slightly-shady (!) junk items. Look for our blowout sales—you just might find some great quality products and incredible deals.

Address: 1-11-3 Soto-Kanda, Chiyoda-ku, Tokyo
Phone: 03-3254-3999
URL: http://www.tsukumo.co.jp/shop/dosv/
Hours: Mon.–Fri. 11:00–20:00/Sat. 10:30–20:00/Sun. & holidays 10:30–19:30; open year round

Huge selection and cost performance

Tsukumo Case Oukoku

The ultimate PC case specialists

You'll find the case for you here!

With over 300 varieties of PC cases, Tsukumo Case Oukoku is the definitive case specialty store. From deep-discount cases to high-end aluminum cases, Tsukumo offers a case for every model you can think of. The store also boasts huge selection in power supply, with more than 80 different varieties. If you're in the market for cases or power supplies, Tsukumo Case Oukoku is the only stop you need to make!

Address: 3-2-14 Soto-Kanda, Chiyoda-ku, Tokyo
Phone: 03-5298-5099
URL: http://shop.tsukumo.co.jp/
Hours: Mon.–Sat. 11:00–19:30/Sun. & holidays 10:30–19:00; open year round

Cases, cases, everywhere!

Tsukumo the 12th Shop

We're the pre-owned PC specialists

A different kind of Tsukumo store

Tsukumo the 12th shop has been revamped and reopened as a pre-owned PC specialty shop, offering mainly pre-owned PCs and monitors. There's incredible variety here, from buy-at-your-own risk "junk" items to manufacturer-serviced top-of-the-line used PCs. We also offer miscellaneous PC related products, including media items, at discount prices.

Address: 3-4-14 Soto-Kanda, Chiyoda-ku, Tokyo
Phone: 03-5298-5299
URL: http://shop.tsukumo.co.jp/
Hours: 11:00–19:30; open year round

A vast variety of used PCs

Tsukumo Robot Oukoku

Tsukumo—the first name in robots

Tsukumo main shop, third floor

If you're into robots, Tsukumo Robot Oukoku is the place for you! You'll find the bipedal walking robots—the flagship products of the robot manufacturers—as well as talking robots, cleaning robots, home security robots and much more. In addition to these, the store also offers some 20,000 related products including everything from electronic engineering kits to robot parts to specialized books and more. In short, we've got everything the robot lover could ever need.

Address: 1-9-7 Soto-Kanda, Chiyoda-ku, Tokyo
Phone: 03-3253-5599
URL: http://shop.tsukumo.co.jp/
Hours: Mon.–Sat. 10:30–20:00/Sun. & holidays 10:30–19:30; open year round

Robots everywhere you look!

Restaurants

Ramen Tenzo

Try our specialty: *ramen* in rich pork bone broth—yum!

Ramen Tenzo is undeniably one of the most popular shops gracing Akiba's Chuo-dori Avenue. It's frequented by company workers on weekdays, and by tourists and couples on the weekends. Located in an underground shopping area, this is a large space where customers can enjoy their *ramen* in a relaxed atmosphere. We recommend our *umatoro ramen* (¥680): once you've sampled this rich, pork-bone flavored broth, you'll keep coming back for more. Get an extra helping of noodles for ¥50, or a large serving for an extra ¥100.

Address: 3-13-7 Soto-Kanda, Chiyoda-ku, Tokyo
Phone: 03-5294-2311, Fax: 03-5294-2311
Hours: 11:00–21:00 (Fri. & Sat. 11:00–22:00); open
    year round

Our Recommendations

Umatoro ramen: ¥680
Pork-bone and soy sauce *ramen*: ¥680
Pork slice: ¥300
Egg, dried laver seaweed, scallions, *sungan*, corn,
    bean sprouts, seaweed: ¥100
Large serving: additional ¥100
Extra helping of noodles: ¥50

Akiba Noodle Sakura

The instant *ramen* museum

A first in Akihabara!

As an instant *ramen* specialty shop, Akiba Noodle Sakura offers not only all kinds of instant *ramen* from around Japan, but from abroad as well. This is literally an instant *ramen* museum featuring over 400 varieties where customers can either eat in or take out (for an additional ¥250). The *ramen* comes with spinach, *sungan*, pork slice and scallion toppings. As of March 14, we launched two new products: instant dipping *ramen* and *dan dan* noodles. This is Akihabara's *ramen* lover's shop, and there's never a dull moment here.

Address: Akibako Tower 2F, 3-15-6 Soto-Kanda, Chiyoda-ku, Tokyo
Phone: 03-3256-1757
URL: http://akiba-noodle.com/
Hours: 11:00–22:00; open year round

Our Recommendations

Akiba's own chameleon ramen: ¥180
Sakura ramen: ¥180
Shirokuma salt *ramen*
    (Asahiyama Zoo limited edition item): ¥200
Ground *natto* (fermented bean) *soba*: ¥180
Kin-chan ramen: ¥140
Topping: additional ¥250

Chameleon ramen:
an Akiba original

Okonomiyaki Yukari Akiba-ichi

Authentic Osaka flavor right in Akihabara!

Okonomiyaki Yukari is located on the third floor of Akihabara UDX. This restaurant's Osaka *okonomiyaki* features a fluffy, light consistency that keeps everybody coming back for more. So when you're in the mood for *okonomiyaki,* make it Osaka-style at Yukari.

A retro look

Address: Akihabara UDX AKIBA-ICHI 3F, 4-14-1 Soto-Kanda, Chiyoda-ku, Tokyo
Phone: 03-3526-3310, Fax: 03-3526-3310
URL: http://www.akiba-ichi.jp/restaurant/detail.php?shopcode=25&floor=3
Hours: 11:00–22:30 (Last call 21:30); open year round

Our Recommendations

Special mix: ¥1,200
Cheese fry: ¥1,200
Pork: ¥900
Scallion: ¥1,150 & up
Akiba-yaki: ¥2,980 (serves 2-3)
Yakisoba (fried noodles): ¥880

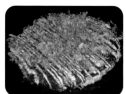

Our special mix—our most
popular dish!

Café Torionpu

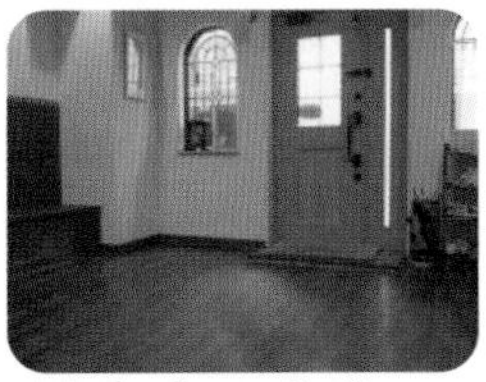

Divider-free flat seats ideal for events

Create your very own event at this unique café

Akihabara's café-for-rent features a romantic, antique-look atmosphere. It's whatever you want it to be: use the kitchen to cook for your own event, reserve the place for your own catered party or hold your own live concert, exhibition or photo session—the sky's the limit. On regular business days, it's a calm-and-relaxing little café complete with classical music, making it the perfect place to sit and enjoy a book, meet friends after work, chat with our manager at the counter—whatever you're in the mood for, this café is simply a great place to be.

Address: Metro Bldg. 1F, 5-6-4 Soto-Kanda, Chiyoda-ku, Tokyo
Phone: 03-6380-9540 URL: http://sweettrip.biz/
Hours: Weekdays 11:30–22:00/Sat. & holidays 13:00–21:00; closed Mon. (with some exceptions)

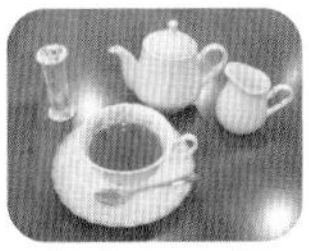

Watch your tea brew luxuriously in the pot.

Our Recommendations

Tea: ¥550 & up; Coffee: ¥500 & up
Weekday lunch specials
Looking for a way to celebrate a birthday? Try our stunning "Anniversary Parfait" in a Baccarat glass: ¥1,800 (reservations required)
Cocktails: All ¥700 (leave it to our manager: he'll bring you a surprise!)
Early bird gets the worm: space rentals are dirt cheap in the morning!
You can even make us your own maid cafe for a day: this is the only place where you can design your event and leave the food up to us!

Sand Suzuka

Take a jaunt around Akiba, apple croquet in hand!

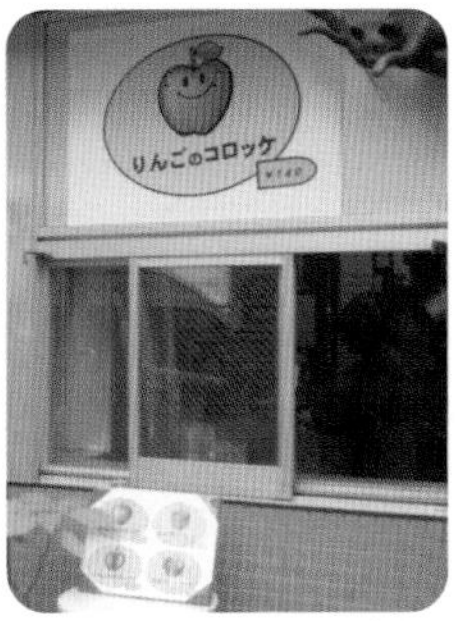

Located near Kanda-myojin shrine.

We're famous for our apple croquets, courtesy of TV. But there's lots of other good stuff here, too! The potatoes are the *danshaku* variety that come all the way from Hokkaido, while the roast pork—which really makes the flavor—is from Ibaraki Prefecture. If you're in the mood for hardy food, these croquets are what you want! The mincemeat cutlets and ham cutlets are also great choices.

Address: 3-1-2 Soto-Kanda, Chiyoda-ku, Tokyo
Phone: 03-3251-5361
URL: http://homepage2.nifty.com/sandosuzuka/
Hours: 11:00–18:30; closed Sat., Sun. & holidays

Our Recommendations

Apple croquet: ¥140
Mincemeat cutlet: ¥180
Ham cutlet: ¥160
Hot dog: ¥90
Barbecued pork (100 g): ¥290
Pork fillet cutlet: ¥570

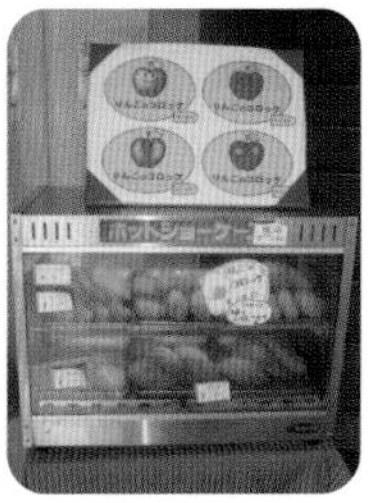

We recommend our mincemeat and ham cutlets.

Magurotei

Servings so generous, they're too big for the bowl!

Check out Magurotei, but make sure you're good and hungry—we're known for our incredible portions: there's a whole lot of happiness in every single bowl! Our special *maruki-don* is loaded with all kinds of seafood delights, including *chutoro* and *otoro* tuna, salmon caviar, sea urchin and more. And at night customers are in store for another pleasant surprise: the place turns into an *izakaya* (Japanese-style bar). Try the delectable sashimi with your favorite sake. Magurotei is a dream for seafood lovers!

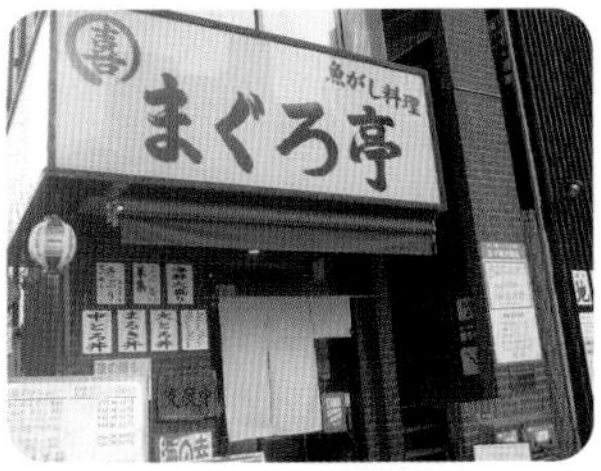
まぐろ亭

Just cross the Mansei Bridge and we're right there!

Address: 2-1-16 Soto-Kanda, Chiyoda-ku, Tokyo
Phone: 03-5295-3338, Fax: 03-3807-2285
Hours: 11:00–15:00, 17:00–23:00 (Sun. & holidays 11:00–17:00); open year round

Our Recommendations

Chutoro-don: ¥1,000
Maruki-don: ¥1,500
Otoro-don: ¥1,500
Sea urchin & salmon caviar-don: ¥1,500
Chutoro sashimi: ¥1,000
Edomae-zuke-don: ¥1,000

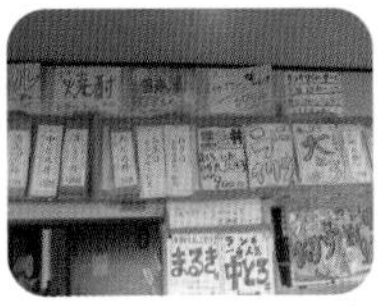

A distinctly Japanese-style atmosphere

Star Kebab Akiba Terrace

The place for Turkish *doner* kebab sandwiches in Akiba: one of the area's signature delights

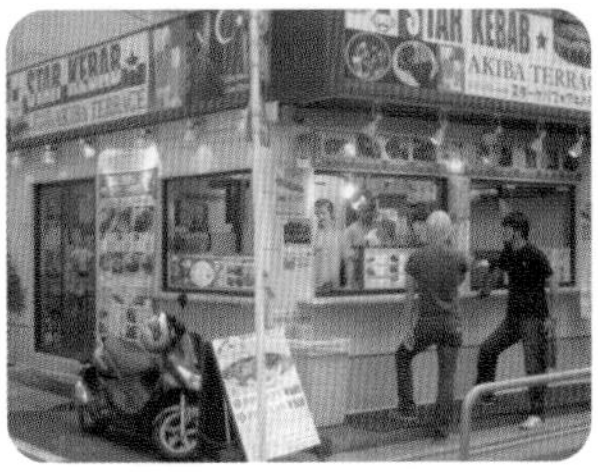

You can't miss the red-and-white shop!

Star Kebab Akiba Terrace is the second shop of this popular restaurant launched in 1999. Authentic Turkish kebabs are a delight for the customer on two counts: price and serving size! You can take out or eat in and enjoy the Turkish-style atmosphere of the place. Have a chat with the friendly staff as you dig in!

Address: 3-10-7 Soto-Kanda, Chiyoda-ku, Tokyo
Phone: 03-3255-0004
URL: http://www.kebab.co.jp/index.html
Hours: 11:00–21:00; open year round

Our Recommendations

Star *doner* sandwich: ¥500
Doner kebab plate: ¥600
Shish kebab plate: ¥700
Shish kebab: ¥500
Kofte kebab plate: ¥600
Big kebab plate: ¥1,100

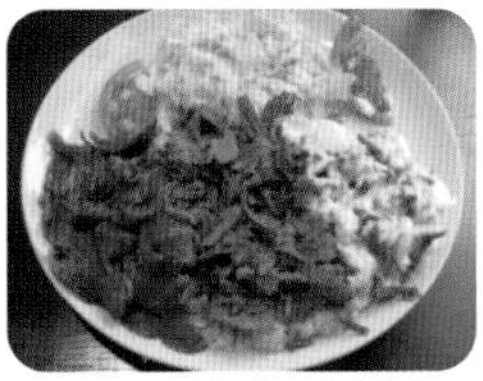

Our very popular *doner* kebab plate!

Dragon Ice

A new kind of snow cone that lives up to its name: experience the delightful texture of new-fallen snow

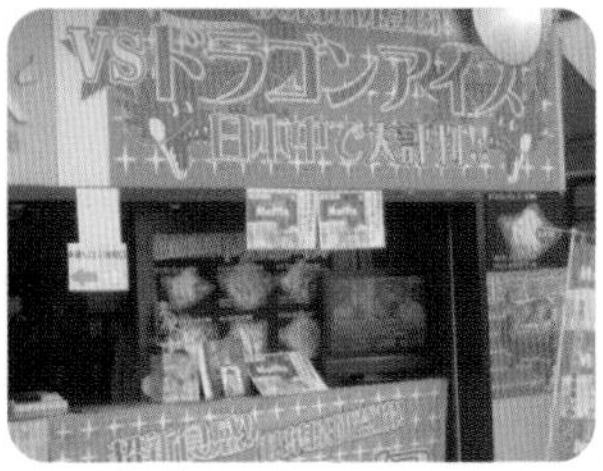

We're a hit all over Japan.

Dragon Ice is hands-down one of the most popular ice cream shops in Akihabara. All eyes are on the mango at the moment, and the delectable Dragon Mango makes this luscious fruit even better. Once you've tried this incredible combination of shaved ice with milk and condensed milk, you'll keep on coming back for more. And there are a number of other great items on the menu too.

Address: Akibako Tower 1F, 3-15-6 Soto-Kanda, Chiyoda-ku, Tokyo
Phone: 03-3256-2505
URL: http://akibaice.com/
Hours: 11:00–19:30; open year round

Our Recommendations

Dragon Mango: ¥500
O.K.O. Special: ¥500
Boken-o Special: ¥500
Dragon Chocolate: ¥500
Dragon Orange: ¥500
The Pure Dragon: ¥400

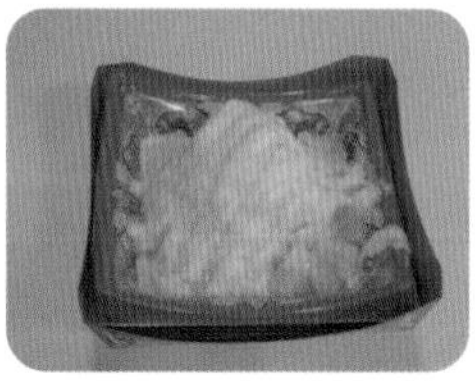

Our Dragon Mango: number one on our menu!

Fluf deu sezon

Akihabara's fruit oasis

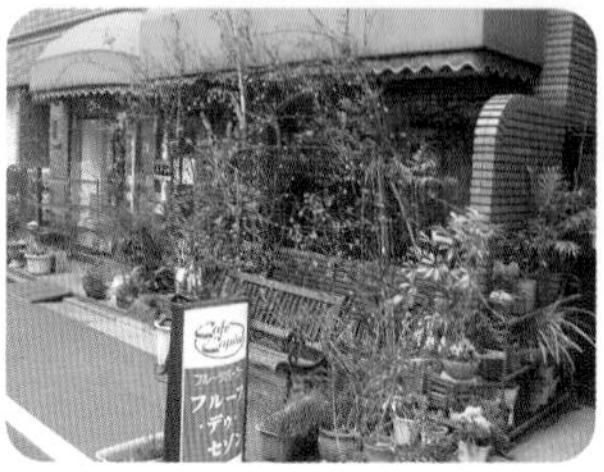

An oasis in Akihabara!

The Fluf deu sezon fruit parlor is a wonderful refuge from the busy streets of Akihabara, so when you've had enough shopping, stop in for some fresh fruit and fresh-baked bread! Just three minutes' walk from Suehirocho Station on the Tokyo Metro Ginza Line, it's also easy to get to. Featuring a cute exterior and interior reminiscent of the nostalgic cake shop, and a menu chock full of all kinds of sweets, Fluf deu sezon is especially popular with the girls. Besides the regular menu, we also offer limited-time-only items and specials, so check us out from time to time! The best little escape in Akihabara.

Address: 4-11-2 Soto-Kanda, Chiyoda-ku, Tokyo
Phone: 03-5296-1485
URL: http://www.geocities.co.jp/Foodpia-Olive/2728/
Hours: Mon.–Fri. 9:00–19:00/Sat., Sun. & holidays 12:00–19:00; closed Thurs.

Our Recommendations

Fruit parfait: ¥1,000
Strawberry parfait: ¥1,300
Banana milk: ¥700
Chocolate banana parfait: ¥900
Blueberry juice: ¥700
Croissant sandwich set (A): ¥800

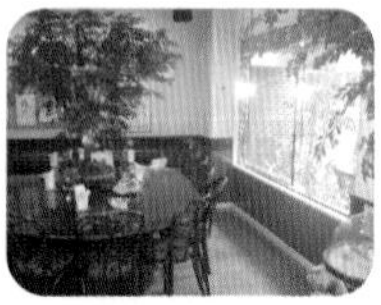

Stylish-and-sweet decor

Bengal

A curry specialty shop

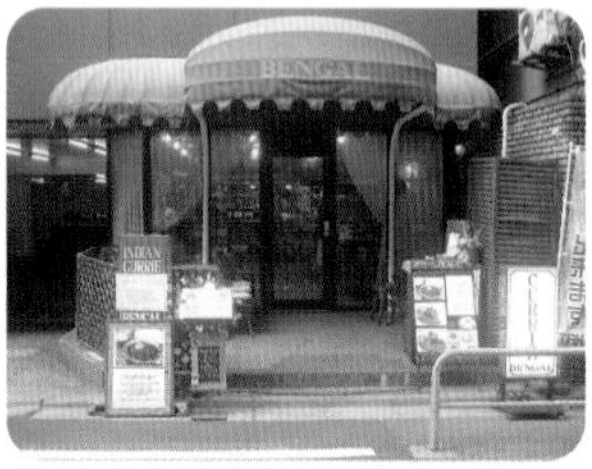

The longest-running curry shop in Akihabara!

Bengal is the oldest curry shop in Akihabara. A favorite with customers is the super-spicy curry, made from a powder blend of 20 spices aged for a period of two years. The menu offers a variety of choices including the usual beef curry, as well as not-so-ordinary bean or mutton curry. We highly recommend the special-of-the-day for both its generous portion and rich flavor. On the way out, customers can pick up some curry power or spices to make their own curry at home! Give Bengal—the curry specialists—a try!

Address: Nikka Sekiyu Bldg. 1F, 3-10-12 Soto-Kanda, Chiyoda-ku, Tokyo
Phone: 03-3255-4410, Fax: 03-3255-4410
Hours: 11:00–15:00, 16:00–19:30; closed Mon.

Our Recommendations

Beef block curry (mild, medium or spicy): ¥1,100
Mutton curry: ¥1,000
Bean curry: ¥1,000
Special-of-the-day: ¥1,300
Spicy potato salad: ¥500
Lassi: ¥450

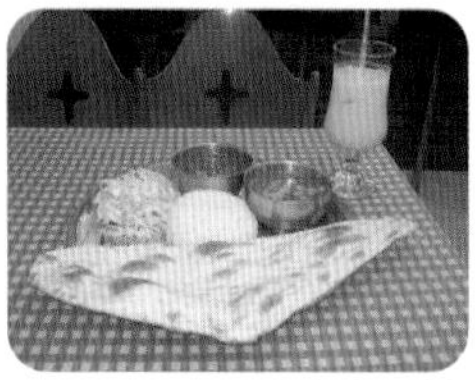

Today's special!

Matsuya

Bring home something uniquely Akihabara!

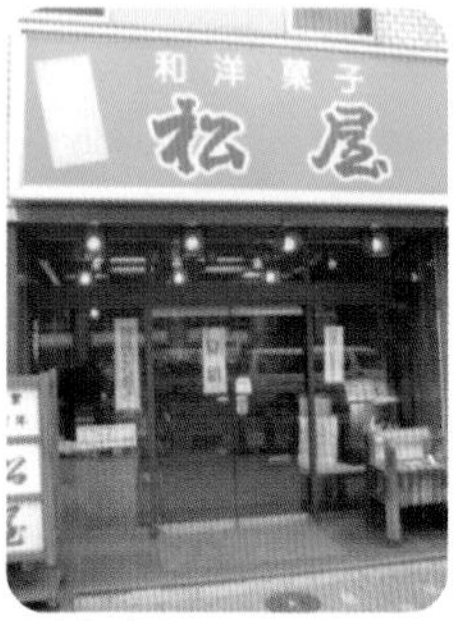
和洋菓子
松屋

Look for the green sign!

Matsuya has been a welcoming presence in Akihabara for 120 years. While it remains true to its traditional flavors, items come wrapped in original Akiba-style prints; it's got the best of both worlds, and maybe that's the key to its popularity. The coffee *dorayaki* (bean jam pancake, ¥210), featuring bean jam and coffee cream sandwiched between pancake layers, is not to be missed. Just one minute on foot from the Showa-dori Exit of Akihabara Station facing the main road, it's also quite easy to find.

Address: 1 Kanda-Matsunagacho, Chiyoda-ku, Tokyo
Phone: 03-3251-1234
URL: http://www.wagashi.or.jp/tokyo/shop/0201.htm
Hours: Weekdays 8:30–19:00/Sat. 9:00–16:00; closed Sun. & holidays

Our Recommendations

Dorayaki: ¥210
Coffee *dorayaki*: ¥210
Kasutera rasuku: ¥170
Akiba sable: ¥210
Matsu-monaka: ¥189
Original print: additional ¥20 & up

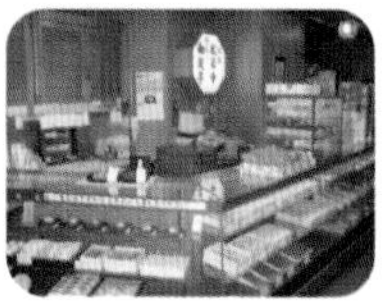

Hard to decide...!!

PCs

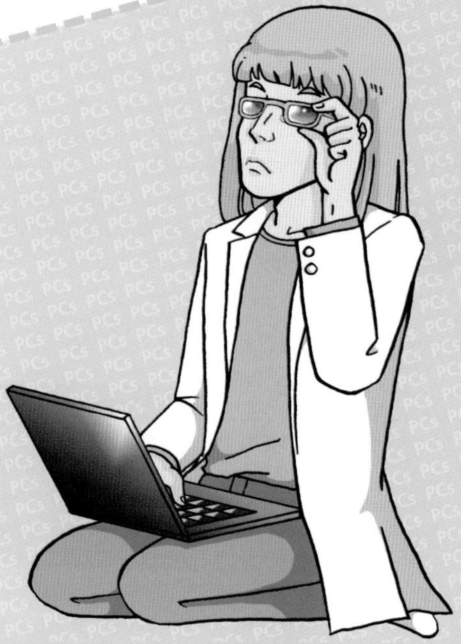

Two Top Akihabara the Main Shop

Akihabara's premier PC shop

Two Top carries everything from PC parts including CPUs, memory products, HDDs, etc. to complete products such as PCs, liquid crystal monitors and more. We also take orders for custom-made PCs. Estimates are free, so stop in anytime to get yours. Our selection includes a variety of items only available as imports, and we sell and take orders on rare parts as well. We even have some things that you'd never expect to see in a PC shop! With our vast inventory, special events and fun staff, we've got something for every customer. Come on in for a good time shopping!

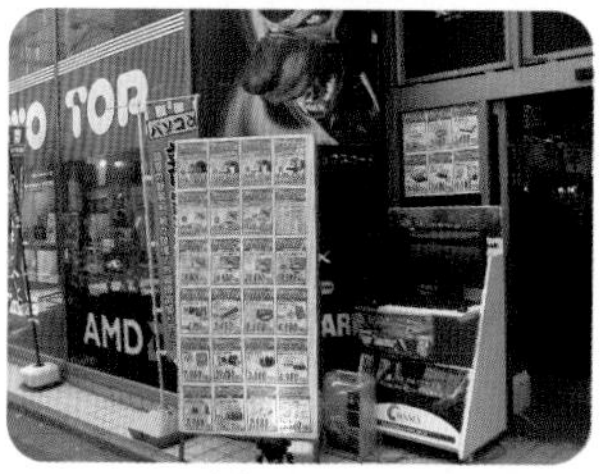
AMD
Look for the Two Top red banner.

Address: Akihabara HF Bldg. 1F, 3-14-10 Soto-Kanda, Chiyoda-ku, Tokyo
Phone: 03-5209-7330
URL: http://www.twotop.co.jp/
Hours: 11:00–20:00; open year round

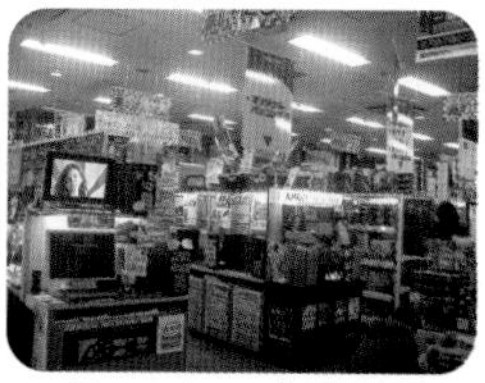
Tons and tons of great products

PC Shop Wakamatsu

We've been part of the Akihabara scene for a very long time

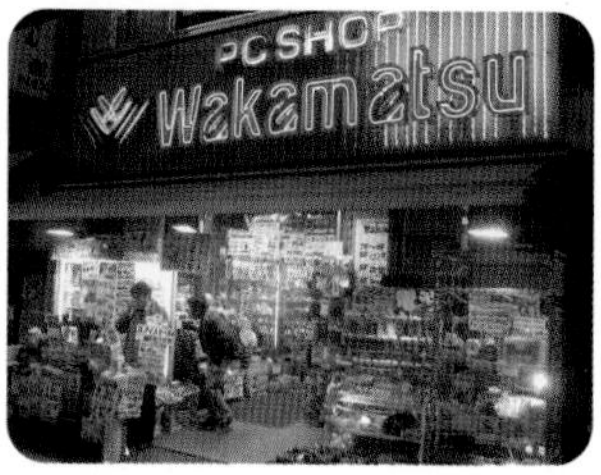
PC SHOP
Wakamatsu
Our eye-catching signboard: you can't miss it!

Wakamatsu is one of Akihabara's oldest and most well-established PC shops. Our bright neon signs stand out, even amongst the sea of neon of Akihabara. The first through sixth floors are specialty floors offering electronics parts, flash memory cards, an array of PC items and more. Look for our friendly staff at the first floor entrance, and welcome to our exciting store!

Address: 4-7-3 Soto-Kanda, Chiyoda-ku, Tokyo
Phone: 03-3257-0601
URL: http://www.wakamatsu.co.jp/
Hours: Mon.–Sat. 10:30–20:30/Sundays & holidays 10:30–20:00; open year round

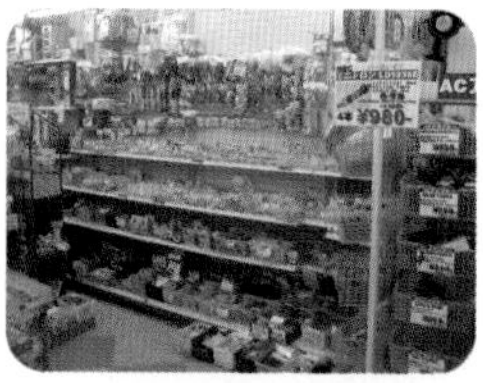
We're known for our incredible selection.

Akibakan

Mac fans, look no further than Akibakan

Akibakan is just a two-minute walk from the Electric Town Exit of Akihabara Station. We're easy to find—just look for the yellow building on Chuo-dori Avenue. with the Akibakan sign. For all of you Mac users out there, we offer your favorite Macs and peripherals at friendly Akihabara prices. The first floor houses peripherals and electronic parts, while the second floor is chock full of Mac products. Head down to B1 for the trade-in counter and customer support center. We provide estimates and take inquiries at all times, so if you're thinking of making your next computer a Mac, Akibakan is the place to look.

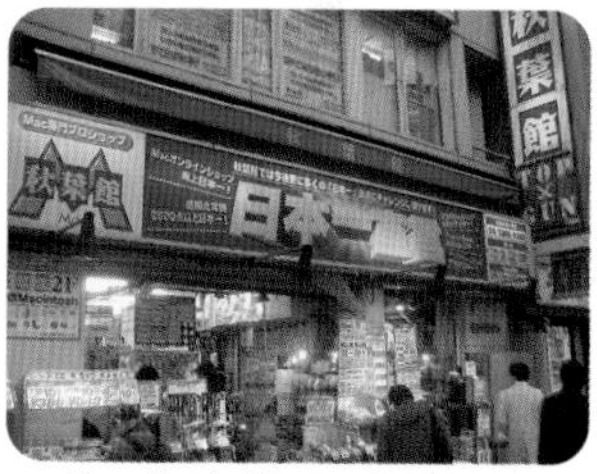
The yellow building on Chuo-dori Avenue

Address: Dai-ni Chuei Bldg., 1-11-9 Soto-Kanda, Chiyoda-ku, Tokyo
Phone: 03-3255-8252
URL: http://www.akibakan.com/
Hours: 11:00–20:00; open year round

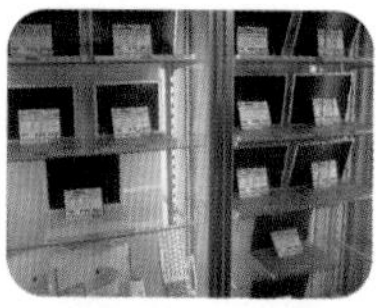
Back-to-back Mac items!

Ark

We're the PC parts and game software specialists: look for the memory-chip signboard

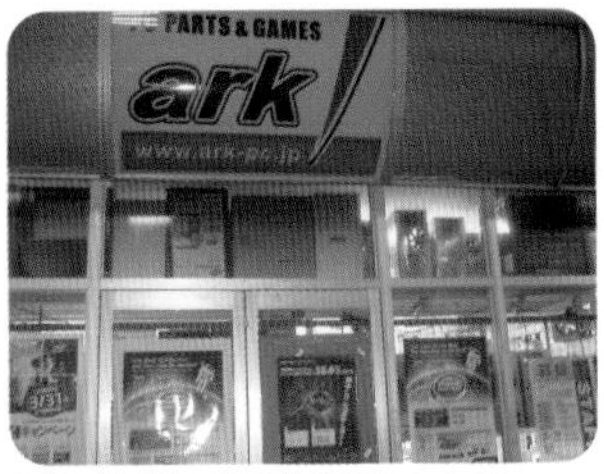
PARTS & GAMES
ark
www.ark-pc.jp
Our unique signboard

Ark is conveniently located just one minute from Suehiro Station on the Ginza Line, and you can't miss our unique memory-chip sign. Our product selection includes PC parts, PC game software, built-to-order PCs, a variety of game devices, speakers, headphones and much more. If you like PCs or PC games, you're in for a treat in our store. But don't worry if you live too far away to stop in: we've also got an online store!

Address: Tsuun Kaikan 1F, 3-16-18 Soto-Kanda, Chiyoda-ku, Tokyo
Phone: 03-5298-7020
URL: http://www.ark-pc.co.jp/
Hours: Weekdays 11:00–19:00/Sat., Sun. & holidays 10:30–19:00; closed on year-end and New Year holidays

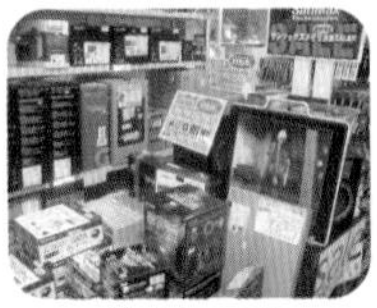
The PC and PC game lover's paradise

Clevery the 1st Shop

We're the authority in PC parts. Look for our bright red signboard!

On the streets of Akihabara, our red sign stands out among the rest, and fittingly we're the area's first name in PC parts. Our store's signature product is VGA cards, and we carry all kinds of them, from retail to bulk lots. Other items include an extensive selection of I/F cards and optical drives. Our knowledgeable staff give you all the information you need on the products, so you can shop with confidence even if you know nothing about PCs. Stop in when you're in Akihabara!

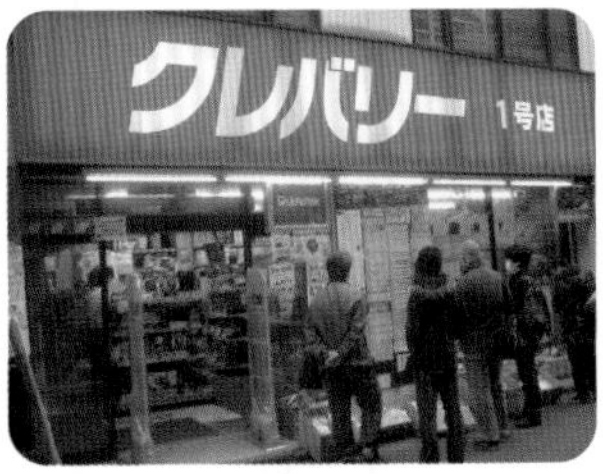
クレバリー 1号店
You can't miss our red sign.

Address: 3-13-4 Soto-Kanda, Chiyoda-ku, Tokyo
Phone: 03-5294-2088
URL: http://www.clevery.co.jp/shop/
Hours: 11:00–20:00; open year round

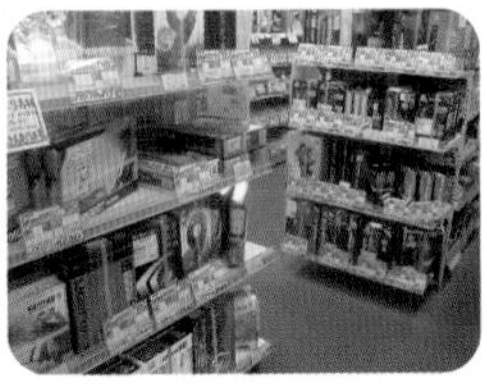
Check out our VGA cards!

Clevery the 2nd Shop

The ultimate specialty store for keyboards and mice

This is Akihabara's new place to be! For keyboards and mice, look no further. At Clevery the 2nd Shop, we're more interested in helping you type faster than boosting your PC speed, and we're more into utilities like chatting than complicated stuff like editing film. We've got an unrivalled selection of English-language keyboards, keyboards for special applications, super-slim keyboards and everything from pantograph to mechanical keyboards.

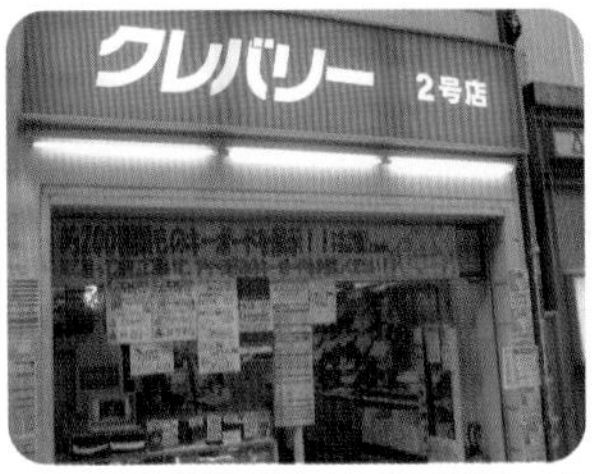
クレバリー 2号店
We're Akihabara's new hot spot!

Address: 3-13-2 Soto-Kanda, Chiyoda-ku, Tokyo
Phone: 03-5296-1775
URL: http://www.clevery.co.jp/shop/shop-2.html
Hours: Weekdays 11:00–20:00/Sun. & holidays 11:00–19:30; open year round

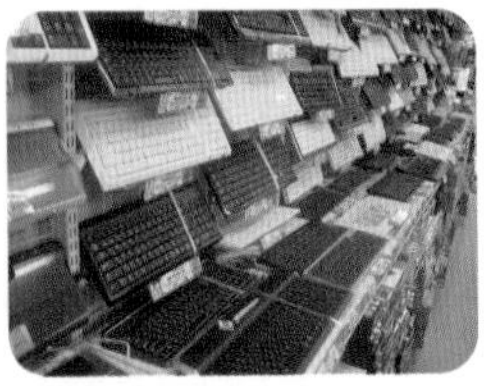
Go nowhere else for keyboards or mice.

Clevery Internet Kan

Making the Internet even better

Our goal at Clevery is to help make the Internet the most optimal tool it can be for you. We provide everything you need to download, store and use Internet content, all under one roof! We have everything from the usual standard items to incredible bargains, and we get the latest products in fast. We especially recommend our HDD cases, flash memory, and Windows DPS. In addition to other brands, we also offer our very own shop brand, COORDY'S, so don't forget to check it out!

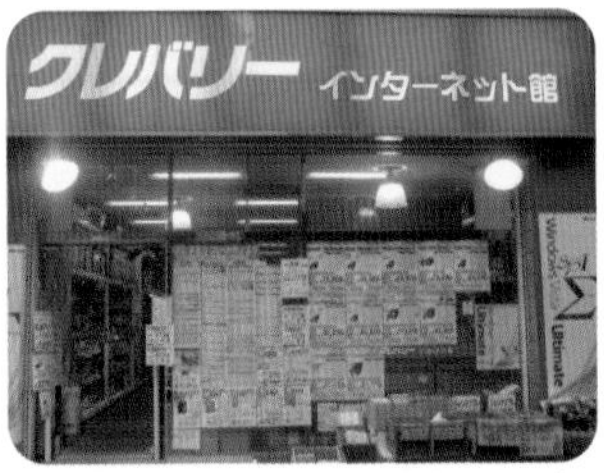
クレバリー インターネット館
The best your Internet experience can be.

Address: 3-14-3 Soto-Kanda, Chiyoda-ku, Tokyo
Phone: 03-5296-1770
URL: http://www.clevery.co.jp/shop/net-annex.html
Hours: Weekdays 11:00–20:00/Sun. & holidays 11:00–19:30; open year round

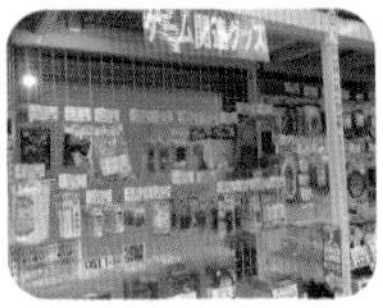
All the current hit products

Sellsta R-1

The deep discount store for pre-owned PCs

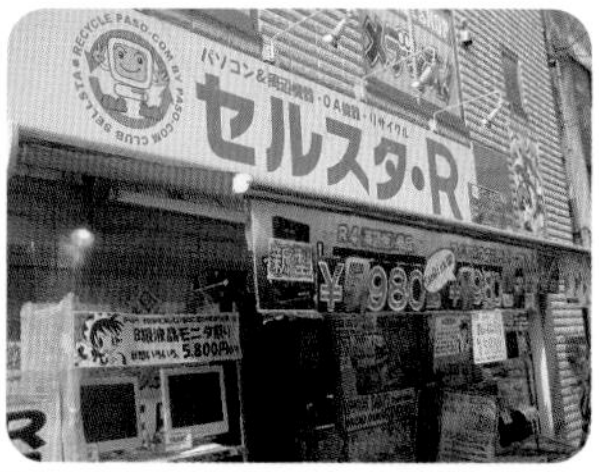
セルスタ・R
This is the place to find your pre-owned PC.

Sellsta R-1 carries primarily pre-owned personal computers, as well as pre-owned peripherals, parts, accessory products and more. Our store is very attractively decorated, and our products are arranged so that you can easily find what you're looking for. Yet that's not all—we're known for our very reasonable prices, which can go as low as ¥10,000-plus, and we're experts on pre-owned PCs. To top it all off, we've even got lots of underground-style game products.

Address: MY Bldg., 3-7-14 Soto-Kanda, Chiyoda-ku, Tokyo
Phone: 03-3253-8130
URL: http://www.sellsta.net/
Hours: 11:00–20:00; open year round

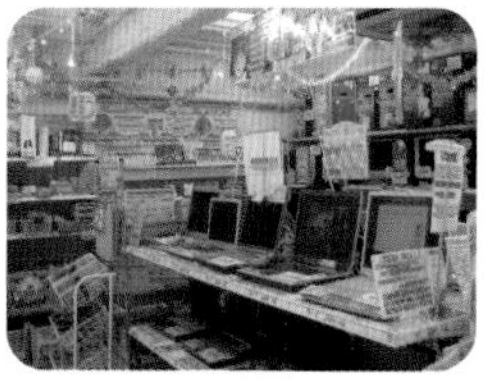
Terrific interior decor!

Figures

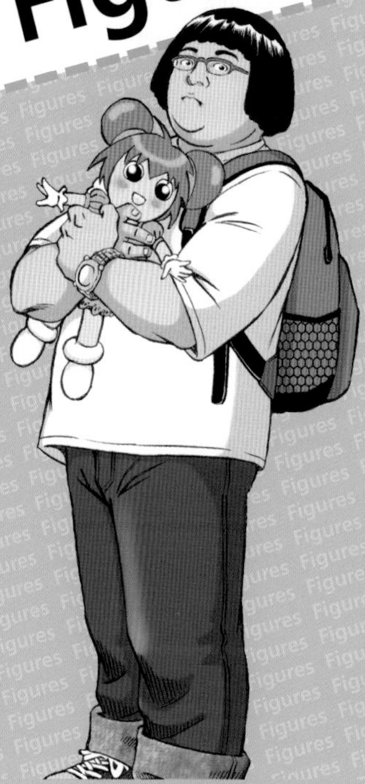

Sellsta R-3

Besides bargain prices on PCs, we've also got tons of game products, too!

Another very unique shop has made its appearance in this competitive district: we're Sellsta R-3, a hot new player in the pre-owned PC business. Besides PCs on the first floor, we also offer underground-style game products on the second floor. Venture to the back of the first floor and you'll find desktops, while the other half of our computer selection is notebook PCs. There are even some available for the unbelievably low price of just ¥10,000. In addition to PCs and games, we've also got digital products and peripherals. We're well worth a look!

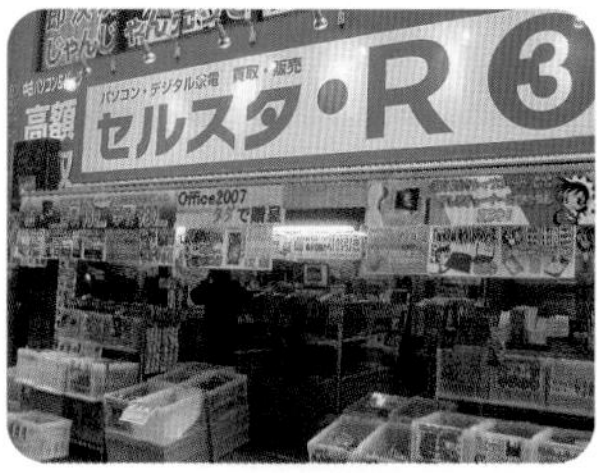
セルスタ・R 3
Akihabara's great new PC store

Address: TK Nishikan Bldg., 3-13-3 Soto-Kanda, Chiyoda-ku, Tokyo
Phone: 03-3526-6996
URL: http://www.sellsta.net/
Hours: 11:00–20:00; open year round

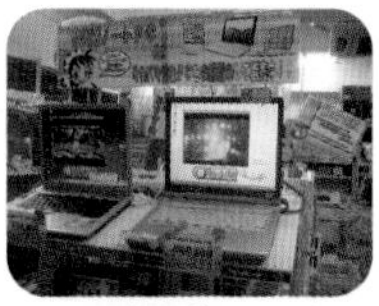
Looking for a used PC? Check out our first floor.

Asobit Chara City

A virtual department store for character goods!

Asobit Chara City has such an amazing selection of character goods, it's more like a department store than a shop. One of the largest stores specializing in character goods in Akihabara, we carry everything from *gampura* (*Gundam* models) to *bishojo* figures (girls collection figures), *anime* characters, *tokusatsu* (special effects film/TV drama) hero figures and much more. Featuring popular items and new products, our first floor storefront is always crowded with visitors. One of the store's most impressive features is the population of life-size figures on the fifth floor—a bizarre scene that can only be witnessed here!

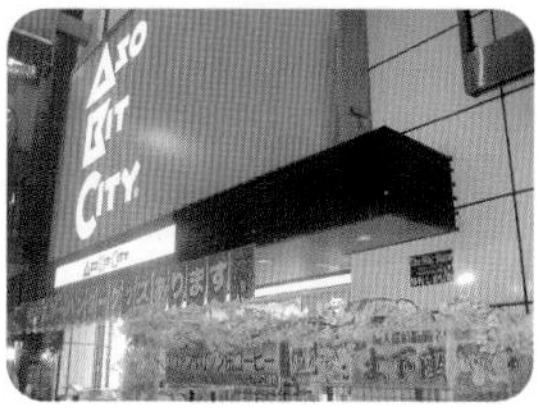
Character items everywhere you look!

Address: 1-8-8 Soto-Kanda, Chiyoda-ku, Tokyo
Phone: 03-3257-2590
URL: http://www.akibaasobit.jp/
Hours: 10:00–22:00; open year round

Floor Guide

1F TV games, trading cards, figures & new products
2F Robot characters
3F *Tokusatsu* hero figures
4F *Moe* figures and *bishojo* games software
5F Character goods and cosplay items

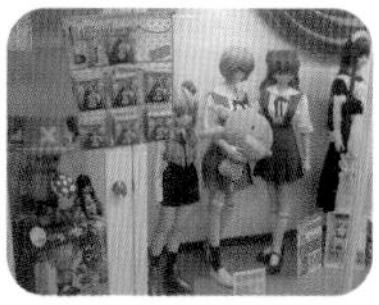
Life-size figures

Asobit Hobby City

The hobby specialty shop

This comprehensive hobby shop is full of a wide variety of items from all sorts of genres, including radio-controlled models, model railroads and model guns, as well as plastic models including *Gundam* models, navy ships, racing cars and more. The fourth floor features a mini 4WD course, and on the seventh floor, there're even shooting ranges for air guns (two 12-meter and one 13-meter ranges). So even if there's nothing specific you're looking to buy, you can still have lots of fun in this store!

Address: 1-15-8 Soto-Kanda, Chiyoda-ku, Tokyo
Phone: 03-5298-3581
URL: http://www.akibaasobit.jp/
Hours: 10:00–22:00; open year round

Floor Guide

B1F	Adult
1F	*Gundam*
2F	TV games and game software
3F	Scale models, color paint, tools
4F	Car hobby goods and radio-controlled models
5F	Model railroads
6F	Guns and military gear
7F	Shooting range

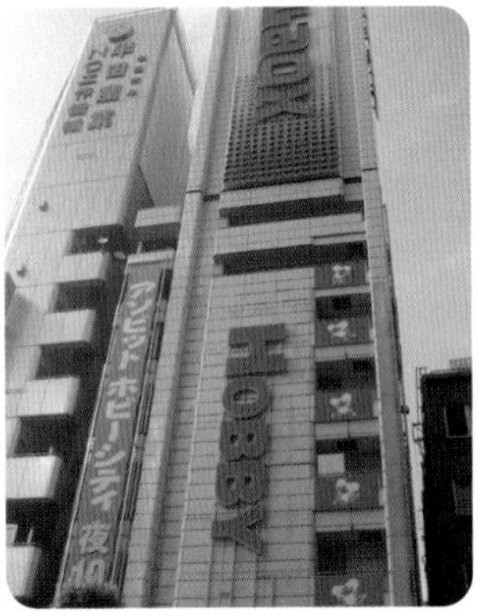
HOBBY
The total hobby shop

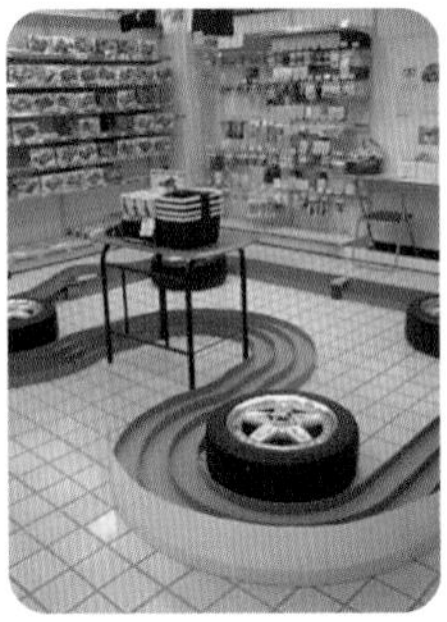
Check out the mini 4WD course on the 4th floor!

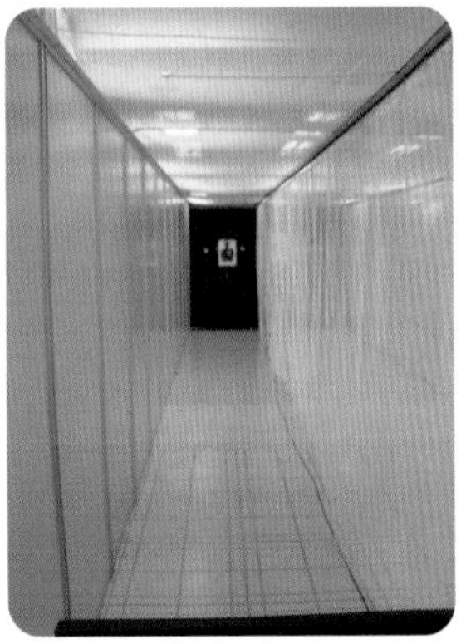
Our super-popular shooting range

Kaiyodo Hobby Lobby Tokyo

Come see our life-sized Kenshiro figure!!

This is none other than model manufacturer Kaiyodo's retail store, and we've got tons of the popular low-priced steerable figure Revoltech. We're also home to life-sized figures Rei Ayanami, Kenshiro and *Aa! Megami-sama*, and visitors can even take pictures with them! Also on display are more than 2,000 of Kaiyodo's previously sold items, such as miniature animals, Godzilla, *bishojo* and *tokusatsu* (special effects film/TV drama) hero figures, and more.

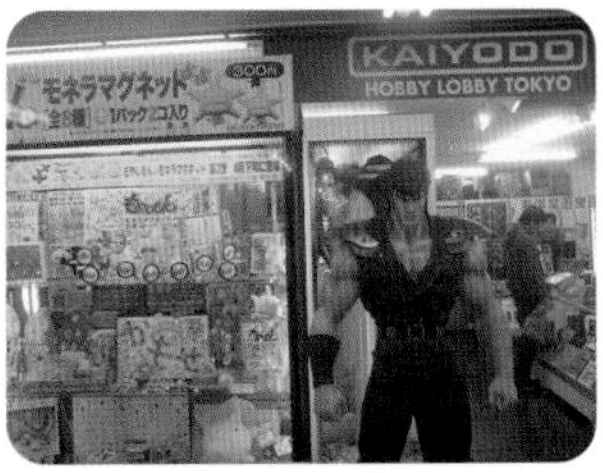
KAIYODO
HOBBY LOBBY TOKYO
A life-size Kenshiro figure greets you!

Address: Rajio Kaikan 4F, 1-15-16 Soto-Kanda, Chiyoda-ku, Tokyo
Phone: 03-3253-1951
URL: http://www.kaiyodo.co.jp/kaiyodo_HB/TK_topics/
Hours: 11:00–20:00; closed Wed.

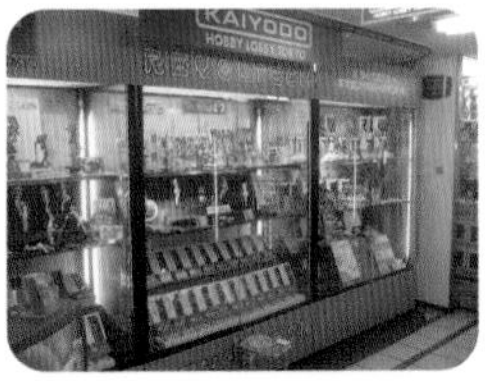
More than 2,000 Kaiyodo figures to choose from—all the time!!

Robot Hero Kan

We specialize in your favorite robot animation and *tokusatsu* hero figures

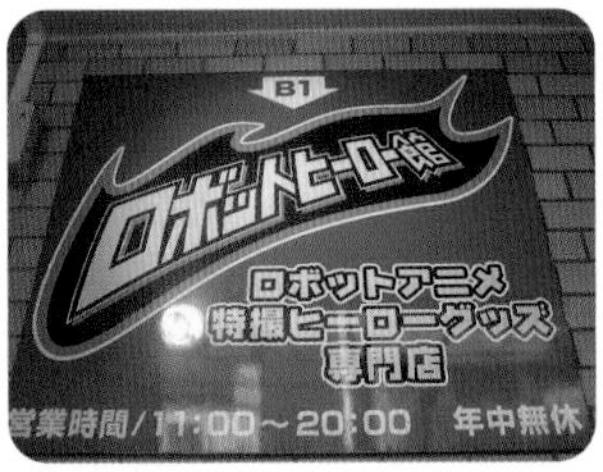
B1
ロボットヒーロー館
ロボットアニメ
特撮ヒーローグッズ
専門店
営業時間/11:00～20:00 年中無休
Take a look in our basement floor!

This store is an absolute must-visit for fans of robot *anime* like *Gundam, Macross, Transformers,* etc. and *tokusatsu* (special effects film/TV drama) heroes like *Masked Rider* and *Ultraman.* Something truly special about this store is that it has something for everyone regardless of age group—everything from out-of-production premier goods to the latest items. We're a great stop for families.

Address: Maruwa Bldg. B1F, 3-10-6 Soto-Kanda, Chiyoda-ku, Tokyo
Phone: 0120-135-163
URL: http://www.robot-herokan.com
Hours: 11:00–20:00; open year round

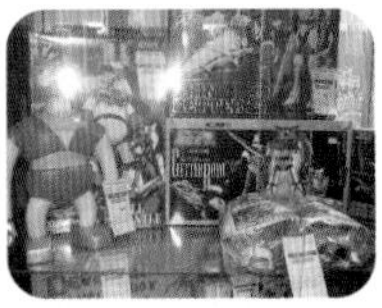
Robot and *tokusatsu* hero figures

Toys & Figure Uchusen

A character toy specialty shop

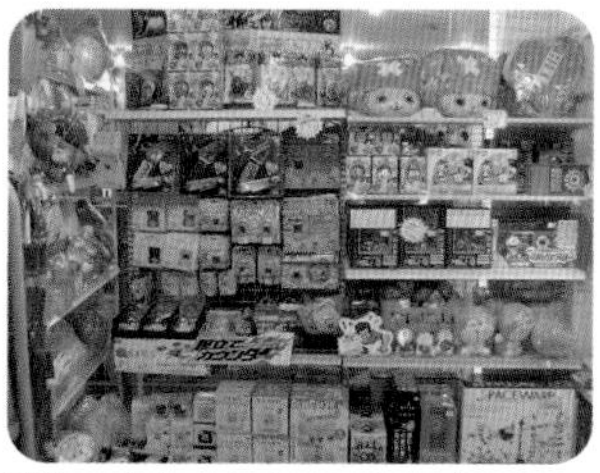

Millions of character toys to choose from!

Uchusen is a character toy specialty shop offering astonishing selection with everything from widely available character toys to highly specialized items. We are constantly getting in new stock, both of made-in-Japan items and imports. This is the place for toys in Akihabara!

Address: Akihabara Rajio Kaikan 4F, 1-15-16 Soto-Kanda, Chiyoda-ku, Tokyo
Phone: 03-3258-8031
URL: http://www.uchusen.co.jp/
Hours: Weekdays 11:00–20:00/Sat., Sun. & holidays 10:00–20:00; closed occasionally at irregular times

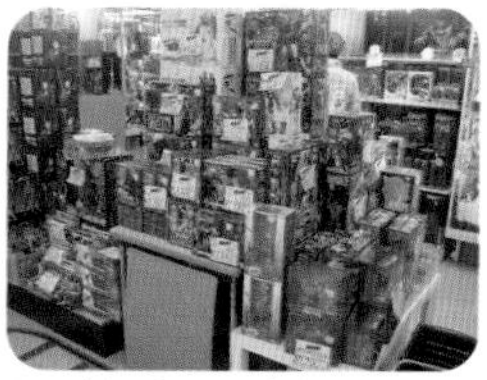

Everything from made-in-Japan items to imports

Yellow Submarine Akihabara G-SHOP

As a large specialty store, we've got the most impressive selection of figures around!

The Yellow Submarine is a prominent presence amongst hobby shops. We're located on the fourth floor of Rajio Kaikan, right next to the Electric Town Exit of Akihabara Station. We carry anything that can be categorized as a figure, including *gachapon, gampura* (*Gundam* models), garage kits and more. We see customers every day who make the trip from far away, just to get their favorite figures!

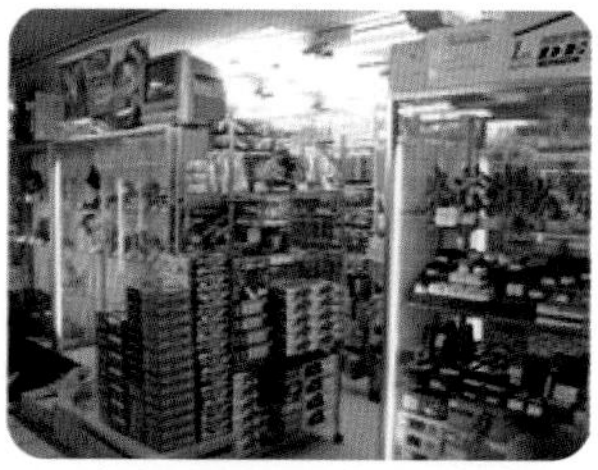

We're the large-scale specialty store for figures.

Address: Akihabara Rajio Kaikan 4F, 1-15-11 Soto-Kanda, Chiyoda-ku, Tokyo
Phone: 03-5298-3123
URL: http://www.yellowsubmarine.co.jp
Hours: 11:00–20:00; closed January 1

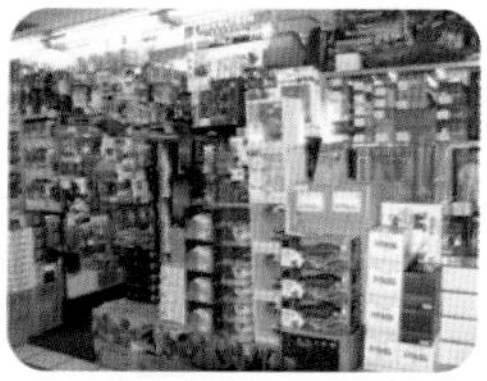

For selection, we simply can't be beat!

PORD Akihabara Shop

PORD is the place to buy your favorite items together—for even better value!

PORD carries a massive selection of toys-in-a-capsule, *shokugan* (toys with supplement to eat), prizes and trading figures, as well as ample *moe-kei* figures such as *bishojo* figures (girls collection figures), game characters and more. We have incredible inventory, and we're always getting in new products. In fact, we get new items in faster than other stores in Akihabara, a fact that's made us very popular with customers.

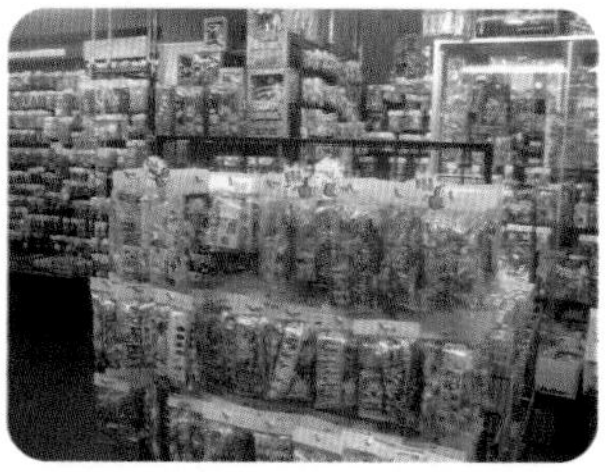

Check out our vast array of figures and items.

Address: MN Bldg. 3F, 3-15-5 Soto-Kanda, Chiyoda-ku, Tokyo
Phone: 03-5209-6664
URL: http://www.pord.co.jp/
Hours: Weekdays 11:00–20:00/Sun. & holidays 11:00–19:00; closed January 1

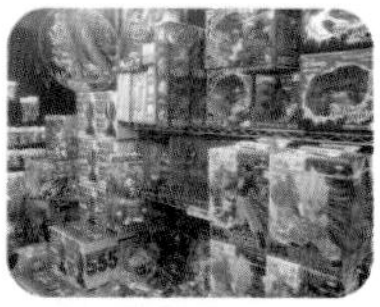

We get the goods in our store incredibly fast.

PORD Rental Showcase

Tons of display cases everywhere you look!

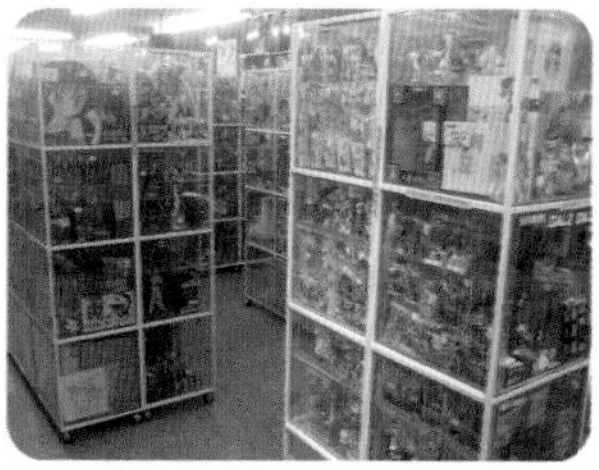

Gachapon Hall, 4th floor

We're on the fourth floor of the famous Akihabara Gachapon Hall. Our cases display figures, *anime* items, limited-time-only event items, *gachapon,* cards and more. We have a special service where we rank our cases by sales earnings, and offer half off on rent depending on performance. We even hold special events where we auction the use of our display cases for month-long periods. And because our cases are set up so beautifully, we're like visiting a unique museum.

Address: MN Bldg. 4F, 3-15-5 Soto-Kanda, Chiyoda-ku, Tokyo
Phone: 03-5259-6664
URL: http://www.pord.co.jp/
Hours: Weekdays 11:00–20:00/Sun. & holidays 11:00–19:00; closed January 1

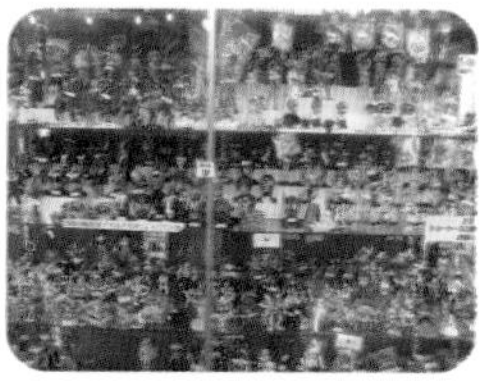

Display cases

Games

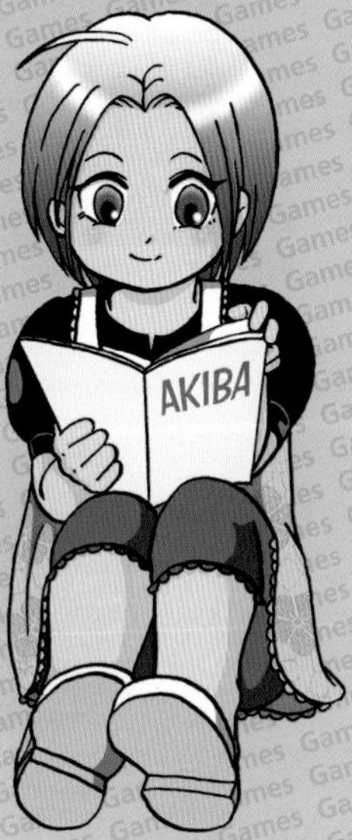
AKIBA

Super Potato Retro Kan

We're the specialists in retro games: come in for a bit of nostalgia!

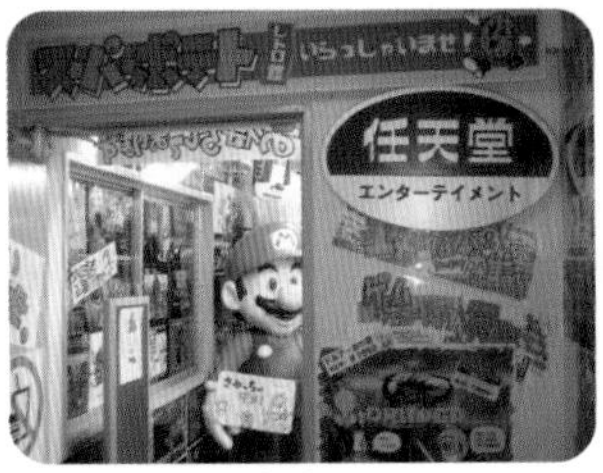
任天堂
エンターテイメント

A retro game specialty shop

Super Potato is the one-and-only retro game specialty shop. We carry pre-owned games including family computer games, and to complement our theme, our store is decorated with tons of old-fashioned games and character dolls—for a vibrant and unique atmosphere. If retro games are your thing, remember to stop in at Super Potato.

Address: Kitabayashi Bldg., 1-11-2 Soto-Kanda, Chiyoda-ku, Tokyo
Phone: 03-5289-9933
URL: http://www.superpotato.com/
Hours: Weekdays 11:00–20:00/Sat., Sun. & holidays 10:00–20:00; open year round

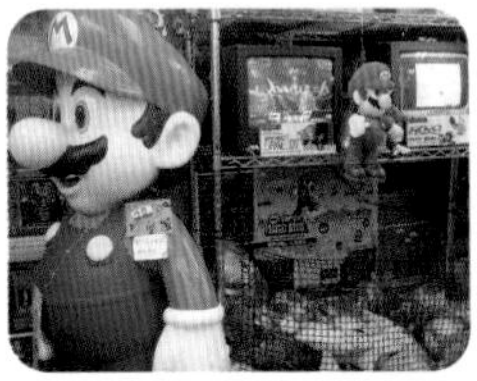

Come and see life-sized figures.

Asobit Game City

Asobit: the ultimate stop for games galore!

We're a specialty store offering TV games, PC games and DVD software. Our fourth-floor PC game area boasts the most fabulous selection in all of Akihabara. We've also got demonstrations and campaigns happening on our first floor each and every day. Our sister stores include Asobit Chara City, Asobit Hobby City and the big retailer Laox. If you're looking for games or any kind of related products, stop in at Asobit Game City and you'll find what you're looking for.

Address: 1-13-2 Soto-Kanda, Chiyoda-ku, Tokyo
Phone: 03-3251-3100
URL: http://www.akibaasobit.jp/
Hours: 10:00–22:00; open year round

Floor Guide

B1F Adult (Windows games & DVD software)
1F Video games (PS2, PSP)
2F Video games (Nintendo & Xbox)
3F Video, music
4F PC games
5F Books, documents
6F Special events

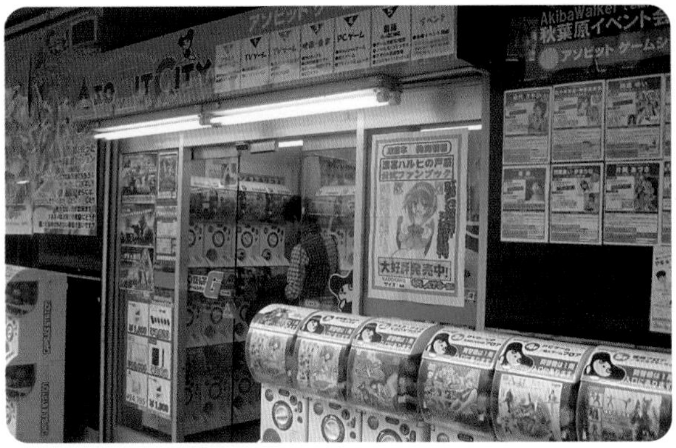

The biggest name in game shops

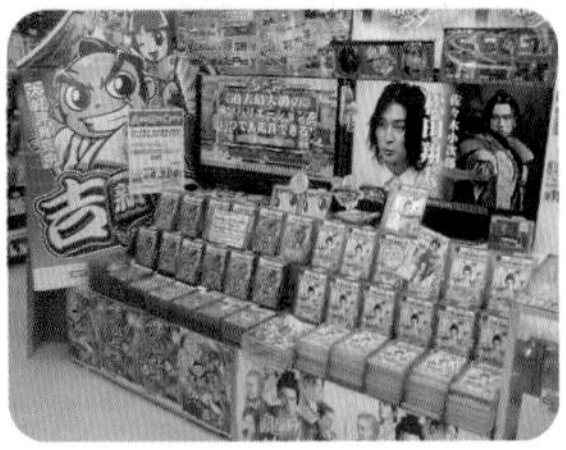

Attractive interior decor

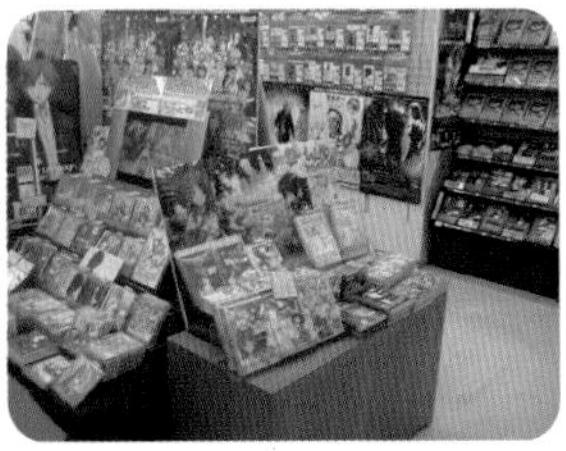

We get new products in fast!

Gamers the Main Shop

We've got every kind of character item you can think of!

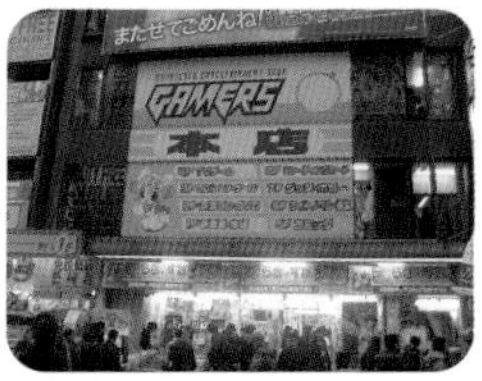
GAMERS
本店
Gamers the main shop

You can find Gamers locations all around the country, but this is the main store. The first through eighth floors house a host of popular character items including games, books, CDs, DVDs, figures and more. Whatever it is you're looking for, you're in for a treat with the astonishing selection here. We're also easy to find: just step out of the Electric Town Exit of Akihabara Station and we're right in front of you. Our store is always a lively place with lots of customers. If you're in the market for character items or games, you've got to stop in and see us!

Address: Takarada Bldg., 1-14-7 Soto-Kanda, Chiyoda-ku, Tokyo
Phone: 03-5298-8720
URL: http://cgi.broccoli.co.jp/gamers/honten2/main.html
Hours: 11:00–21:00 (1F 9:00–22:00); open year round

Floor Guide

- 1F Magazines, newly published comics & new products
- 2F New DVDs & CDs, animation DVDs
- 3F CDs & DVDs (*tokusatsu* [special effects film/TV drama])
- 4F Game software & strategy guides
- 5F Comics, novels, magazine books & painting collection books
- 6F Character items, T-shirts, trading cards, giveaway exchange, girls' comics & novels
- 7F Plastic models, figures, *shokugan* (toys with supplement to eat) & hobby items
- 8F Card games & space for duels

Digi Fan

The *moe* fan's delight!

Digi Fan, the *bishojo* game (girls game) and *bishojo* items specialist, now has stores all around Japan. In addition to our *bishojo* game forte, we also carry tons of *moe-kei* items like phone cards, posters, T-shirts, costumes and much more. *Moe* shop Digi Fan is the place to make *moe* dreams come alive!

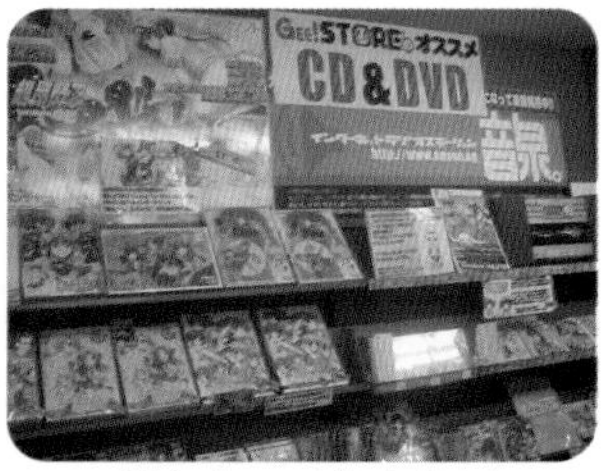
CD&DVD
We're the specialists in *bishojo* games and items.

Address: MN Bldg. 2F, 3-15-5 Soto-Kanda, Chiyoda-ku, Tokyo
Phone: 03-3526-6877
URL: http://www.digifan.jp/
Hours: 11:00–20:00/Sat., Sun. & holidays 11:00–19:00; closed for the year-end and New Year holidays

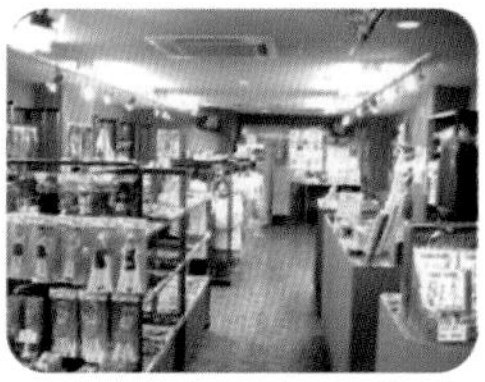
Look no further for your favorite *moe* stuff.

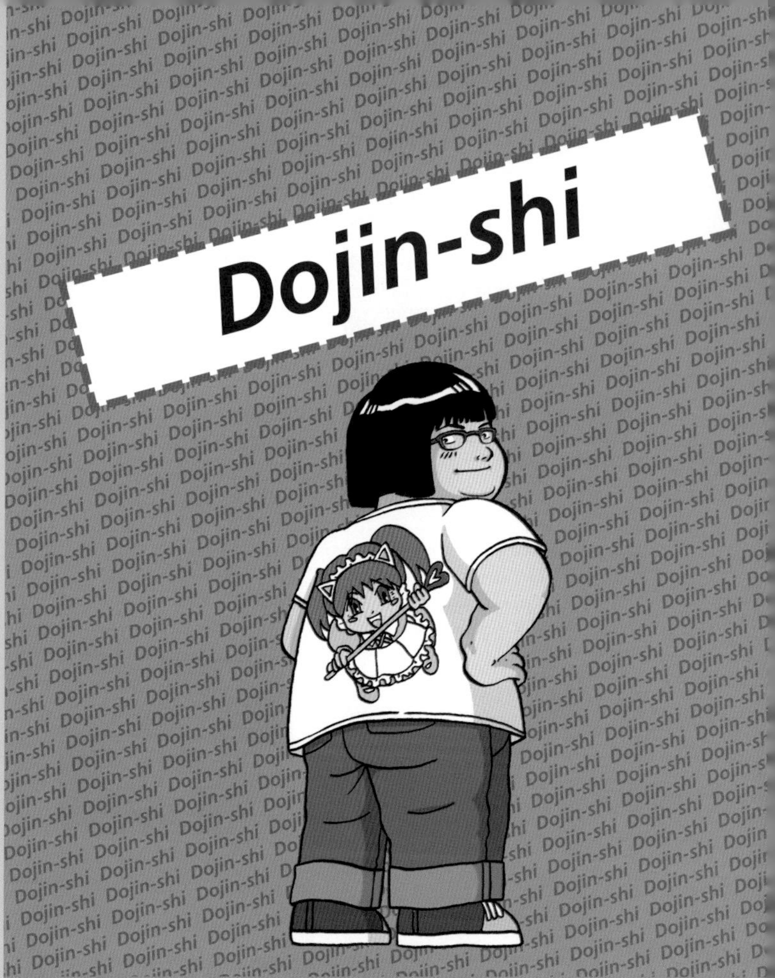
Dojin-shi

K-BOOKS Akihabara Shop

Akiba's leading thrift shop: we've got everything under the sun

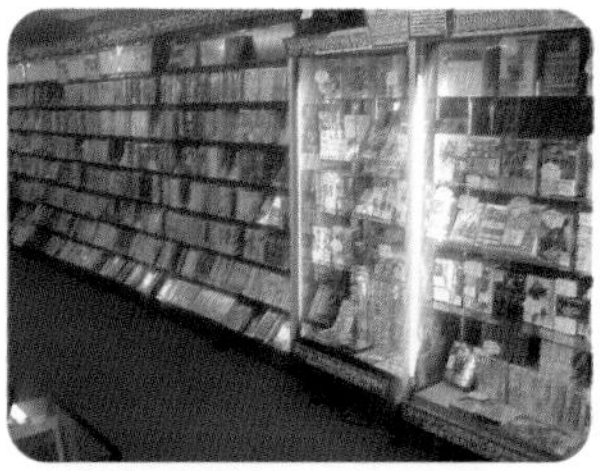
A thrift shop that has everything you want

K-BOOKS has three different sections: comics, *dojin-shi* (self-published manga) for men, and other items. Thanks to our incredible variety of offerings including not only *dojin-shi* and *dojin* items, but also CDs, DVDs, phone cards, trading cards, card games, character goods, gift items, figures, toys, cosplay costumes, comics, magazines, strategy guides, illustration collections and more. With such amazing selection, it's no wonder our customers keep on coming back for more.

Address: Akihabara Rajio Kaikan 3F, 1-15-16 Soto-Kanda, Chiyoda-ku, Tokyo
Phone: 03-3255-4866
URL: http://www.k-books.co.jp/
Hours: 11:00–20:00; open year round

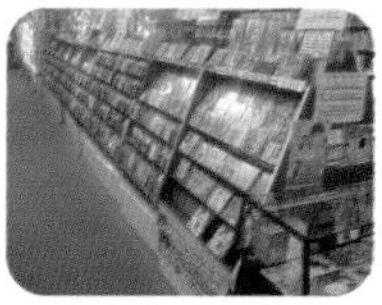
The best selection in all of Akihabara!

K-BOOKS Akihabara Shin Kan

More comics than you ever dreamed in one place!

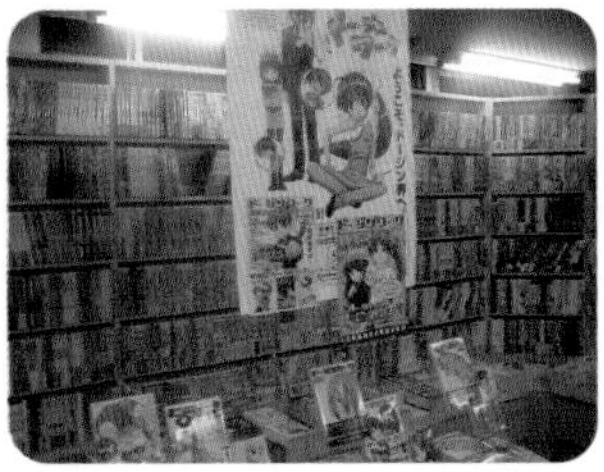

A treasure trove of comics!

Shin Kan is located on the third floor of the Akihabara Rajio Kaikan, right next to the K-BOOKS Akihabara shop. Our vast shelves hold some 120,000 volumes of comics, illustration collections, novels and more. We have lots of interesting items including everything from the newly-published to nostalgic old comics.

Address: Akihabara Rajio Kaikan 3F, 1-15-16 Soto-Kanda, Chiyoda-ku, Tokyo
Phone: 03-5297-5065
URL: http://www.k-books.co.jp/
Hours: 11:00–20:00; open year round

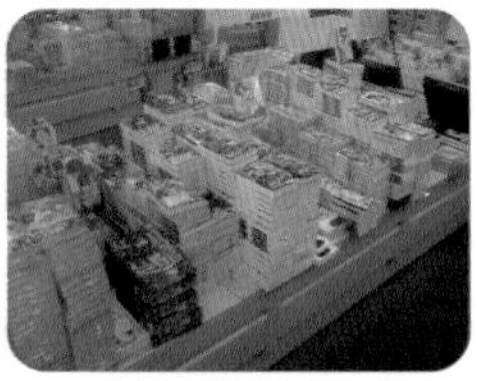

Unbeatable selection of some 120,000 items

COMIC TORANOANA Akihabara the 1st Shop

For comics and *dojin-shi,* look no further!

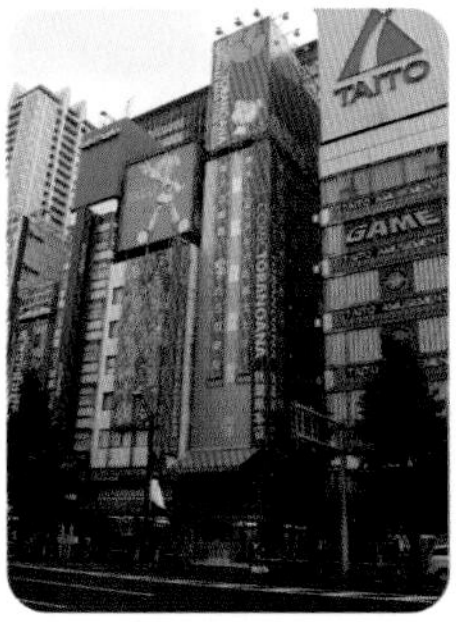
TAITO

COMIC TORANOANA Akihabara the 1st shop

For *dojin-shi* (self-published manga), TORANOANA is the eminent specialist. Some of our products even have original special features like message cards. We also stage events such as voice actor talk shows and short live shows. Check out our Website for details, and be sure to stop in!

Address: 4-3-1 Soto-Kanda, Chiyoda-ku, Tokyo
Phone: 03-5294-0123
URL: http://www.toranoana.co.jp/
Hours: 10:00–22:00; open year round

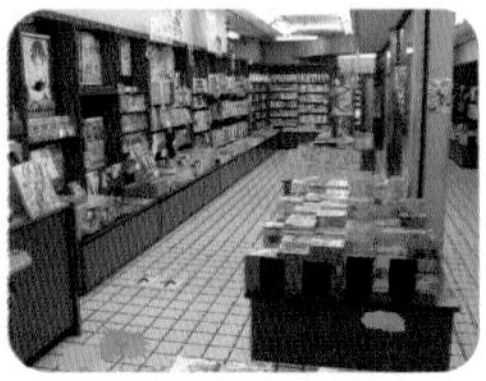

Loads of new magazines on the 1st floor!

COMIC TORANOANA Akihabara the Main Shop

When in Akiba, first come to the Tora!

At the COMIC TORANOANA Akihabara the main shop, we offer hobby items such as CDs, DVDs, PC games and millions of other hobby items. The third and fourth floors feature tons of items for female audiences, including comics, *dojin-shi* (self-published manga), PC games and much more. For those of you new to Akihabara, come to the Tora to experience the Akiba culture for yourself, and see what everyone's talking about!

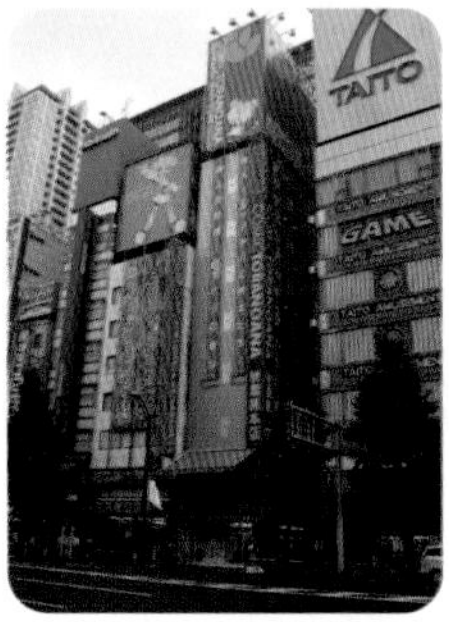
TAITO

COMIC TORANOANA Akihabara the main shop

Address: 4-3-1 Soto-Kanda, Chiyoda-ku, Tokyo
Phone: 03-3526-5551
URL: http://www.toranoana.co.jp/
Hours: 10:00–22:00; open year round

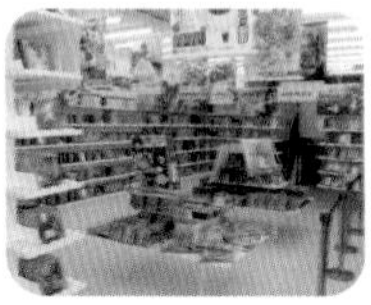

Our 1st floor—full of CDs and DVDs

White Canvas the Main Shop

Welcome to White Canvas!

Welcome to White Canvas in Akihabara. We carry loads of items designed to make your life more fun! We have *dojin* (self-published) software, *dojin* music CDs, *dojin-shi, dojin* items, comics, *bishojo* (girls game) PC software and a whole lot more. Many customers purchase products from our website as well. In addition to our main store, we've got the 2nd shop, the Osaka Namba shop and the Kanazawa shop. We look forward to seeing you!

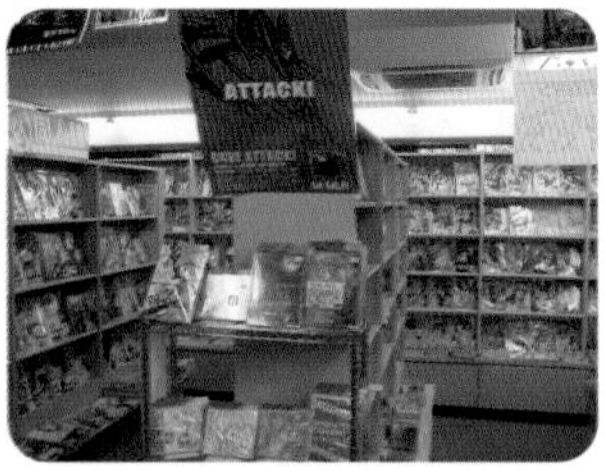

You'll be glad you came in.

Address: Toyo Bldg. 2F, 3-9-8 Soto-Kanda, Chiyoda-ku, Tokyo
Phone: 03-5298-4451
URL: http://www.w-canvas.com/
Hours: Mon.–Thurs. 12:00–20:00/Fri.–Sun. & holidays 11:00–20:00; open year round

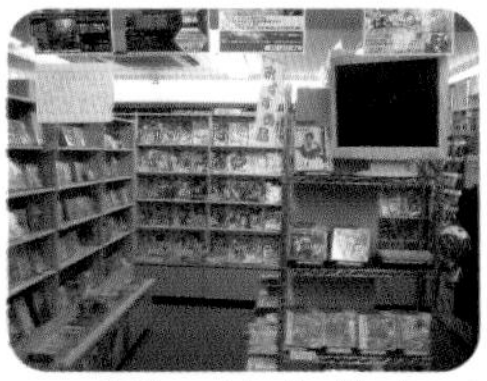

We've got loads of fun items!

Audio Equipment

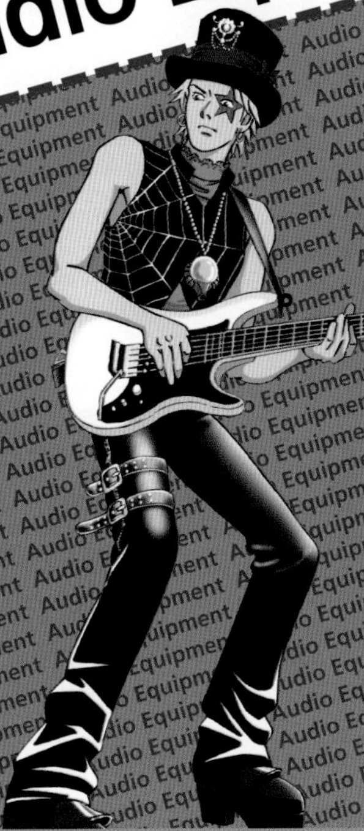

Fal

We're the place for advanced-technology speakers

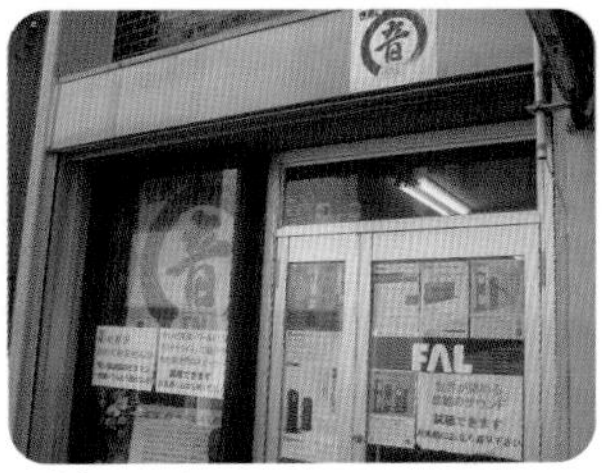

FAL

Look for our sign.

Scientific theory predicted that flat speakers would provide the ultimate sound reproduction. Fal's flat speakers achieve sound quality free of phase shifting, utilizing our own specially developed powerful magnetic circuit, all without a network. This innovative speaker system re-creates the quality and depth of sounds produced by musical instruments and voice, as well as balanced orientation. Come in and give a listen to anything you're interested in!

Address: 3-6-11 Soto-Kanda, Chiyoda-ku, Tokyo
Phone: 03-5298-2221
URL: http://www.fal.gr.jp/
Hours: 11:00–19:00; closed irregularly

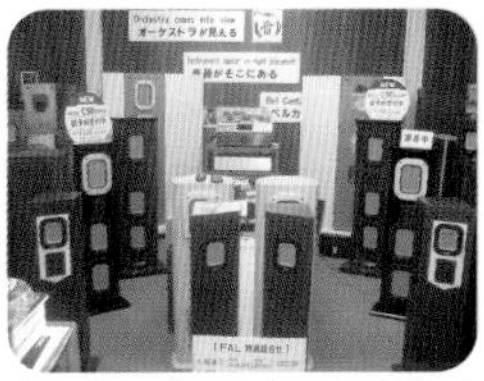

Listen first—then make your choices!

White Canvas the 2nd Shop

White Canvas' 2nd shop—more of a great thing!

White Canvas the 2nd shop is located on the first floor of the main shop, just a three-minute walk from Suehirocho Station on the Ginza Line. Just look for the rainbow-colored campus signboard and you're there! We've got all the *dojin* (self-published) items you can think of, including *dojin* software, *dojin* music CDs, *dojin-shi*, *dojin* goods, comics, *bishojo* (girls game) PC software and more. Stop in, or try our popular mail order service.

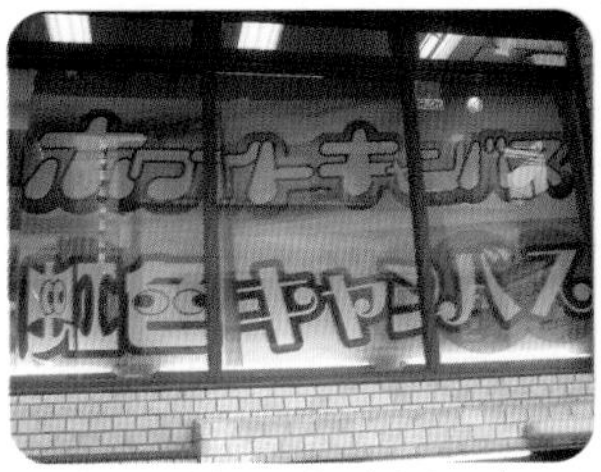

Look for our rainbow-colored signboard.

Address: Toyo Bldg. 1F, 3-9-8 Soto-Kanda 3-9-8, Chiyoda-ku, Tokyo
Phone: 03-6808-9920
URL: http://www.w-canvas.com/
Hours: Mon.–Thurs. 12:00–20:00/Fri.–Sun. & holidays 11:00–20:00; open year round

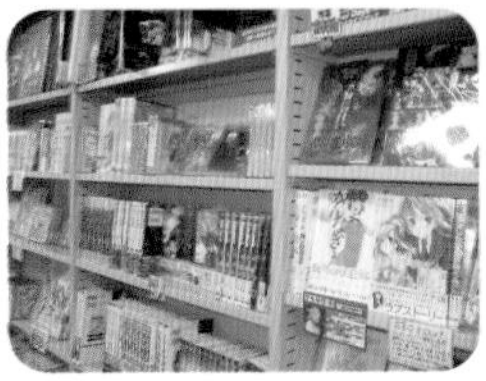

Better *dojin* selection than anyplace!

Azabu Audio

We're in the business of making more and more fans of audio

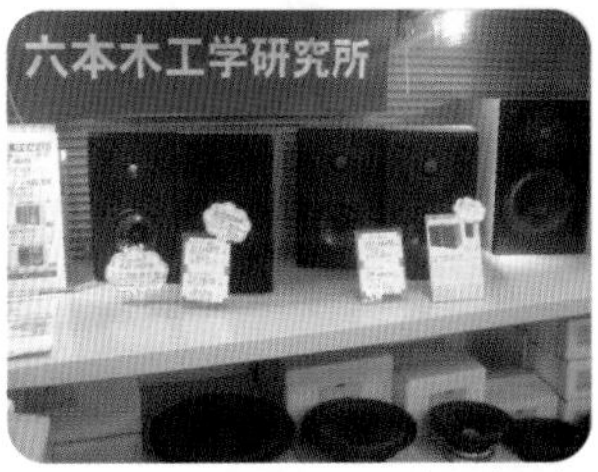

六本木工学研究所

Making more fans of audio.

The Roppongi Institute of Technology is constantly engaged in a process of trial and error to make audio quality the absolute best it can be. One result of these initiatives is Azabu Audio, right here in Akihabara. Azabu Audio consistently supports the audio industry in the form of three concepts: 1) making more audio fans, 2) conveying the incredible fun of manufacturing and 3) providing terrific products through direct channels. The Roppongi Institute of Technology and Azabu Station continue to develop new ways of manufacturing. Check us out now and then and see what great things we're up to!

Address: Adegawa Bldg. 1F&2F, 3-6-17 Soto-Kanda, Chiyoda-ku, Tokyo
Phone: 03-5294-0327
URL: http://www.ritlab.jp/shop/
Hours: 12:00–20:00; closed Tues.

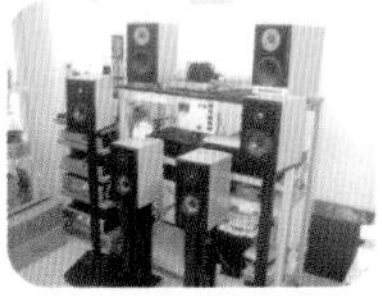

Lots and lots of your favorite audio items

Cosplay

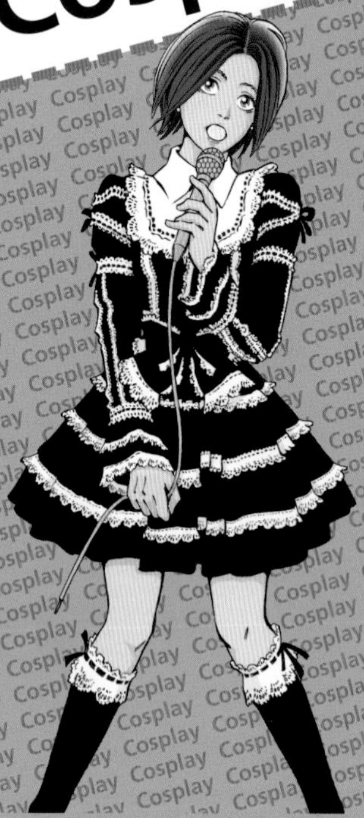

Cosren

The cosplayer's paradise

Cosren is a quiet store located inside Nagomi style café. It's well worth coming in to take a look at the colorful array of cosplay outfits on display—we are truly the cosplayer's paradise. Our collection has something to please every otaku, including specialty items and services. Stop in and see us.

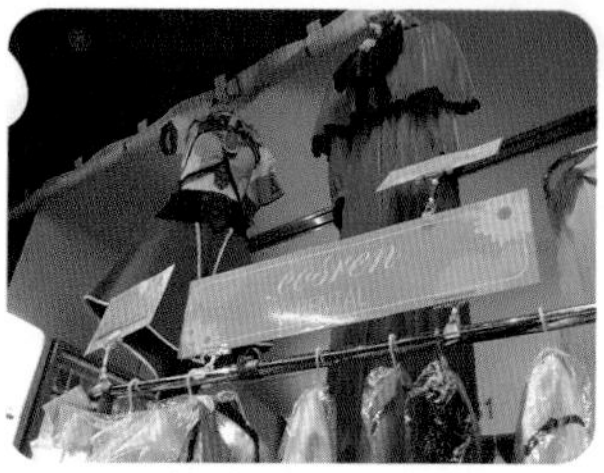
You'll find any cosplay outfit you could possibly want, right here!

Address: Sakai Suehiro Bldg. B1F, 6-14-2 Soto-Kanda, Chiyoda-ku, Tokyo
Phone: 03-5812-9753
URL: http://www.cosren.city-connection.co.jp
Hours: Open 24 hours a day, year round

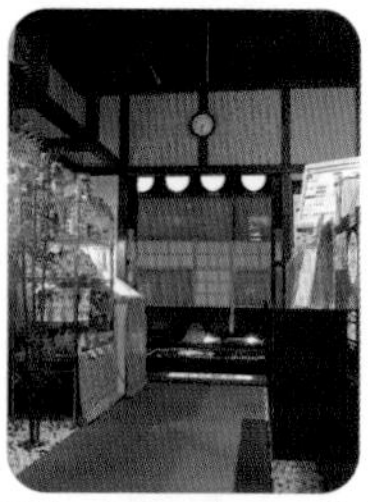
We're at Nagomi style café.

Cosmode

Whether you want order-made or copyrighted items, we're all about excellent quality

Cosmode is the store for both order-made and official costumes. We are known for making highly accurate, excellent quality cosplay costumes with full manufacturer supervision. For customers who want a one-of-a-kind costume, we do it with incredible accuracy at a reasonable price, and we offer free estimates. We can provide estimates based on any reference materials you bring, but that's not required either—if you know the name of your character, we can even base your estimate on that.

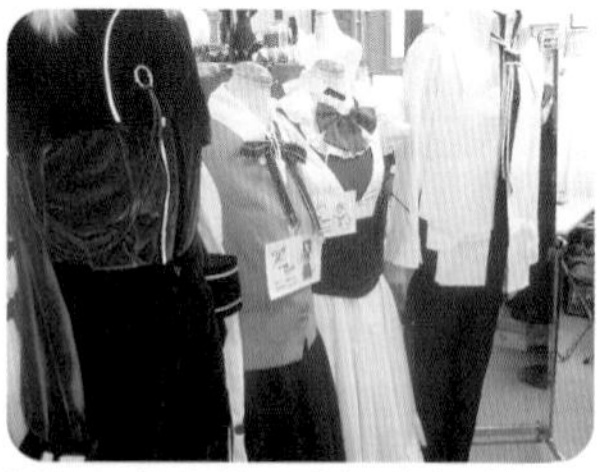
We're on the 3rd floor of the Chubu Bldg.

Address: Chubu Bldg. 302, 3-7-14 Soto-Kanda, Chiyoda-ku, Tokyo
Phone: 03-3255-8138
URL: http://www.cosmode.jp/
Hours: 11:00–19:00; closed Sun., Mon. & holidays

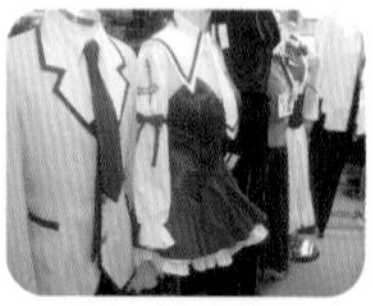
Tons of superior-quality cosplay outfits

Bukiya

Decorate your home with world-class weapon replicas—it's all here!

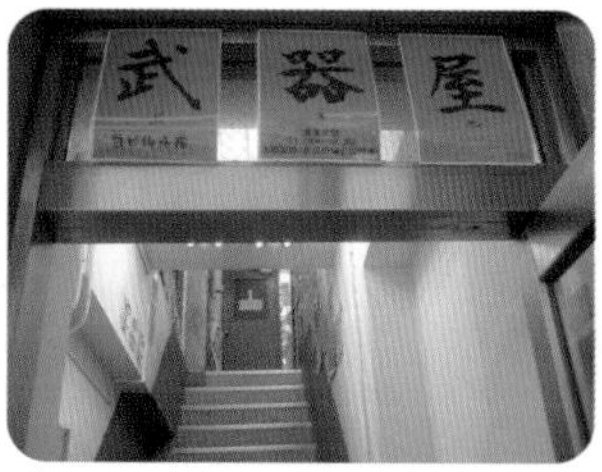
武 器 屋
When you need that weapon, come on over to Bukiya!

Our store features a variety of unusual cosplay items including weapons and protective gear from around the world—swords, armor, helmets and much, much more! We get lots of weapons enthusiasts from all over, every single day, to see the one-of-a-kind weapons specialty shop Bukiya.

Address: Takara Bldg. 4F, 1-5-7 Soto-Kanda, Chiyoda-ku, Tokyo
Phone: 03-3254-6435
URL: www.wbr.co.jp
Hours: 11:00–19:30; closed Wed.

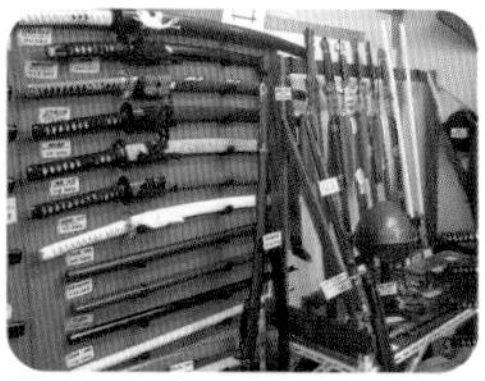
Weapons and protective gear from all over the world—all under one roof

Arcades

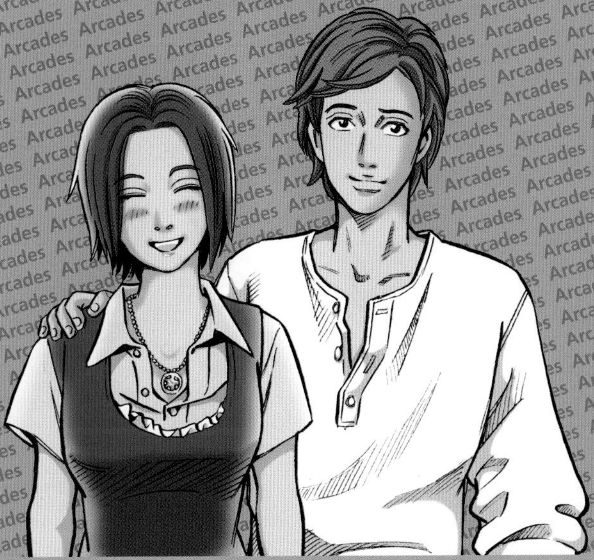

Club Sega

Welcome to the world of games!

This is Sega's arcade. The basement through fifth floors are loaded with *kakugei* (fighting games) and other games. Each floor offers a different genre of game, so visitors can try their hand at all different kinds in this one place. And since we are in Akihabara, we've got tons of crane games, UFO Catcher games and much more, where otaku can get the gift items they love, so come and try for your favorites! You've got to witness this Akiba-style amusement park.

Address: 1-10-9 Soto-Kanda, Chiyoda-ku, Tokyo
Phone: 03-5256-8123
URL: http://location.sega.jp/loc_web/cs_akihabara.html
Hours: 10:00–1:00; open year round

Floor Guide

B1F *Kakugei*
1F Prize games
2F Large sensory video games
3F *Kakugei*
4F Video Games
5F WORLD CLUB Champion Football (WCCF)

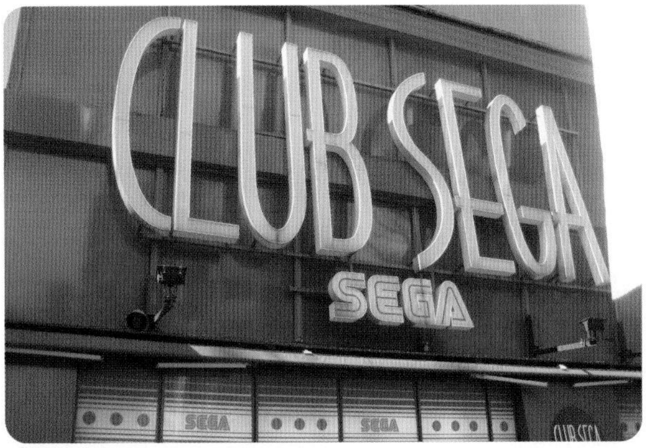
CLUB SEGA
SEGA
We're right on Chuo-dori Avenue.

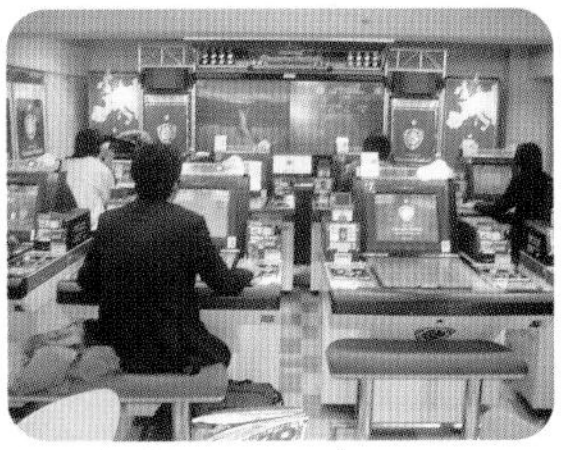
Come check out our popular soccer games.

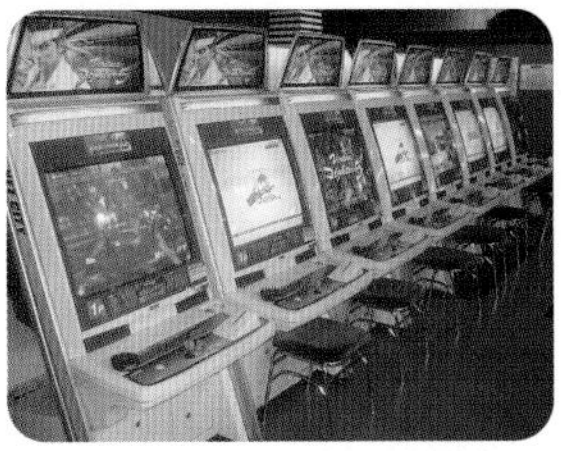
The *kakugei* everybody loves!

Cospatio

We're number one in cosplay costumes

We're known as the best in cosplay costume design, recreating costumes with our extensive experience, knowledge and technology, and offering the best in comfort as well as quality. Yet we don't stop with costumes—we also develop cosplay-related items, and we're proud of our incredible selection. Use our order-made service to create the exact costume that you want—all estimates are absolutely free!

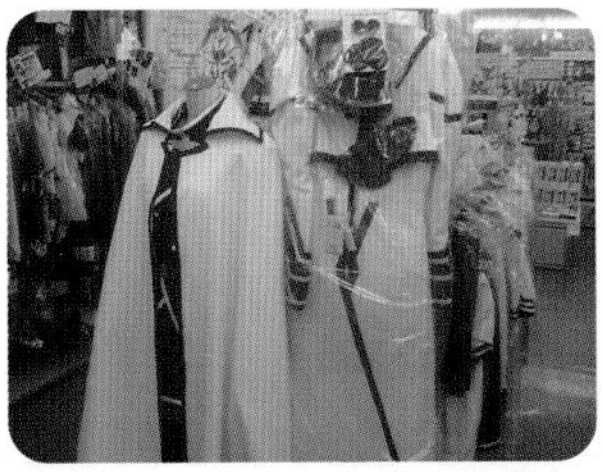
When it comes to cosplay costume design, nobody beats us!!

Address: Gee Store Akiba, 3-15-5 Soto-Kanda, Chiyoda-ku, Tokyo
Phone: 03-3526-6877
URL: http://cospatio.com/
Hours: 11:00–20:00/Sun. & holidays 11:00–19:00; closed for the year-end and New Year holidays

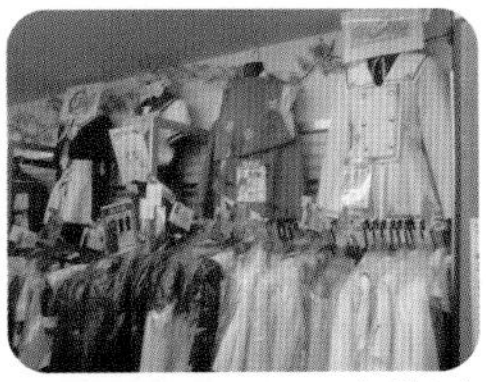
Cosplay costumes and all kinds of accessories

Sega Gigo

The place to be for Akiba's own special brand of entertainment

We're Sega's other arcade in Akihabara, just one minute on foot from Akihabara Station. Together with Club Sega, we're in the business of entertaining tons of customers every single day. In addition to the newest games including large-sized card games, we also have many unusual games for enthusiasts and otaku. On the first and second floors, our girls dressed in cosplay outfits come out to greet you. This is the ultimate in entertainment, and we're unquestionably the leading Akiba-kei arcade.

Address: 1-15-1 Soto-Kanda, Chiyoda-ku, Tokyo
Phone: 03-3252-7528
URL: http://location.sega.jp/loc_web/akihabara_gigo.html
Hours: 10:00–24:00; open year round

Floor Guide

1F Prize games
2F Prize games and card games for kids
3F Large games
4F Large games
5F Large games
6F Video games

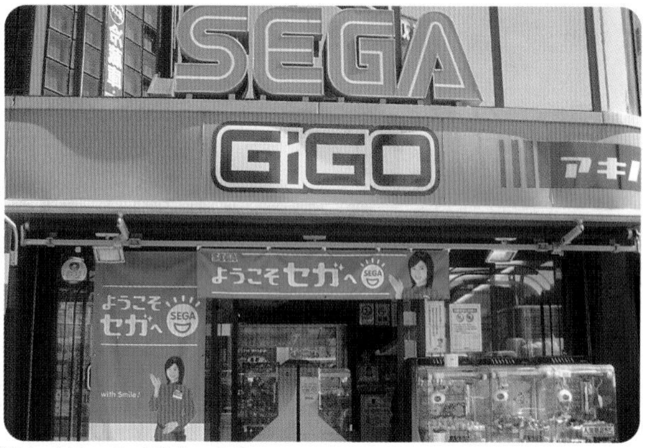
SEGA
GiGO
ようこそセガへ
ようこそセガへ
We're right next to Akihabara Station.

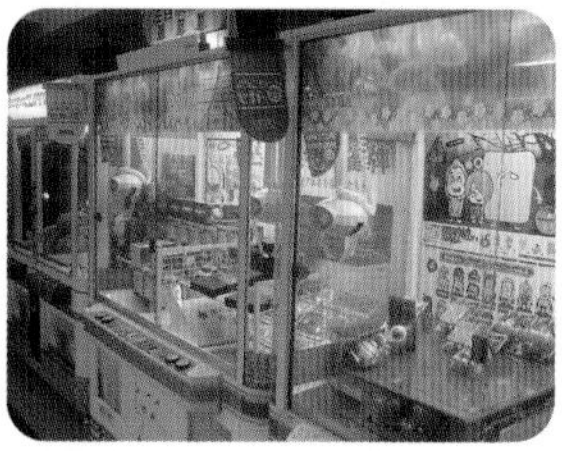
UFO catcher: everyone's favorite

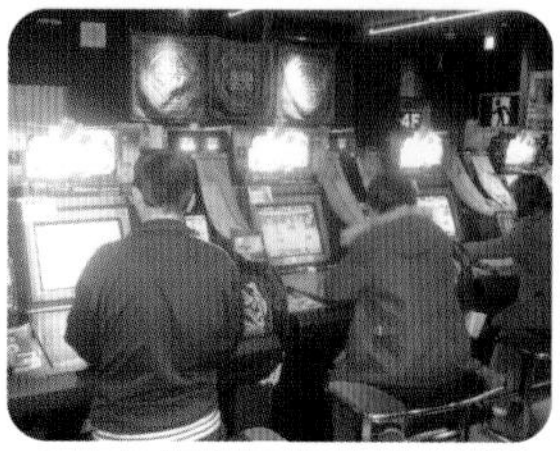
Sangokushi-taisen gains much popularity.

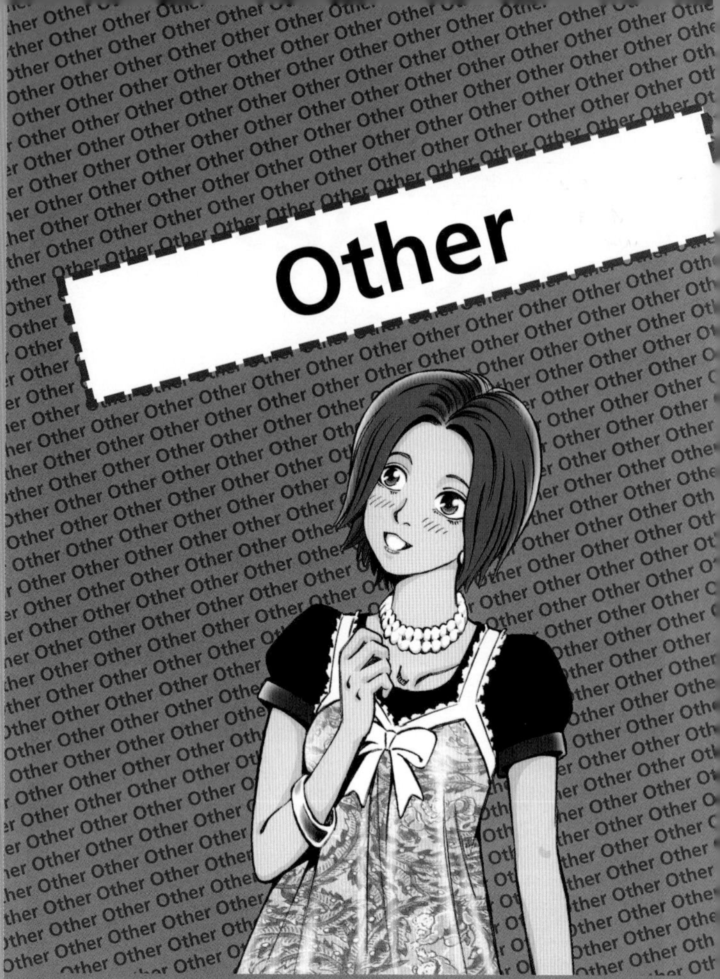
Other

Gachapon Hall

With over 350 machines, we're definitely the *gachapon* specialists

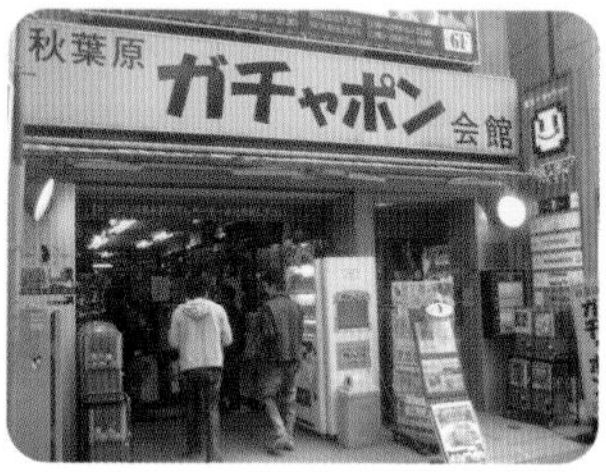
秋葉原
ガチャポン会館
We're one of Akihabara's most popular stores.

With *gachapon* left and right, you might have some trouble deciding which one you want to try! We've got an astonishing total of over 400 machines, making us a *gachapon* specialty shop by any standard—in fact, we're a *gachapon* museum! We carry major manufacturer Carddas, figures and even food! As one of the most well-known stores in Akihabara, we're a popular destination for tourists, who love to stop in and check out this unusual spot.

Address: MN Bldg. 1F, 3-15-5 Soto-Kanda, Chiyoda-ku, Tokyo
Phone: 03-5209-6020
URL: http://www.akibagacha.com/
Hours: Weekdays 11:00–20:00/Fri., Sat. and the day before holidays 11:00–22:00/Sun. & holidays 11:00–19:00; closed January 1

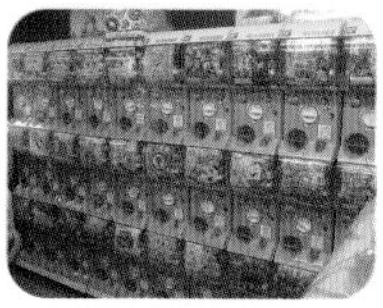
Gachapon fans will never want to leave!

Mudaya

We're a cool little shop that helps people communicate

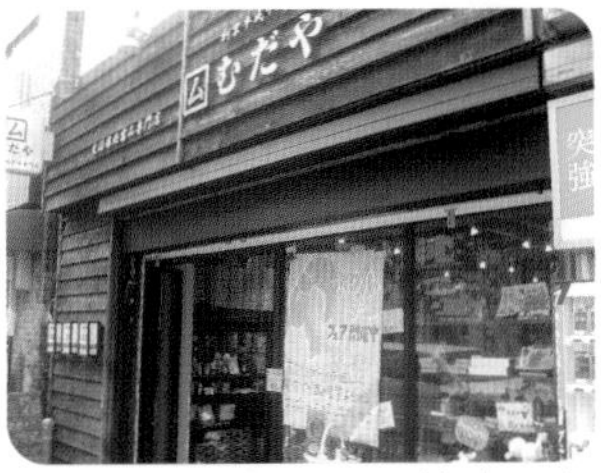

Our welcoming wood-look exterior

"Muda" means "frivolous." We've been living the "frivolous life" for 30 years, and this store is our way of telling the world about the "usefulness of frivolousness!" People nowadays have lots of problems with communication, and we consider it our mission to make it easier for people. Though we know that we can't always make people better communicators, we can give them something to communicate about! We're pleased to offer products that people can talk about, and we're really glad when our stuff leads to lots of good conversation, and a little more happiness in the world!

Address: 4-6-7 Soto-Kanda, Chiyoda-ku, Tokyo
Phone: 03-5298-3696
URL: http://mudaya.com
Hours: 11:00–20:00; open year round

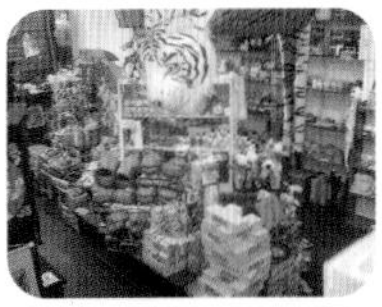

Everything you need for day-to-day life

Puroresu Shop BackDrop

Specializing in professional wrestling goods

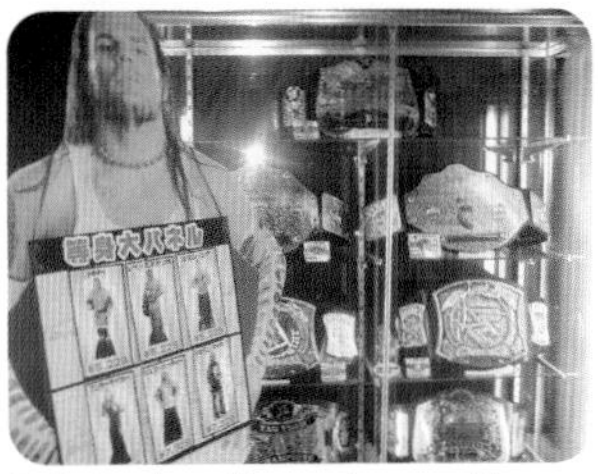

Professional wrestling goods are our thing.

Puroresu Shop BackDrop specializes in professional wrestling items, and American pro wrestling in particular. Just look for the yellow sign that says "Akibakan"—we're on the fourth floor. Our products include figures, magazines, clothing, DVDs and lots of other items, as well as rare pieces and specially-for-fans items that you can only get here. We've got a total of more than 3,000 different items, so we're lots of fun to come and look at. We offer Internet shopping as well.

Address: Dai-ni Chuei Bldg. 4F, 1-19-9 Soto-Kanda, Chiyoda-ku, Tokyo
Phone: 03-3255-8701
URL: http://www.b-drop.com/
Hours: 11:00–20:00; open year round

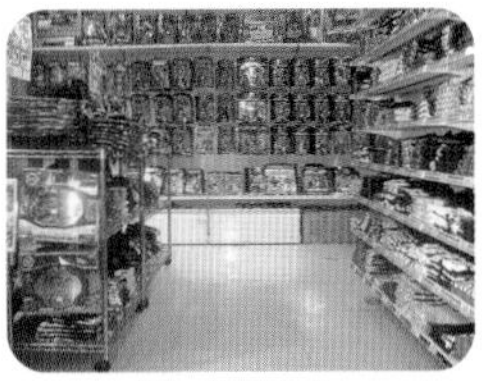

Wrestling stuff everywhere

Rock Goods Shop BackDrop

The specialty shop for rock music lovers: we've got more than music!

BackDrop carries a variety of specialty goods related to rock musicians. Come in and you'll find imported T-shirts and figures, DVDs and a lot more. We've got so much fascinating stuff—including rare products and items for true enthusiasts—that we could even be mistaken for a museum. We're also inexpensive, so you can get the things that keep you connected with the musicians you love for less than you might think!

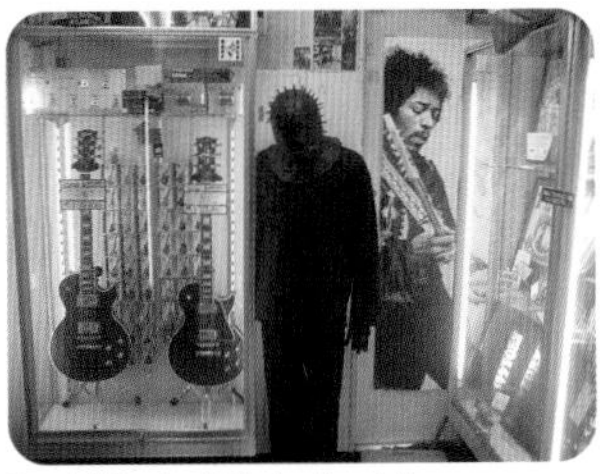

Specializing in all kinds of rock items

Address: Dai-ni Chuei Bldg. 3F, 1-11-9 Soto-Kanda, Chiyoda-ku, Tokyo
Phone: 03-3255-8702
URL: http://www.rakuten.co.jp/b-drop/
Hours: 11:00–20:00; open year round

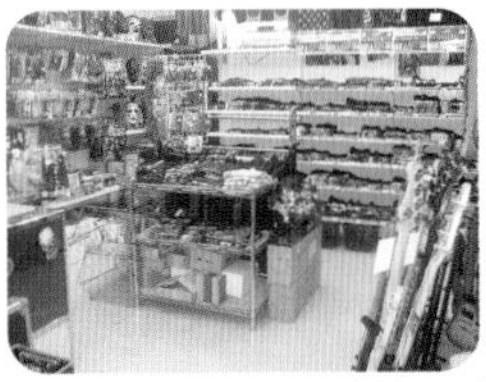

Tons of novelty goods for fans of foreign musicians

Nagomi Style Café

The modern and the traditional come together: an Internet café with Japanese decor!

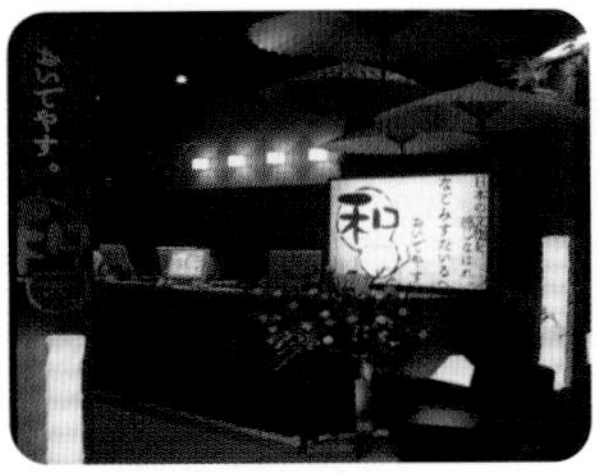

Pure traditional Japanese decor!

The delightfully traditional Japanese atmosphere of our shop is complete with kimono-clad staff. This unique café has 20,000 comic books, 140 magazines, 20 kinds of online games, and free drinks and ice cream. All seating is separate-compartment, and we even have places where customers can take a nap, as well as a shower room. If you like, we can offer you a futon in the tatami room. For a truly one-of-a-kind Internet café experience, try the Nagomi style café.

Address: Sakai Suehiro Bldg. B1F, 6-14-2 Soto-Kanda, Chiyoda-ku, Tokyo
Phone: 03-5812-9753
URL: http://www.nagomi-cafe.com/
Hours: Open 24 hours a day, year round

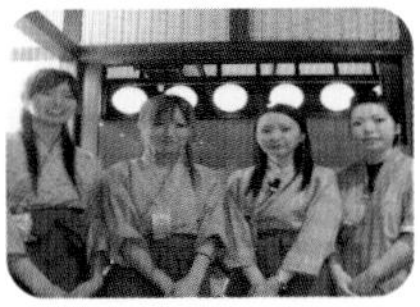

Our friendly staff welcome you.

Shosen Book Tower

The entire building is one big book store!

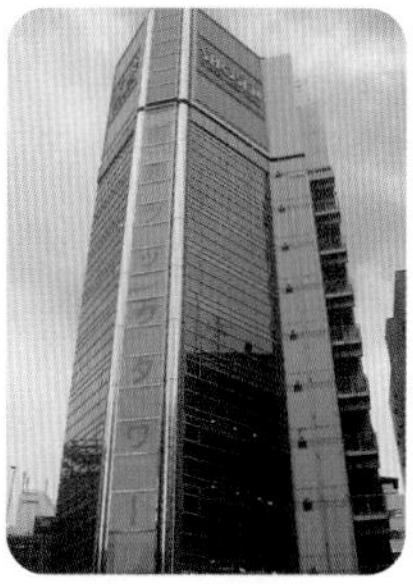

Our Book Tower: a towering symbol of Akiba!

Shosen Book Tower is the biggest bookstore in Akihabara. We're just a one-minute walk from the Showa-dori Exit of Akihabara Station, and our building really stands out! The store is full of books, magazines and comics of all kinds. In fact, the entire place is one big department store for books, from the first through eighth floors. In addition to comics and computer-related items, we also offer general interest books and specialty books. Whatever kind of book it is you're looking for, head on over to the Tower!

Address: 1-11-1 Kanda-Sakumacho, Chiyoda-ku, Tokyo
Phone: 03-5296-0051 URL: http://www.shosen.co.jp/
Hours: 10:30–21:00; open year round

Floor Guide

1F New publications, popular publications and maps
2F Computer-related books
3F Paperbacks, new books and specialty books
4F Business books
5F Transportation, linguistics and hobby books
6F Photo collection books, music and sports books
7F Strategy guides and novels
8F Comics

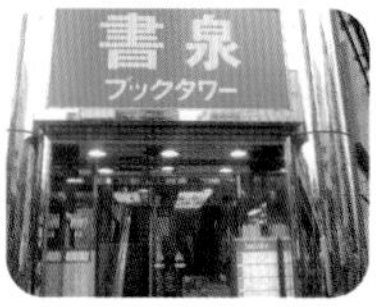
書泉
ブックタワー

Our entrance

Cospa Gee Store Akiba

Character goods and apparel—it's all here!

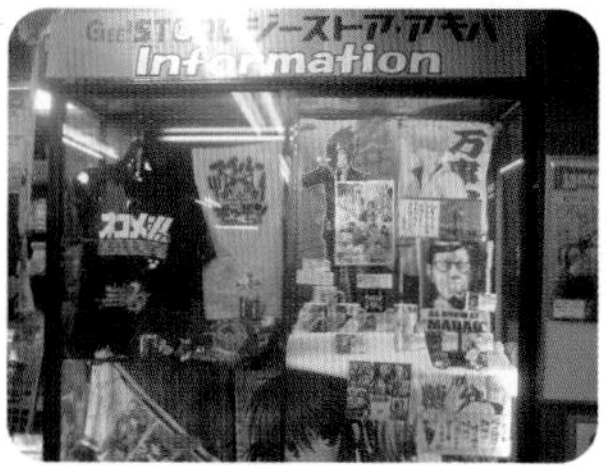

Gee Store Akiba 2nd floor

We're the specialty store for manga, *anime* and game character items. Our apparel items include T-shirts, pants, wristbands, caps and more, plus our special *Gundam* costumes and maid outfits! Recently, we've added the latest *Dragon Ball Z* design T-shirts to our collection. In a sign of changes to come in Akiba-kei fashion, we offer a stylish touch for the genre that everyone feels comfortable wearing. Stop in and see us.

Address: Gee Store Akiba 2F, 3-15-5 Soto-Kanda, Chiyoda-ku, Tokyo
Phone: 03-3526-6877
URL: http://www.cospa.com/
Hours: 11:00–20:00/Sun. & holidays 11:00–19:00; closed for the year-end and New Year holidays

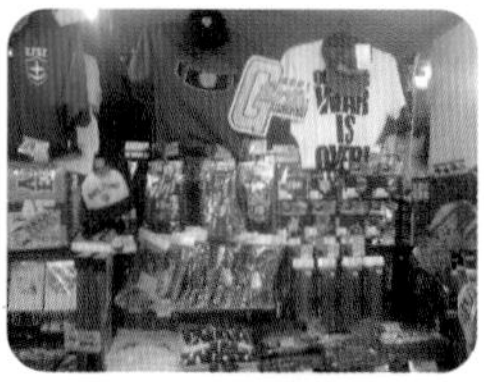

Lots of apparel complete with your favorite character logos!

Little World Gee Store Akiba

The place to find what you love to do most!

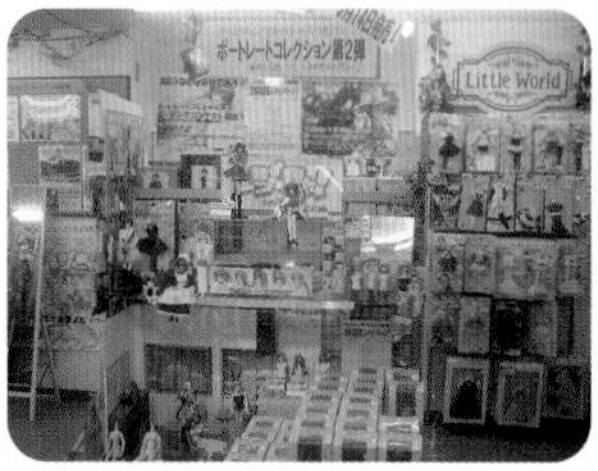

All your favorite dolls and figures

Welcome to our Little World! This is the place to find just the thing to make your life even more fun. Of course we've got dolls and figures, but we've also got a small photo-shooting area, custom figure displays, doll clothes, order-made small items and more, for one various-and-sundry collection of products and services. This addition to the Cospa group represents a new style in Akihabara fun.

Address: Gee Store Akiba 5F, 3-15-5 Soto-Kanda, Chiyoda-ku, Tokyo
Phone: 03-3526-6877
URL: http://www.little-world.net/
Hours: Weekdays 11:00–20:00/Sun. & holidays 11:00–19:00; open year round

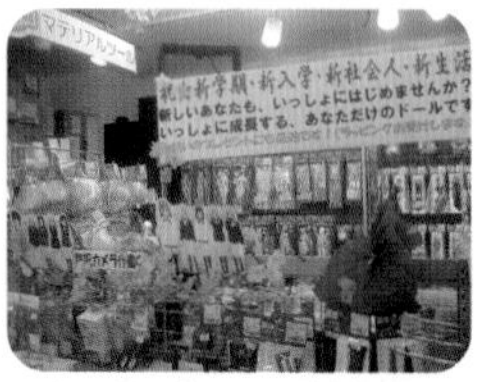

Stop in and see us—this is an easy way to add more fun to your life!

Nijigen Cospa

Just for *moe* fans!

Just for *moe* fans. At Nijigen Cospa, we're delighted to bring you *moe* specialty items, *moe bishojo* (girls) characters and other characters that fans go crazy for. We love the items we create, and we want to make them even more popular, and for fans to have even more fun with them! We're the brand that makes these items with love—for fans that adore them as much as we do.

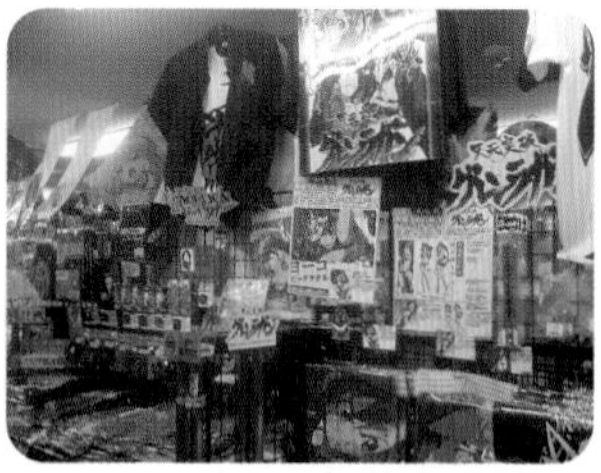

Especially for fans...

Address: Gee Store Akiba, 3-15-5 Soto-Kanda, Chiyoda-ku, Tokyo
Phone: 03-3526-6877
URL: http://www.nijigencospa.com/
Hours: 11:00–20:00/holidays 11:00–19:00; closed for the year-end and New Year holidays

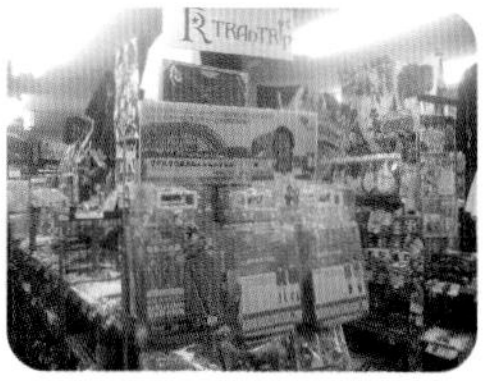

Adorable characters await you!

Akihabara a year after ILY's legendary street performance

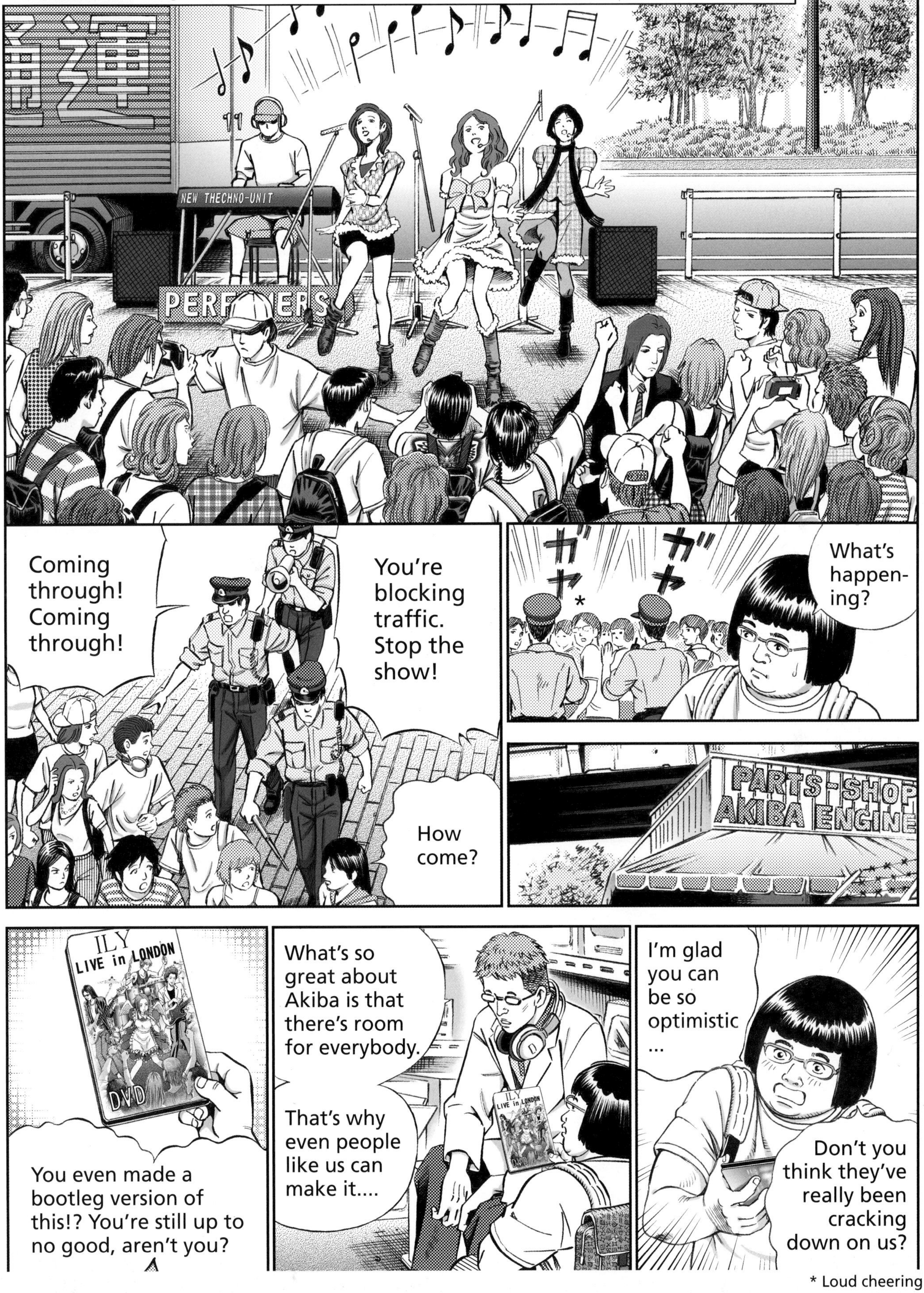
NEW THECHNO-UNIT
Coming through! Coming through!
You're blocking traffic. Stop the show!
How come?
ガヤ*
ガヤ
What's happen-ing?
PARTS-SHOP
AKIBA ENGINE
ILY
LIVE in LONDON
DVD
You even made a bootleg version of this!? You're still up to no good, aren't you?
What's so great about Akiba is that there's room for everybody.
That's why even people like us can make it....
ILY
LIVE in LONDON
I'm glad you can be so optimistic ...
Don't you think they've really been cracking down on us?

* Loud cheering

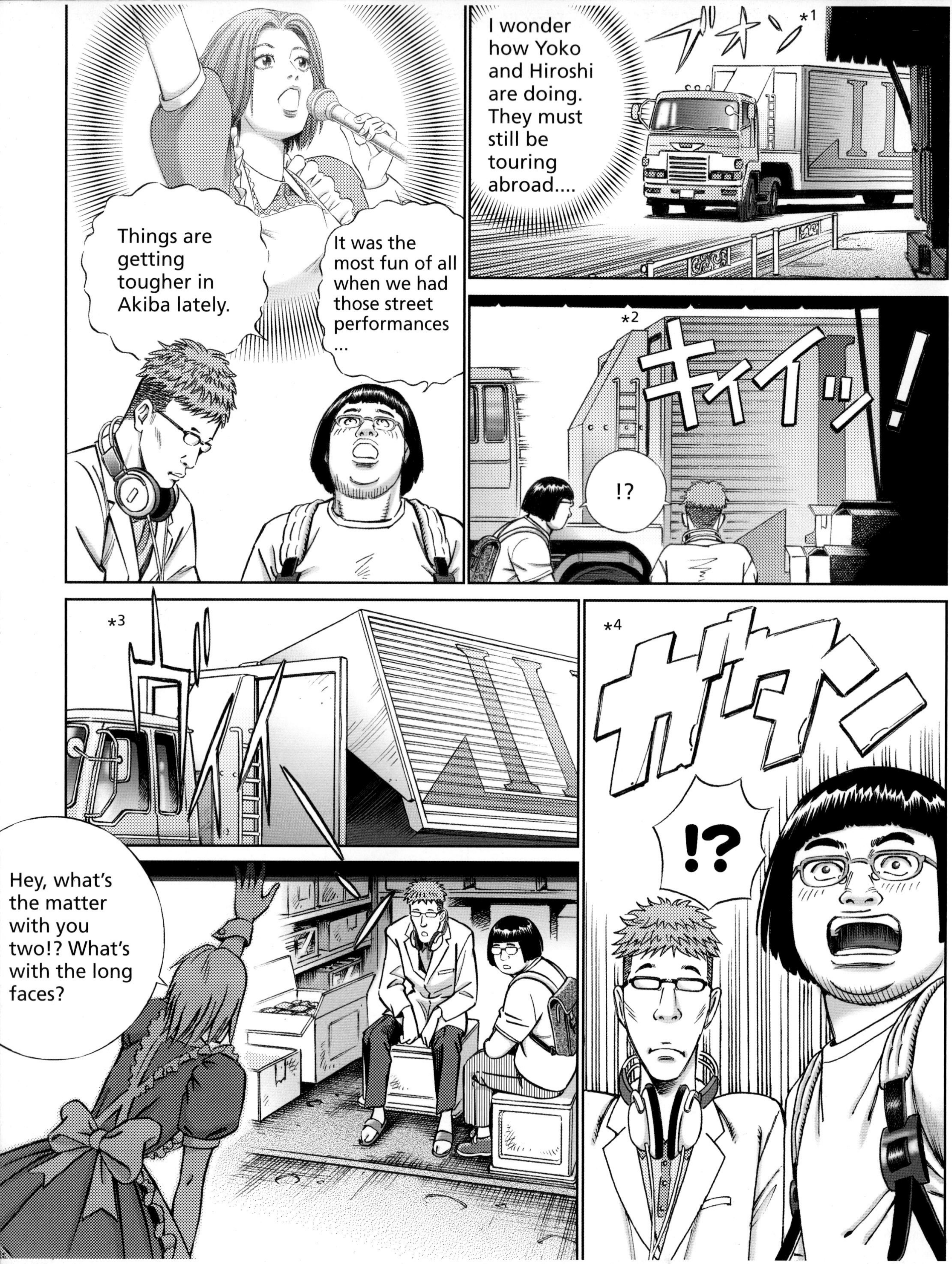

Things are getting tougher in Akiba lately.
It was the most fun of all when we had those street performances ...
I wonder how Yoko and Hiroshi are doing. They must still be touring abroad....
ブオン *1
*2 キイイッ!
!?
*3
Hey, what's the matter with you two!? What's with the long faces?
*4 ガタン
!?

*1 Vroom-vroom *2 Screech! *3 Shutter opens *4 Bang!